Advance Praise for
Thirty Days to Hope & Freedom for Sexual Addicts

This positive, practical book will help those in recovery reclaim their lives in a non-shaming way. Following Magness' guidance will insure the discovery of a vital, healthy self and a life worth living.

Alexandra Katehakis, MA

Author of *Erotic Intelligence: Igniting Hot, Healthy Sex While in Recovery from Sex Addiction*

We are in desperate need of exceptional books in our field of sexual addiction. Dr. Magness has provided us with such a book. He has been a leader in the field for many years. Great leaders lead from their own experience of being treatment providers and teachers. Dr. Magness has a sound clinical mind as well as a gentle and caring spirit. You will be blessed by this book.

Mark Laaser, PhD,

Author of *Healing the Wounds of Sexual Addiction* and *Faithful & True*

Any individual hoping to manage his or her sex addiction must have both motivation and skills to maintain recovery. In *Thirty Days to Hope & Freedom*, Dr. Magness provides a wonderful road map to do just that. Not only does he describe symptoms of sex addiction and the possibility of cross addiction, he also proposes ways to increase spirituality as a way to sustain hope. This book is packed with practical tips such as managing internal and external triggers that challenge early recovery, utilizing Twelve Step groups, and finding a sponsor. He clearly outlines the components of a reasonable recovery plan. *Thirty Days to Hope & Freedom* is a great way to begin the healing journey.

M. Deborah Corley, PhD,

Co-author of *Disclosing Secrets: When, to Whom, & How Much to Reveal*

Thirty Days to Hope & Freedom from Sexual Addiction provides those suffering from problematic sexual behaviors a practical and comprehensive guide to a healthier and fulfilling sexual life. Dr. Magness uses his years of clinical experience and leadership to distill the recovery process into thirty days, with each day offering practical exercises, resources, and hope brought to life by true stories. For the sexual addict, this book makes recovery real and possible by breaking down each step into units with worksheets and reflections designed for personal growth. For clinicians, this book provides the cognitive, behavioral, and spiritual guidance and resources for clients in all phases of the recovery process. I would consider this workbook to represent the current standard in the field.

Charles P. Samenow, MD, MPH

Editor of *Sexual Addiction and Compulsivity: The Journal of Treatment and Prevention*

Early recovery from sexual addiction can feel overwhelming and confusing. In his book, *Thirty Days to Hope & Freedom from Sexual Addiction*, Dr. Magness' comprehensive thirty-day plan gives concrete answers for the challenges the recovering individual faces. I highly recommend this book to promote and sustain healthy sexual recovery.

A solid and comprehensive book with a thirty-day plan gives the recovering addict a concrete guide to recovery. Dr. Magness leaves no stone unturned as he guides the reader through early stages of sexual sobriety. This book is a must have on the list of anyone's recovery resources.

Maureen Canning, MA
Author of *Lust, Anger, Love: Understanding Sexual Addiction and the Road to Healthy Intimacy*

Dr. Magness has added yet another useful resource for those facing the rigors of daily recovery from sexual addiction. *Thirty Days to Hope & Freedom from Sexual Addiction* reflects the compassion, structure, and challenge many have benefited from in working with Dr. Magness. This book is for individuals looking for a comprehensive, practical, and daily focus during those early and often difficult days of recovery.

Therapists will find *Thirty Days to Hope & Freedom from Sexual Addiction* an extremely helpful complement to their work with sexual addicts. This resource will decrease the pressure of managing details of an addict's first days of recovery.

Marcus Earle, PhD
Co-author of *Sex Addiction: Case Studies and Management*

Thirty Days to
hope & freedom
from Sexual Addiction

*The Essential Guide to
Beginning Recovery and
Preventing Relapse*

Milton S. Magness, D.Min.

Thirty Days to
hope & freedom
from Sexual Addiction

The Essential Guide to Beginning Recovery and Preventing Relapse

Milton S. Magness, D.Min.

Gentle Path
PRESS

Carefee, Arizona

Gentle Path Press
P.O. Box 3172
Carefree, Arizona 85377
www.gentlepath.com
Copyright © 2011 by Gentle Path Press

First Edition: 2011

For more information regarding our publications, please contact Gentle Path Press at 1-800-708-1796 (toll-free U.S. only).

Book edited by Marianne Harkin
Book interior designed by Serena Castillo
Cover designed by Mikall Hill
Author photo by Giddings

ISBN: 978-0-9826505-5-4

For Those I Love
Who Are No Longer Here

C.R. "Pappy" Magness, my grandfather
Elizabeth "Beth" Magness, my mother
Marilyn Magness Brittain, my sister

Contents

Acknowledgments

I am grateful for the very significant help of my sister Bonnie Zinn, who through multiple readings has helped me refine the manuscript. She also has written me scores of notes throughout the manuscript trying to get me to remember the grammar lessons our English teacher mother taught us. Bonnie, being the better student, learned all the rules. But I, to my chagrin, was content with just learning to use proper grammar in speech.

Once again, I am thankful to my wife Kathie who has endured my absence during writing retreats. She also put up with my mental absence throughout the past many months during our visits to our home in Canada. I also appreciate her insights and guidance in preparing the manuscript.

Finally, I appreciate the great folks at Gentle Path Press. My thanks to Serena Castillo for another great book design. And my special thanks to Marianne Harkin who took a special interest in this project, gave up several weekends for editing the manuscript, and made all of the pieces come together.

Introduction

Sexual addiction is on course to destroy your life. It may start by destroying your self-esteem, your relationship, your job, or your health. The destructive power of sexual addiction will permeate everything that is dear to you.

This book is intended as a step-by-step guide to recovery from sexual addiction. This is not to say that this is the "right way" or the "only way" to recover from sexual addiction. Other sexual addiction therapists may provide a similar or different path. However, I have used these techniques with my clients for a number of years with great success. Everything you will read about has been tried and tested.

Whether the person who struggles with compulsive sexual behavior is you or is someone you love, the focus of this book is to lead readers to recognize that there *is hope* for sexual addiction. Using this book as a guide, you or your loved one will find hope and, ultimately, *freedom*.

You will notice that, contrary to the norm of speaking of compulsive sexual behavior as *sex addiction*, throughout this book, as well as the book that precedes this, I use the term s*exual addiction* to describe the compulsive sexual behavior that may typically lead to a path of destruction and ruin. The term *sexual addict* is a bit softer, lacking the edge of the term *sex addict*. This does not minimize the very negative impact of the behavior, but rather is to spare persons who are affected by this disorder the stigma that may be associated with identifying themselves as a *sex addict*.

My therapy clients routinely go through a check-in at the beginning of each session that begins with them giving their name and saying, "I am a precious child of God who struggles with compulsive sexual behavior." No term—either *sexual addict* or a *person who struggles with compulsive sexual behavior*—may adequately describe the plight of persons who find themselves repeatedly returning to behavior that they loath. Labels are not helpful. Descriptive terminology about behavior is. For this reason, I see my clients as persons of special value who happen to struggle with sexual addiction. Their addiction does not define them. Neither does it diminish their value as human beings.

Sexual addiction is not a benign disorder to be laughed at or ignored. For those who are not affected by sexual addiction, they may jokingly say that if they were to be saddled with any addiction, they would choose this one. But for persons suffering with sexual addiction, as well as those in a relationship with them, they know this addiction is an all-encompassing, life-altering condition that leaves a vast trail of destruction.

Most of the people I have worked with have a history of repeating demoralizing compulsive sexual behavior over a period of years. They make numerous valiant efforts to stop the behavior. Some have made promises to their spouse or partner. Others have made vows to God. Still others have gone to extraordinary lengths to remove themselves from things that they perceive as a threat to their sexual sobriety. Regrettably, some have even sought to harm themselves—with a few inflicting fatal harm on themselves—in order to stop behavior that is inconsistent with the person that they truly are.

Such efforts do not get to the root of the problem. And they do not provide a process for recovering from what they may consider to be reprehensible behavior. Instead, they represent more well-intentioned self-help efforts at stopping a true addiction, failing to recognize the hold that sexual addiction has on them.

Sexual addiction is often called a disease. And as a clinician, I treat clients using a medical model to address their sexual addiction. While calling sexual addiction a disease is technically correct, I personally never refer to it as such. Instead, I call it an addiction, a pathology, a disorder, or I use some other term to describe the condition short of calling it a disease. The reason for this is twofold. First, I believe that some sexual addicts gravitate to the word *disease* to relieve them of responsibility for their egregious behavior. It is almost like a "get-out-of-jail-free" card for them. For others, it is a way of escaping personal responsibility for behavior in which they chose to engage and have perpetuated through multiple ruined relationships, past several sexually transmitted diseases (STDs), and across destroyed careers. For this group of people who are looking for someone or something else to blame other than themselves, calling their predicament a disease eases their conscience, so they can evade responsibility for their actions.

The second reason I do not refer to sexual addiction as a disease is out of respect for the victims of sexual addicts. Victims fall into two categories: those with whom sexual addicts engaged in their compulsive sexual behavior and the partners of sexual addicts who have been traumatized by their behaviors.

This book is addressed directly to the sexual addict. If you are in love with someone who is a sexual addict, this book is still helpful for you because it tells you the path that your loved one can take to find hope and freedom. However, it is significant to note that you cannot take this journey for your partner or loved one. You can offer your encouragement, challenge them to get help for their addiction, motivate them to keep moving forward in recovery, and perhaps even threaten them with severe consequences if they do not continue recovery. But ultimately you cannot do their recovery for them. They have to choose which path they want to travel—continuing in their addiction or choosing recovery from it. And they must continue to make that choice daily.

The suggestions contained in this book are part of the journeys of many men and women who have fought their way out of the pit of sexual addiction. I believe the suggestions are sound, but I also realize that everyone is an individual and will respond better to some things than to others. The suggestions made here are not meant to be an all-encompassing list of activities, which if followed, will automatically result in recovery from sexual addiction. Rather, this book contains a step-by-step approach to sexual addiction recovery that establishes a path of new behavior. I am grateful to say that I have seen it work with many clients.

If you diligently follow the plan laid out in this book, you should be able to achieve freedom from all compulsive sexual behaviors. But the journey does not end at thirty days. In order to continue living in freedom, you have to be willing to make recovery a lifestyle. Every day for the rest of your life, you have to make a decision to live in recovery in order to achieve hope and freedom. When recovery becomes an integral part of your life, you will know you have made the changes necessary to support lifelong sexual sobriety. Following the suggestions in this book can prevent relapse.

Impossible? Actually, it is something that you *can* achieve. When recovery routines are taking place multiple times a day without conscious thought, you will know you have made recovery a part of your daily life. These routines do not end in a year, or ten years, or for that matter in fifty years.

The things suggested here are not easy, not a quick cure, and will not be followed by all who read them. But if you are serious about recovery, this is a primer that will get you started on the road to freedom. This will mark the beginning of recapturing integrity, self-esteem, hope, happiness, joy, peace, and new meaning in the most important relationships of your life.

I would like to say a word to those who have been in recovery for a while and have achieved a level of sobriety. Do not become complacent. When a person gets too relaxed about recovery, he or she is in a dangerous place. When he or she slacks off on meeting attendance, working the steps, being accountable, or reaching out to others with program calls, a slip or relapse is possible.

On Day 30, you will be introduced to the *iRecovery™—Addiction Recovery Tracker iPhone™ App*. I encourage you to go to the Apple Store and download the iRecovery app to take full advantage of this book.

All of the forms and worksheets in this book can be found at www.ThirtyDaysTheBook.com. There is no charge for using the forms on this site. They are "fillable" PDF files that you can complete on your computer and then print out for your own use. None of your information is stored. You are the only one who will see it or have access to it. The Recovery Tracker information can be found at www.RecoveryApp.com.

You may read this book all at once or read only a chapter a day. If you read straight through it, go back and re-read a chapter each day for the next month. The next thirty days is just the beginning of the recovery journey.

Hope begins now. Freedom awaits.

Day 1: Start the Journey

Geraldo's Story

Geraldo hurt his back in an automobile accident. He was prescribed physical therapy, which he continued for several months. His doctor suggested that he also start getting massages to work on the muscle spasms that he still had in his lower back. He was shocked when at the end of a massage he was asked if he wanted a "happy ending," that is, some sexual relief. At first he declined. However, at his next massage, he eagerly agreed and found that the person giving the massage would masturbate him at the conclusion. Before long, Geraldo got to be an expert at spotting massage parlors that would offer more than massage services. When he finally entered recovery for sexual addiction, he was going to massage parlors an average of three times every week.

If you don't have a goal in mind, how do you know when you get there? You may not know where your out-of-control addiction is headed, but you can take steps to see that your recovery follows a predictable path. Recovery leads to serenity, to hope, and ultimately to freedom.

If you Google the phrase "start your journey" or "starting the journey," you will find there are around one million websites that use that distinct language. Based on that alone, we can conclude that getting started on a journey is an activity of paramount importance.

Perhaps reading this book marks the beginning of your journey toward achieving lasting sexual sobriety. If that describes you, I hope you will affirm yourself for taking this courageous step. For some who are reading this book, your journey may have started some time ago. In fact, this book may be one of a number of recovery-related books that you have read. You may be reading this to glean additional information that will help you succeed in your recovery. However, I realize there are some who are reading this who have determined to make one last attempt to stop their compulsive sexual behavior.

Sure I've Got a Problem, But Am I a Sexual Addict?

Take this short screening test:

- Have you ever been involved in any sexual behavior that harmed you or someone else?
- Did you do it again?
- If you answered yes to both, you may have a problem.

So I like sex. Does that make me an addict? Not at all. In fact, it is possible for a person to have a very active sex life and not be a sexual addict.

What is the definition of sexual addiction? One of the simplest definitions of sexual addiction is the inability to manage or control one's sexual behavior. It has also been called hypersexual behavior or sexual compulsivity. Sexual addiction specialists typically look for signs of addiction which may include an escalation of behavior over time, continuing behavior in the face of loss or significant negative consequences, engaging in high-risk behavior, loss of time due to pursuing compulsive sexual behavior, and unsuccessful efforts to stop the behavior.

Are you a sexual addict? Do you really want to know the answer to that question? It is possible to take a brief screening exam online to see whether sexual addiction may be present. A screening exam developed by Dr. Patrick Carnes, the world's preeminent authority on sexual addiction, can be found at www.SexHelp.com.

Make a Commitment to Recovery

The attitude with which you approach recovery will be partially responsible for your success or lack thereof. What does it mean to make a commitment to recovery? First, it is not a promise to never act out again. Such declarations do not work. Likely, you have tried these before. How many times have you vowed never to repeat some behavior that you detest?

A commitment to recovery is not the same as making a promise that you will work recovery perfectly. Many of the sexual addicts I have worked with were raised to expect personal perfection. And a significant number of this group have achieved remarkable things in life and have truly made a difference in the world. However, all of us fall short of perfection. So if your standard has been to expect perfection from yourself, it is time to lay that unachievable goal aside and recognize that even in recovery, you will not be perfect. You will not always follow your recovery plan to the letter. There will be days when you simply do not measure up to the goals that you have set for your recovery.

That does not mean you can be assured of a slip or a relapse. Based on many people I have worked with, I know it is possible for a person to live the rest of his life without acting out again. You may find that you can live an imperfect life and do a less-than-perfect job of recovery but still live in sexual sobriety and enjoy the gifts that hope and freedom from sexual addiction bring.

Most people find their way into recovery because of a crisis caused by the addiction. Some have created a burden of debt that they can no longer handle and cannot hide from their spouse. Others are caught in an affair or having sex outside of their committed relationship. Some get caught looking at pornography on the Internet while at work and are threatened with the loss of their job—or perhaps they got fired for their addiction. Still others find their way into recovery after being arrested.

Can you relate to any of these situations? Were you involved in some behavior that threatened to upset your world? Did a crisis drive you into recovery or at least to reading this book?

What if you could change the circumstances? What if you could turn the clock back and keep your spouse or your boss from finding out? Perhaps a more plausible scenario would be to ask yourself what you would do if you could repair your marriage, save your job, or get out of the legal entanglements in which you find yourself. How would you feel about recovery then? Would you still be interested in finding relief from your sexual addiction?

Before buying into a belief that recovery is going to solve all of your problems, consider another scenario. Suppose you get into recovery and your spouse decides to divorce you. Or you get into recovery and find out that your employer no longer has any use for you. Still another possibility to consider is, what if you get into recovery and believe you are making good progress but your legal problems don't go away. In spite of all that you have done to bring about a change in your life, your career, your marriage, and perhaps everything you hold dear continues to come unraveled. What would you do?

Would you continue in recovery? Would you still be interested in getting free from your compulsive behavior if your marriage ended in divorce? Would you continue to seek freedom from your addiction if your job ended or if your freedom were taken away from you?

For many sexual addicts who finally come into recovery because of some great crisis in their lives, recovery does not reverse their circumstances. Sexual addiction has already exacted a price in terms of ending a relationship, a job, or freedom, or ruining one's health. That is the simple reality of the cost of sexual addiction.

The question comes down to one of personal motivation. For every recovering sexual addict, the moment of truth comes when they ask themselves, "If I knew recovery would not change the circumstances of my present situation, would I still be in recovery?" Another question to ask is, "If my spouse still leaves me, or if I get fired for my acting out, or if I go to jail for my acting out, do I still plan on staying in recovery?"

It is indeed a question of motivation. A person has a chance of finding relief from sexual addiction only when he can honestly say that regardless of what may happen concerning his present circumstances, he is going to stay in recovery. At that point he knows that he is in recovery not to save a job or a relationship, but rather to find hope and freedom.

But for a person to stay in recovery, they will require more motivation than keeping their job or their relationship. That kind of motivation echoes the words of my mother when I was a child. On occasion, she would tell me, "You're not sorry for what you did. You are sorry you got caught!" Bingo! In my child's mindset, the greatest motive I had for doing what I was told was to avoid the punishment that came from misbehaving.

If a sexual addict does not move beyond being motivated to stay in recovery to keep from getting in trouble with his or her boss or partner, little real progress will take place. And a lack of progress in recovery inevitably leads to the end of the job or relationship. If the only thing keeping a person in recovery is to appease others, recovery motivation disappears when the job or marriage goes away.

As hard as it seems, a sexual addict has to make a commitment to recovery that is not conditional on staying employed or keeping a relationship. Some people have found that even success in recovery could not mitigate the damage done to their relationships. But regardless of whether the relationship is saved and the job or career is salvaged, the addict will want to seek recovery and be committed to staying in recovery whatever the outcome of personal relationships.

Does that mean that a person's commitment to recovery must be stronger than his commitment to the relationship? That is exactly what it means! The road to recovery is the road to hope and freedom. When sexual addicts enter recovery, they are fighting for their very life because a continuation of compulsive sexual behavior leads to the destruction of everything that is important to them—and perhaps even life itself!

Are you willing to do whatever it takes, pay whatever it costs, sacrifice whatever you have to in order to restore your integrity and live in continuous sexual sobriety? There will be temptations to try to find short cuts and an easier path. In my opinion, recovery from sexual addiction will be the hardest thing you have ever done. I have listened to people who were also recovering crack cocaine addicts say that it was easier to kick the crack habit than it was to find continued sobriety from sexual addiction. I do not say this to discourage you but rather to help prepare you for your journey.

Before embarking on this road, you should know that to be successful in recovery means that you can never take a vacation from recovery. You will never get a day off or be able to coast without your addiction exacting a price. The penalty for slacking off is a slip or a full-scale relapse into the most degrading of your compulsive behaviors.

There will be times when you may want to take a holiday from recovery. You may even think that a period of sobriety should grant you some extra measure of protection and allow you to slack off for a few days. However, completing a day of sober living does not give any hedge against the struggles of tomorrow. Sobriety is not like a savings account where you invest in sobriety; then, in a weak moment you are able to draw on the account. Sobriety must be fought for every day, every hour, and, especially in the first months of recovery, every moment of the day.

All around us, the world is making jokes about infidelity, casual sex, sex with multiple partners, and sexual addiction. The evening television sitcoms use sex as a recurrent theme. Late night talk show hosts toss out one-liners about celebrities and their addictions. Most movies have at least some sexual theme running through them. Even the music you listen to may seem to be permeated with themes that one might suppose emanated from the mind of a sexual addict.

It may be that part of the cost of recovery for you will be that you cannot watch some (or a lot) of the television shows you used to watch. You may have to drastically alter your selection process for movies. And you may even find that there are certain kinds of music that are not healthy for you.

Music in particular is a powerful conduit to our minds. And who doesn't like music? Before entering recovery, a person may listen to music throughout the day without giving much thought to the lyrics, the beat, or the mood that the music elicits. But when a person begins recovery, he soon finds that he wants to have more careful control over his thoughts. The first indication of this may be the realization that you are continually reviewing a song in your mind that you heard several days before. As you consider the message to the song, you realize that it is a message that you associate with past acting-out behavior or may cause you to fantasize about acting out.

A commitment to recovery means a fundamental altering of your life. Priorities must change. Your interests, traffic patterns, time use, spending habits, attitudes—indeed every part of your life—must change. When you are ready to make a commitment to recovery, you can know that you have started moving toward the goal of being completely free from all compulsive sexual behaviors.

Decisions During the First Year

As you begin your recovery journey, you will likely see many things about your life that you want to change. There will certainly be behavioral changes. And you will be learning healthy boundaries and how to avoid things that have previously led you toward compulsive sexual behavior.

However, I strongly suggest that you do not to make *any* major decisions during the first year of recovery. Give yourself time to get into a normal recovery routine and restore some semblance of order to your life. For some, this is not a time of restoring order but of finding order for the first time as an adult.

Some significant changes may be unavoidable. For example, if you lost a job due to your acting out or even if you were simply laid off due to company downsizing, you will have to find a new job. However, decisions that are optional should be postponed for at least a year. These include but are not limited to making major purchases (including vehicles), moving to a new city, purchasing a home, changing jobs, starting a new romantic relationship, or getting a divorce.

You should build some extended time completely free from all acting-out behavior to allow your thinking to get clear. Your brain will begin to settle down from the neurochemical explosions that accompany sexual acting out. Only when you have been free from your addictive highs for several months can you reliably make good decisions. So postpone all major decisions. If your partner is pushing you for a divorce, do what you can to buy time. Besides, when you have been in recovery for several months and learn to put greater value on your relationship, your partner may find that you are the person he or she wants to be in relationship with after all.

My Commitment

While the recovery journey may seem overwhelming, do not lose heart. If you are diligent about recovery, freedom from all of your addictive behaviors is within reach. Many who follow this path find that they are able to live the rest of their lives without acting out.

My Commitment

I admit that I have made some poor choices in the past that have negatively impacted my life and the lives of those I love. I realize that today I may not be able to rely on my current thinking to make major decisions.

Today, _____ , I commit myself to postponing all major decisions for twelve months. I make this commitment believing that my focus during this next year will be on my recovery and not on coping with the aftermath of major change.

Signed _____

Day 2: Identify Your Enemy

What is your enemy? The short answer is: addiction. But there are multiple factors, multiple opponents that you will face. Some of these are subtle. Others are more easily recognized. But they are all enemies that must be acknowledged and dealt with if you are to find hope and freedom.

Sol's Story

Sol can clearly recall the first pornographic images he saw. When he was in grammar school, he would watch the scrambled cable channels that continuously showed adult movies. He would watch the "Picasso porn" for hours, hoping for a glimpse of some recognizable body part. Long hours of watching and waiting marked this compulsive behavior.

Through the years he has been involved in many similar voyeuristic behaviors where he would wait for an opportunity to glimpse an image that would fuel his addiction. Most recently, Sol has been spending hours each night in his darkened room watching neighbors' houses with binoculars, hoping for a glimpse of flesh. He finds it ironic that his current behavior is so similar to what he was doing when he was in the fifth grade.

Isolation

The first enemy (and these are in no particular order) is that of isolation. Even for persons who would describe themselves as extroverts, sexual addiction often drives them into extreme isolation. Even if their acting out is with other people, sexual addicts often live separated from others. Their time is spent in individual pursuits. They often withdraw from family and friends, choosing instead to spend their time engaging in addictive behavior.

Can you find examples of how you have isolated yourself from others? Think through how you have pulled away from those you love. Have you made excuses to miss various functions so you could act out? Do family members or friends complain that you are not as available as you have been in the past? Have you complained of non-existent health problems to get out of events that in the past you would have enjoyed?

Spend a few minutes with the list on page 12. See how many examples of isolation you can recall. Start with the most recent example you can remember. Continue to scrutinize your recent past until you have listed several examples. If necessary, go back a few months to find additional examples.

Isolation

I have been isolating myself in the following ways: _____

_____

_____

_____

_____

_____

_____

Dishonesty

The next enemy of recovery is dishonesty. Childhood habits of shading the truth are hard to break. Lying may have started as an effort to escape an abusive parent or harsh teacher. You may have used it to cover for a learning disability or to provide an alibi for an alcoholic parent.

Hiding your compulsive sexual behavior has led to sharpening your skills of prevarication. No longer are you using dishonesty to cover up for not understanding how to solve a problem in school or to escape punishment for some childhood infraction. It is likely that you have continued to lie to those you love and those you work with. Some of your deceit may be to cover your unhealthy sexual behavior. But you may find that you have been dishonest about things that are so irrelevant that they do not really matter to you or others.

The price of dishonesty is the loss of integrity. No one can take integrity from you. Integrity is something a person gives away. If you are not a person of integrity, there is only one person to blame—you!

Can you think of examples of how you have been dishonest in the recent past? Have there been times when you have told a lie automatically before you could even consider if you wanted to tell the truth? Can you think of instances where you told a lie one minute and wished you could take it back the next?

Spend a few minutes completing the list below. This is not a list for anyone else to see. If you are having problems thinking of occasions of dishonesty, perhaps it would be useful to probe deeper and ask if you are being honest with yourself.

Dishonesty

In the past month I have been dishonest in these ways: _____

_____

_____

_____

_____

_____

Secrecy

The next enemy is secrecy. Secrecy goes hand-in-hand with dishonesty. Most sexual addicts want to keep their behavior hidden and will go to extraordinary lengths to do so. Secrecy is not to be confused with privacy. You always have a right to privacy. Recovery does not mean that you have to be the latest person to "come out" on the Internet and admit that you are a sexual addict. You will, however, find that in recovery you can live your life in the open with trustworthy people.

Can you summon the courage to dig into your past and resurrect those secrets you have never told another person? Are there things that you have done that you have vowed never to divulge? There may be things that you have not only kept from others but that you have pushed from your own thoughts.

Spend a few moments remembering those things that no one else knows. What are the things that carry such shame that you wish you had never done them? What are the things you have done you hope no one ever finds out? Make a list of your secrets. If you fear someone will discover this list, use a few key words so that you know which event you are referencing but others will not.

Secrecy

I have the following secrets I have never told anyone: _____

_____

_____

_____

_____

_____

_____

Selfishness

The next enemy of recovery is selfishness. Selfishness is at the heart of sexual addiction. For sexual addicts who are not in recovery, the only thing that matters is what they want, what they like, and what makes them feel good. Partners of sexual addicts will often identify this selfishness as narcissism and may even conclude the sexual addict has narcissistic personality disorder. My experience has been that is seldom the case, but the fact remains that sexual addiction can cause a person to act in self-centered ways.

The extreme of selfishness is narcissism.[1] And sexual addiction certainly is narcissistic. What are examples of narcissism you can see in your life? The presence of narcissistic traits doesn't mean that you are a narcissist or that you have narcissistic personality disorder. Rather those examples indicate that you have much in common with other sexual addicts. Sexual addicts want what they want and care mostly about what makes them feel good, often without regard to how their behavior may impact others. They may like to set the agenda and be first to say which restaurant or movie they prefer. And they may be either blind to others' needs and wants, or dismiss them as being secondary to their own needs and wants.

Can you find examples of when you have been selfish during the last few months? If you have trouble with this list, ask someone you are close to for some insight.

---

1. More on narcissism is found in Day 13.

Thirty Days to Hope & Freedom for Sexual Addicts

Selfishness

Examples of my selfishness: _____

_____

_____

_____

_____

_____

_____

Denial

Another enemy of recovery is denial. Are you really a sexual addict? Some people are immediately repulsed by the idea that the term may describe them. Breaking through denial is not an easy process and may take years to complete. Your partner, other family members, or close friends may have mentioned things about your behavior that was troubling, but you ultimately dismissed their comments because you did not believe that you had a problem. I hope you have already begun to recognize your struggle with denial and are ready to break through that layer of self-deception and face your sexual addiction.

Felicia's Story

When Felicia went for her annual gynecological exam, she was horrified to find that she had contracted an STD. Her doctor calmly explained to her that the only way she could have received the infection was through sexual contact with someone who was also infected. The physician explained that both she and her husband should be treated.

At the conclusion of the exam the physician's nurse gave her a supportive hug, knowing that Felicia would want to confront her husband for his infidelity. However, Felicia did not have the heart to tell the nurse that what was going to make the confrontation so difficult was that she was the one who had engaged in high-risk sexual behavior with multiple sex partners. Unfortunately, it took Felicia two more years to admit to herself that her problem was not "bad morals" but sexual addiction. When she finally

entered recovery, she felt as if she had come home for she found many other men and women who were
basically good people but who struggled with compulsive sexual behavior.

Sometimes denial is subtle. It is common in Twelve Step meetings to hear people say, "My addict wanted to…" or "My addict made me…." While this may communicate well in recovery meetings to other addicts, using the phrase "my addict" may be used by some to avoid taking personal responsibility. Your spouse may hear this as a total shifting of blame.

Can you think of examples of how you may have been denying that you have a problem? Take a few minutes and record examples of denial that you have observed in your life.

Denial

My denial list: _____

_____

_____

_____

_____

_____

_____

Resistance

The twin of denial is resistance. Even when a person breaks through denial he is not ready to get help until he can break through the wall of resistance. Getting help means that many things in life must change. Entering recovery requires a change in priorities, a reordering of your schedule, altering your traffic patterns, and perhaps spending money for therapy or longer treatment. Recovery will mean giving up dysfunctional coping mechanisms for dealing with stress. It will not only mean a change in your behavior but a change in your thought patterns.

Thirty Days to Hope & Freedom for Sexual Addicts

Adrian's Story

Drug use ruined Adrian's marriage. That was a wakeup call for him. He quit his drug use on his own and was proud that he did so without help from others. Adrian said he just realized he wanted to stop using and figured he did not have to go to meetings like people he considered weaker. After his divorce Adrian started dating women he met on Internet dating sites. He found single life on the Internet surprising because there were lots of willing partners.

Adrian's sexual addiction was soon in full swing. He realized things were really out-of-control when he found he was not capable of being monogamous in any relationship. What happened with Adrian? Rather than get into recovery because of his drug use, he traded his drug addiction for sexual addiction.

Adrian did not like thinking of himself as a sexual addict. He fought the idea that he should work a program of recovery for all of his addictions. Finally he surrendered and began inpatient treatment. He said he could no longer deny the addiction that was ruining his life.

What are the evidences of resistance that you see in your life?

Resistance

Examples of my resistance to recovery: _____

_____

_____

_____

_____

_____

_____

Procrastination

A final enemy of recovery is procrastination. How often have you decided that you will start a diet tomorrow? Or clean a cluttered garage or closet? Recovery cannot wait until tomorrow. It must begin today. Now is the time. If you have identified yourself as a sexual addict, what is keeping you from entering recovery today?

Procrastination

What are the things that are more important than my starting recovery now? _____

_____

_____

_____

_____

_____

Hopefully there are not many things that you believe are more critical than your entering recovery today. You may have a demanding job, but is your job truly more important than recovery? Sadly, I often encounter someone who has just entered recovery after losing his job due to acting-out behavior. In every case, those men and women wished they had realized earlier that recovery had to receive greater priority than their jobs.

Perhaps you are concerned that your relationship with your spouse or partner is more essential than your recovery. But if you continue acting out, will your relationship survive? Some people may think that entering recovery is too expensive. While it is true that therapy and other longer-term treatment alternatives can be costly, you do not have to spend a great deal of money to begin recovery.

Things that May Change in Recovery

There are numerous things that may change in recovery. Some of these changes will be intentional. Others will be a natural outgrowth of participating in healthy recovery activities.

In recovery you will see a change in your spending habits. Rather than spending money on pornography or sex partners, you may find yourself spending money on recovery-related things. That may mean spending money on therapy, psychiatric care, workshops, and seminars. Since you are reading this book, you have started to spend money on recovery-related reading materials. Whatever the cost, you must be willing to spend what it takes to get the help to succeed in recovery.

But not every person who enters recovery goes into therapy or treatment. If you have the opportunity and resources to utilize the help of mental health professionals who have expertise in treating sexual addiction, your recovery may progress more rapidly. However, many who struggle with compulsive sexual behavior never get into therapy. Instead, they increase the number of Twelve Step meetings that they attend and read everything they can find about sexual addiction.

The way you use your time will change. If you are used to spending uncounted hours in front of a television, you will instead turn off the television so that you can attend Twelve Step meetings. Hours in front of a computer scanning for provocative images will give way to hours of research about sexual addiction and ways to stop the destructive behavior. The level of commitment demanded by recovery will begin to hit home when you realize that you may have to give up participation in a favorite activity or regular evening commitment.

As recovery progresses, you may notice a change in your traffic patterns. You may intentionally avoid certain parts of town that were favorite acting-out haunts. The route you typically would walk in your office building may be altered if it means avoiding someone that you have casually flirted with in the past.

You may find your attitude and outlook on life changing. For some people this means putting an end to feelings of superiority. For others, it means leaving behind negative thoughts of being inferior to others. Anger and resentments are often moderated. Pessimism is blunted as a more positive outlook on life emerges. Negative self-talk is replaced with positive messages. Self-loathing is replaced with feelings of love for self and gratitude for the progress made in recovery.

In addiction, you may have spent a significant amount of energy trying to control other people, their thoughts and feelings about you, or the outcome of certain situations. In recovery you will find you no longer find it necessary to control others but can allow other people to conduct their own lives without interference from you.

Expectations

What are you expecting of your recovery? Are you expecting your recovery to be marked by slips and relapses? You will find people who have attended Twelve Step groups for years and have never had more than a few weeks or months of sobriety, followed by a slip or two and then a full-blown relapse. Since you will likely hear this from many people, you may tend to think this is normal.

This does not have to be the norm! True, many people do slip as they get started in recovery. A slip or even a relapse does not doom a person to never being able to live a life of sober serenity. But slips and relapses do not have to mark your recovery. If you expect you are going to slip, you will probably meet your expectation. (We will look at the subject of slips and relapse more on Day 26.)

Psychotherapists refer to this phenomenon as a self-fulfilling prophecy. Often this is discussed in connection with raising children. Parents are cautioned not to place an expectation of failure in front of their children. A child who is told, "You are so stupid," or "You can't do anything right," will live down to that expectation. On the other hand, when a child is told, "I'm proud of you because you always do your best in school," or "I can always count on you to make the best decision," they live up to their parent's hopes.

What are your expectations of your recovery? Do you expect to work hard, perhaps struggle, but ultimately succeed in your recovery? Or do you expect that you will be sober for a few weeks and then fall back into the same self-defeating behaviors that you have followed through your years of addiction? Will you live up to or live down to your expectations? One choice. Two roads. Which will you take?

As Robert Frost said in his poem, *The Road Not Taken*, "Two roads diverged in a wood, and I—I took the one less traveled by, And that has made all the difference."[2]

Will you make a commitment that you are going to begin recovery today? Are you prepared to pursue recovery with your best efforts? If you are ready to make your commitment to recovery, sign your name below as evidence of your decision.

My Commitment

Today _____, I commit myself to diligently continue the journey of recovery from sexual addiction. Further, I commit myself to continuing the journey in pursuit of both hope and freedom.

Signed _____

---

2. (Frost, 1920)

Thirty Days to Hope & Freedom for Sexual Addicts

Day 3: Twelve Step Meetings—
Isn't There a Better Way?

Eddie's Story

"'Hello, my name is Eddie. I'm a sex addict.' What a startling statement! How did this happen? How could someone with so many things going for himself become a sex addict? When I first heard myself say those words, I didn't feel like it was the end of the world. For me, those words brought hope. I felt like I was finally going to be all right. For years, I knew there was something different about me. I was sure I was the only person who fought with thoughts of things that were inappropriate.

"Even though I felt hope from the beginning, I also had a great deal of fear. I wasn't sure I was headed in the right direction. I didn't like the idea of meeting with other sex addicts. To hide my identity, I wore a ball cap and dark glasses. In order to build enough courage to go to that first meeting, I fortified myself with the false courage of a double shot of booze.

"I was one of about sixty men in that room. My worst fears were realized when I looked around the room realizing that the rest of those in attendance were probably perverts! I thought I could tell by looking. 'They're not like me. I'm in the wrong place,' I told myself. In spite of that concern, I continued attending meetings because I made a commitment to my wife to go each week. What had I gotten myself into?

"I told my wife about how I was sure the room was filled with perverts and surprisingly, she was sympathetic and told me I probably shouldn't go to the meetings. That startled me. If I didn't go to the meetings—even though I thought they were not right for me—where would I go for help?

"I continued going week after week. And I didn't need any liquid courage. I dropped the dark glasses after the first meeting and the ball cap after the third or fourth meeting. Then something happened that shocked me. One evening as I looked around that room filled with men that a few weeks ago I had labeled as being perverts and 'not like me,' I realized they were just like me! Our backgrounds were different. Our acting-out behaviors may have been similar or different, but I realized that I had something in common with every person in that room—we desperately wanted to stop all of our acting-out behaviors forever!"

What Happens in Twelve Step Meetings?

Meetings similar to the one that Eddie attended take place in cities around the world. Most meetings are significantly smaller than the meeting he attended. Some of the meetings are open for both male and female sexual addicts. Some, like Eddie's meeting, are strictly for men and others are strictly for women.

There are some similarities in Twelve Step meetings regardless of the fellowship to which they belong. All Twelve Step meetings follow the model first set forth by Alcoholics Anonymous in 1935.[3] Basically they are peer-led meetings rather than professionally facilitated therapy groups. Membership is voluntary and limited to persons who acknowledge they struggle with compulsive sexual behavior.

Cameron's Story

Cameron watched people getting sobriety "chips" in a Twelve Step meeting. After the meeting he openly voiced his belief that the idea was "dumb." He saw some people getting a "desire chip" (indicating a desire to remain sober). They were just entering recovery or had just experienced a slip or relapse.

Cameron knew he was not going to pick up a chip. By the time he had achieved sixty days of sobriety, he realized he had been sober for the longest period in his adult life. Still he could not bring himself to pick up a plastic poker chip that was embossed with some nice platitude. But when he achieved ninety days of sobriety, he surprised himself by holding up his hand to indicate his sobriety milestone. Applause that he previously thought was half-hearted now seemed heart-felt when he picked up his chip. What surprised him the most was his thought later that the piece of plastic in his pocket meant more to him than if it had been a gold Krugerrand.

Chips do not convey status but only acknowledge sobriety milestones. Rather than giving honor to the recipient, chips convey hope to the rest of the group. Sobriety is possible. The chips that are awarded mark sobriety milestones.

Members go by first names only and take a pledge not to talk about what happens in meetings with anyone outside of the meetings. Most meetings do not allow feedback, typically called "cross talk," but let each person's sharing stand on its own. Meeting lengths vary but are usually an hour to an hour and a half.

How meetings are conducted varies based on local or regional differences and from fellowship to fellowship. In some meetings, all persons introduce themselves (using their first name) at the beginning of the meeting. In other meetings, only the person who chooses to share something during the meeting introduces himself.

Most meetings begin with a reading that may involve one or more persons. These readings may include the "Twelve Steps of Recovery," a section from the Big Book of AA called "The Promises,"[4] and some information about that particular fellowship.

Some meetings are topic meetings in which the person who has previously volunteered to chair the meeting suggests a topic for the sharing time. Other meetings are open topic meetings where members may share on any subject. Still other meetings may focus on a daily reading, meditation, or selection from the textbook of that fellowship.

A good practice is to attend several meetings before you decide to share during a meeting. The reason for this is so that you can get a feel for how the meetings are run, can get an under-

---

3. (History of Alcoholics Anonymous)
4. (Alcoholics Anonymous, Fourth Edition) p. 83-84

standing of what is appropriate and inappropriate to share, and also to be respectful of the traditions that may already be in place.

During some meetings, a telephone list is passed so that attendees have an opportunity to write their name and phone number. Some have a place on the list to indicate whether a person is looking for a sponsor or if he or she is willing to be a sponsor. Participation in the phone list is voluntary. Sometimes this list is passed a second time so that members have the opportunity to take down names and phone numbers of people they can call in support of their recovery.

Many meetings have a literature table with information about that particular fellowship and other literature that is helpful in recovery. Some literature tables also have a small selection of recovery books for purchase.

Initially, some people find the atmosphere of a Twelve Step meeting a bit unsettling. They may want to respond to what someone else says and feel stifled that they cannot. Or they may be frustrated when someone shares something that does not seem to support good recovery. But after a few meetings people usually settle into the routine of the meetings and find comfort and reassurance in having a place to share thoughts and feelings and know they are not being judged or censured. And when something is shared that seems really off base, they are able to adopt the wisdom of the meetings that says, "Take what you like and leave the rest."

The purpose of the meetings is for those present to share "their experience, strength, and hope" with others. Some of the time it is sobering just to hear the struggle others may have had as they share their experiences. At other times they gain strength from words shared by someone who has resisted the lure of the addiction that week. And at other times they gain hope when someone receives a sobriety chip marking a period of time that is free from all acting-out behaviors.

The Major "S Type" (Sexual-Addiction Related) Twelve Step Fellowships

The following list gives a bit of background on the various "S type" Twelve Step fellowships. This is a list only of the major fellowships—that is, fellowships that have many meetings in numerous cities in different locales. By checking the websites of the various Twelve Step groups you can find the meetings that are available nearest to where you live or work. The descriptions that follow are how each fellowship describes itself.

Sex Addicts Anonymous (SAA): "Sex Addicts Anonymous is a Twelve Step recovery program. Our primary goal is to stop our addictive sexual behavior and to help others recover from their sexual addiction. Our members define their own boundaries with the guidance of their Higher Power, sponsors and other group members. We encourage our members to discover and explore what healthy sexuality means to them. Membership is open to all who share a desire to stop addictive sexual behavior. There is no other requirement. SAA is supported through voluntary contributions from members. We are not affiliated with any other Twelve Step programs, nor are we a part of any other organization. We do not support, endorse, or oppose outside causes or issues."

www.saa-recovery.org
International Service Organization of SAA: ISO of SAA
P.O. Box 70949, Houston, TX 77270
713-869-4902

Sexaholics Anonymous (SA): "Sexaholics Anonymous is a fellowship of men and women who share their experience, strength, and hope with each other that they may solve their common problem and help others to recover. Our primary purpose is to stay sexually sober and help others to achieve sexual sobriety. In defining sobriety, we do not speak for those outside Sexaholics Anonymous. We can only speak for ourselves. Thus, for the married sexaholic, sexual sobriety means having no form of sex with self or with persons other than the spouse. For the unmarried sexaholic, sexual sobriety means freedom from sex of any kind. And for all of us, single and married alike, sexual sobriety includes progressive victory over lust."

www.sa.org
International Central Office
P.O. Box 3565, Brentwood, TN 37024
866-424-8777

Sex and Love Addicts Anonymous (SLAA): "Sex and Love Addicts Anonymous is a Twelve Step—Twelve Tradition oriented fellowship based on the model pioneered by Alcoholics Anonymous. One of the resources we draw on is our willingness to stop acting out in our own personal bottom line addictive behavior on a daily basis. In addition, members reach out to others in the fellowship, practice the Twelve Steps and Twelve Traditions of S.L.A.A. and seek a relationship with a Higher Power to counter the destructive consequences of one or more addictive behaviors related to sexual addiction, love addiction, dependency on romantic attachments, emotional dependency, and sexual, social and emotional anorexia. We find a common denominator in our obsessive, compulsive patterns which renders any personal differences of sexual or gender orientation irrelevant."

www.slaafws.org
Fellowship-Wide Services
1550 NE Loop 410, Suite 118, San Antonio, TX 78209
210-828-7900

Sexual Compulsives Anonymous (SCA): "SCA is a twelve-step fellowship, inclusive of all sexual orientations, open to anyone with a desire to recover from sexual compulsion. We are not group therapy, but a spiritual program that provides a safe environment for working on problems of sexual addiction and sexual sobriety. We believe we are not meant to repress our God-given sexuality, but to learn how to express it in ways that will not make unreasonable demands on our time and energy, place us in legal jeopardy, or endanger our mental, physical or spiritual health. Members are encouraged to develop a sexual recovery plan, defining sexual sobriety for themselves. There are no requirements for admission to our meetings: anyone having difficulties with sexual compulsion is welcome."

www.sca-recovery.org
Sexual Compulsives Anonymous
P.O. Box 1585, Old Chelsea Station, New York, NY 10011
800-977-4325

Sexual Recovery Anonymous (SRA): "Sexual Recovery Anonymous (SRA) is a 12-step fellowship. The only requirement for membership is a desire to stop compulsive sexual behavior. Our primary purpose is to stay sexually sober and help others achieve sobriety. Sobriety is the release from all compulsive and destructive sexual behaviors. We have found through our experience that sobriety includes freedom from masturbation and from sex outside a mutually committed relationship. We believe that spirituality and self-love are antidotes to the addiction."

www.sexualrecovery.org
Sexual Recovery Anonymous
P.O. Box 1296, Redondo Beach, CA, 90278

Recovery Groups Affiliated with Religious Organizations

Celebrate Recovery (CR): "Celebrate Recovery is a Christ-centered recovery program designed to help those struggling with hurts, habits, and hang-ups. It's a safe place for individuals to overcome addictive behaviors and experience the loving power of Jesus Christ. Celebrate Recovery offers a new and fresh Road to Recovery. No matter what a person needs freedom from, the steps to recovery are the same. By applying twelve biblical steps, with the support of other believers, participants are empowered to let go of the past and reach for a bright future."

www.celebraterecovery.com

Guard Your Eyes: "With the advance of technology and the ease of availability and privacy that the Internet provides, it has become a daily struggle for many religious Jews to remain Erlich (morally and ethically upright) even in their own homes. Jewish Leaders, Rabbis and Experts worldwide, are beginning to speak out about this serious problem more and more. The GuardUrEyes.com web site and forum are a revolution in the Orthodox community today. For the first time ever, a Jew seeking to better himself in the areas that he always felt he can't talk about with anyone else, finally has somewhere to turn! This website puts all the 'taboo' subjects on the table, and offers a whole system of help, group support and recovery."

www.guardureyes.com
Twelve Step meetings are telephone-based

Provident Living: "If you or someone you love struggles with addiction, there is hope. Addiction recovery groups sponsored by LDS Family Services are available to help you and your loved ones overcome addictive behavior and more fully enjoy the blessings of Church participation. Even if you can't attend one of these meetings, you may benefit from the program study guide. In the guide, the Twelve Steps of Alcoholics Anonymous have been adapted into a framework of the doctrines, principles, and beliefs of The Church of Jesus Christ of Latter-day Saints."

www.providentliving.org

Twelve Step Fellowships for Partners

CoSA: CoSA originally stood for "codependents of sex addicts." The organization now simply uses the name CoSA. "CoSA is a recovery program for men and women whose lives have been affected by compulsive sexual behavior. In CoSA, we find hope whether or not there is a sexually addicted person currently in our lives. With the humble act of reaching out, we begin the process of recovery."

www.cosa-recovery.org
CoSA National Service Organization (or CoSA NSO)
P.O. Box 14537, Minneapolis, MN 55414
763-537-6904

COSLAA: "COSLAA is a Twelve Step support group for the recovery of family, friends, and significant others whose lives have been affected by their relationship with someone addicted to sex and love. The only requirement for membership is a desire to stop living out a pattern of codependency to someone who is sexually addicted. We believe that sex and love addiction is a family illness. By looking at our own attitudes and behaviors, we can find a new way of life that will allow us to be happier. "

> www.coslaa.org
> 860-456-0032

Co-Dependents Anonymous (CoDA): "Co-Dependents Anonymous is a fellowship of men and women whose common purpose is to develop healthy relationships. The only requirement for membership is a desire for healthy and loving relationships. We gather together to support and share with each other in a journey of self-discovery — learning to love the self. Living the program allows each of us to become increasingly honest with ourselves about our personal histories and our own codependent behaviors."

> www.codependents.org
> CoDA, Fellowship Services Office
> P. O. Box 33577, Phoenix, AZ 85067-3577
> Phone 602-277-7991 (answering service only)

S-Anon: "S-Anon is a program of recovery for those who have been affected by someone else's sexual behavior. S-Anon is based on the Twelve Steps and the Twelve Traditions of Alcoholics Anonymous."

> www.sanon.org
> S-Anon
> P.O. Box 111242, Nashville, TN 37222-1242
> 800-210-8141

Al-Anon: "Al-Anon (which includes Alateen for younger members) offers strength and hope for friends and families of problem drinkers. It is estimated that each alcoholic affects the lives of at least four other people... alcoholism is truly a family disease. No matter what relationship you have with an alcoholic, whether they are still drinking or not, all who have been affected by someone else's drinking can find solutions that lead to serenity in the Al-Anon/Alateen fellowship." (Partners of sexual addicts who do not have CoSA, CODA, or S-Anon meetings in their area can find a significant amount of support by participating in Al-Anon.)

> www.al-anon.alateen.org
> Al-Anon Family Group Headquarters, Inc.
> 1600 Corporate Landing Parkway, Virginia Beach, VA 23454-5617
> 757-563-1600

Al-Anon Family Group Headquarters (Canada) Inc.
Capital Corporate Centre
9 Antares Drive, Suite 245, Ottawa, ON K2E 7V5
613-723-8484

Twelve Step Groups for Couples

Recovering Couples Anonymous (RCA): "RCA is a twelve-step fellowship founded in the Autumn of 1988. There are groups throughout the United States, as well as worldwide. Although there is no organizational affiliation with Alcoholics Anonymous, The Twelve Steps, 12 Traditions and Principles are adapted from A.A. The primary purpose of RCA is to help couples find freedom from dysfunctional patterns in relationships. By using the tools of the program, we take individual responsibility for the well-being of the relationship, build new joy, and find intimacy with each other. We are couples committed to restoring healthy communication, caring and greater intimacy to our relationships. We suffer from many addictions and co-addictions; some identified and some not, some treated and some not. We also come from different levels of brokenness. Many of us have been separated or near divorce. Some of us are new in our relationships and seek to build intimacy as we grow together as couples."

www.recovering-couples.org
RCA World Service Organization
P.O. Box 11029, Oakland, CA 94611
(510) 663-2312

In some cities there are couples meetings that are joint meetings of SAA and CoSA as well as SLAA and S-Anon. In many of these, they require that both partners be present in order to attend. Additionally, Celebrate Recovery provides an opportunity for the couple to participate in recovery together for half of the meeting time with gender-specific small groups comprising the rest of the meeting.

Virtual Meetings

Many of the fellowships listed above have telephone and e-mail-based meetings. These are especially useful for persons who live in areas where meetings are not available. Also persons who are easily recognized such as celebrities and professional athletes find they are able to have anonymity that they cannot have in face-to-face meetings. Electronic meetings are also helpful for persons who may have to travel a lot and those whose schedules are more restrictive.[5]

---

5. www.SAATalk.org gives a listing of all SAA electronic meetings

Thirty Days to Hope & Freedom for Sexual Addicts

Begin Attending Twelve Step Meetings

Just making contact with a Twelve Step fellowship is not enough. As hard as it was to make that call and find an "S" group meeting to attend, actually going to your first meeting will likely be more difficult. The hardest step may be stepping through the door of a recovery group for your first meeting. *What will the other members look like? Will it be obvious from looking at those in attendance that the room is filled with sexual addicts? I'm not sure I want to be in a room filled with perverts of all descriptions, sexual deviants and sex offenders."*

While there are many sexual addicts who have been arrested for a sexual offence, the terms *sexual addict* and *sexual offender* are not synonymous. In fact, many sexual offenders do not meet the clinical criteria for sexual addiction. Conversely, most sexual addicts are not sexual offenders. The distinction between the two is significant but is usually lost on the general public.

Requirements for joining Twelve Step groups vary, with most requiring that the member have a desire to stop all compulsive sexual behavior. Members go by first names only. Sharing is voluntary, usually around either an assigned topic or in response to something read by the leader at the beginning of the meeting. When someone shares, they begin by stating their name and identifying themselves to the rest of the group as having an addiction. New members are not required to identify themselves as an addict but are allowed to simply give their name and say, "I'm new," or "This is my first meeting."

From the start it is vital to make a commitment to go to meetings regularly. Even if you do not think you fit into that meeting, it is crucial that you go back. I suggest to my clients that they attend the same meeting at least five times before making a decision on whether that is the meeting for them.

How many meetings should you attend each week? The answer depends on your commitment to recovery as well as the other commitments that you have in life. From the time Alcoholics Anonymous started in the 1930s, its members would routinely encourage new members to complete a 90/90, that is, to attend ninety meetings in ninety days. At the time there was no basis for suggesting a 90/90 other than the evidence that it worked well in helping a newcomer firmly establish sobriety and learn a great deal about recovery. Do not think in terms of how few you can get by with but rather how many your schedule will accommodate.

Today there is some evidence that it takes the repetition of doing something ninety days in a row in order to create new neuropathways or to firmly establish new behaviors. Although completing a 90/90 sounded like it made good sense through the years, today we are finding out that there is good reason to consider making a meeting every day for the first three months of your recovery.

If a 90/90 sounds too ambitious to you, commit to attending a meeting every day for a month. At the end of the month reevaluate and see whether that meeting regimen has been beneficial to your recovery. If it has, commit to another month and then consider another month of meetings after that.

You may be wondering, *What is the least number of meetings I can attend each week and still be in good recovery?* If that is your question, I caution you about approaching recovery with the mindset of doing only the minimum. Approach recovery with an understanding that you are affected with something that is threatening your relationships and your life. A better question to ask yourself is, "What is the most aggressive approach that I can take to recovery?"

Let's assume you are willing to do whatever it takes to do good recovery. And you are trying to carve out enough time to make sure you stay on track with your recovery. How many meetings should you make each week to help ensure that you stay in a healthy place? I encourage my clients to make a minimum of two meetings a week. If you can make more than that, the additional meetings will serve to enhance recovery.

It is common for newcomers to "S" meetings to focus on listening for differences in behaviors. They are looking for evidence that they are in the wrong place. As they listen to other people share, they form opinions about them and evaluate themselves against that person's acting out. If they judge others' acting out to be worse than their own, they may falsely conclude by the comparison that they are not a sexual addict.

By focusing on differences, you think you may hope to discover that you do not belong at the meeting. Perhaps you are not really addicted to sex. But after a few weeks, the new member will recognize many of his own behaviors in the sharing of others. It becomes easy to listen for indications of similar struggles. You realize you have more in common with other members of the group than you have differences. Sure, their acting-out behavior may be different from what you have experienced, but the bottom line is that all members have come to recognize that life had become out-of-control and unmanageable. That common denominator bridges all of the differences that previously separated you from other group members.

One of the greatest gifts of "S" group meetings is finding out that you are not the only person who thinks like you, acts like you, and struggles like you. In spite of what you have told yourself all of your life, you are not alone. You are not unique. There are others who are struggling just as you have struggled.

Attend your first meeting today! With a few minutes of research on the Internet you can compile a list of meetings that are available in your area. Also list all of the electronic meetings. If you cannot attend face-to-face, commit to attending online or by phone. This will be especially helpful when you are traveling. I am frequently asked by clients if there is a better way to support their recovery than in attending Twelve Step meetings. While I am open to the possibility that there may be a better way, I do not know of one. Certainly I have heard about, read about, and even visited with "experts" that propose another path to recovery. But I come back to the fact that Twelve Step meetings work, and they have worked for tens of thousands of people since the 1930s.

Share at a Meeting

"Hello, my name is _____, and I'm a sex addict (or sex-and-love addict or a sexaholic)!" That may be the first that you share. In most meetings you will not be asked to identify yourself as being addicted or having a compulsion about sex, love, or relationships until you have attended a few times and know you belong there. Many meetings give members a strict time limit for sharing. Most meetings have members share using the same format that was used when they first introduced themselves at the beginning of the meeting. Some meetings ask that the member end his sharing in the same way as he began: "My name is _____, and I am a sex addict."

Some groups will observe other guidelines around their sharing. In some groups, profanity is not allowed. In other groups, members are requested to do their sharing in such a way that they are not so graphic as to potentially trigger other members. In other groups, a person shares only when called on by the meeting leader or moderator.

One of the skills that may not have been well developed for many sexual addicts is that of listening. Learn to listen. You may be good at telling others what you are thinking or feeling. You may be practiced at making requests for what you think you want, but it is imperative in recovery that you learn to listen to others. This is especially true in meetings. There is a significant amount of material shared during a typical meeting that the new member can use to help stay sober until attending the next meeting. But this information is lost unless the new member learns to listen with new ears—ears tuned to get the nuggets of truth that will make the difference in living another day in victory or living in the defeat of addiction.

One person told me, "Talking for the first time in a Twelve Step group is like bungee jumping. I had to constantly tell myself, 'Do it, do it, do it, do it.' Then before I knew it, I had broken through my silence. I shared for the first time in a meeting—and I didn't die as a result!"

Sexual addiction is selfish. When a sexual addict attends meetings, he may be more focused on what he wants than what is beneficial for the group. There is value in first listening to what others are saying and drawing strength from them. Then it is time to share. When you do share, share from your heart.

Don't Lose Sight of Hope

Since you have made it this far in the book, you are obviously not the kind of person who is inclined to quit something easily. Recovery from sexual addiction is perhaps the most difficult thing you will ever address during your lifetime. However, it is important that you do not lose sight of your objective of living completely free from all compulsive sexual behavior and of the fact that many men and women who have followed the difficult path of recovery have ultimately found freedom from their destructive behaviors. Freedom can be yours if you persevere.

Day 4: Get Educated

How much do you know about sexual addiction? If you have just gotten acquainted with the term, you probably have many questions and a lot of misinformation. Your understanding of sexual addiction may be limited to news stories of high profile persons who have revealed that they are sexual addicts. The place to begin your journey is to consider what it means to be in recovery.

Eli and Paige's Story

Eli and Paige have a game that they play though neither will admit to it. Eli uses the home computer to access porn. He knows Paige suspects what he is doing, so he does his best to hide his tracks using various software programs to erase evidence of his porn use and to wipe the hard drive clean. However, he did not realize Paige installed several software programs that are supposed to monitor all of her husband's activity on the Internet. Eli freely admits that he is hooked on his cybersex behavior. Paige reluctantly admits that her efforts to control her husband's acting out have taken over her life.

What Does It Mean to Be in Recovery from Sexual Addiction?

Being in recovery does not mean that one has conquered sexual addiction. Following the model of recovery pioneered by Alcoholics Anonymous, most people in recovery from sexual addiction believe they will never be "recovered," that is, they do not believe they will ever be at the point where they can say that they have finally bested the problem that once threatened their marriage, their job, their friendships, and even their very lives.

Instead, a person on this journey continues in a condition of "recovering" throughout his life. This does not mean that a person will always struggle with whether or not to act out on a given day. Indeed a person who has been successful in recovery will not grapple with whether to stay in recovery or revert to previous shame-filled behavior. A recovering sexual addict has a healthy respect for the addiction and does not become complacent. Recovering sexual addicts know they must remain vigilant throughout life if they are to remain in recovery.

What word you use to describe your road to health may not be that critical in the grand scheme of things, but it may be an indicator of your attitude toward recovery, as well as a predictor of future sobriety. To be "recovered" indicates one has reached the goal of having conquered impulses, memories, and thoughts. It indicates that a person believes he is cured and beyond falling back into compulsive sexual behavior.

Such thoughts are dangerous for a sexual addict. Most sexual addicts believe they will never be at the point where they can see themselves as cured and not having to work a program of recovery. For those who believe they can arrive at such a destination (or believe they have already arrived), I wish them my best, but I fear for their future.

Recovery from sexual addiction begins as does any other journey—with the first step. For many that first step is realizing that something is very wrong in their lives. There comes a realization that life is not normal. It is not normal to be controlled by sex. It is not normal to masturbate to the point of injury. There is nothing normal about buying pornography or viewing pornography on the Internet and then going to extraordinary means to keep anyone from finding out about that activity.

For the person who has told himself enough lies to last a lifetime—"I just like sex more than other people" or "I just need sex more than the average person"—there comes a moment of clarity when reality sets in. Normal people do not live like this!

A fortunate few sexual addicts take another step when they have that moment of clarity. They look for help. Regrettably, not all who work in the helping professions recognize the telltale signs of sexual addiction. More than a few well-meaning pastors, physicians, psychologists, and counselors are not aware of the reality of sexual addiction.

For the uninformed pastor, a person suffering from sexual addiction "just needs to get right with God." Physicians who are not knowledgeable about sexual addiction may focus attention on safe sex without any understanding that their patient's behavior is compulsive and addictive. Otherwise competent psychologists and counselors may suggest various behavioral or cognitive interventions that are designed to help a client reduce compulsive sexual behavior. Other mental health professionals may listen to the struggle of a sexual addict and tell them, "Don't be so concerned. Lots of people are doing the same things. This is normal."

But sexual addiction is real! It affects at least one in seventeen Americans—and perhaps many more than that.[6] For the person who is trapped in a cycle of sexual acting out, followed by periods or shame, despair, and depression, and then more acting out—they know they need help.

One of the greatest fears of sexual addicts prior to getting into recovery is that they are beyond help. Many are sure they are the only person in the world who is powerless over their self-defeating behaviors. They live in constant fear that their behavior will be discovered by their partner or employer or that they will be arrested.

The first step to recovery is for the sexual addict to admit he has a problem and that he does not have a solution to that problem. Sexual addicts are experts about what does not work in finding sobriety from compulsive sexual behavior. They have made promises to themselves or to their partners saying, "I will never do that again—I promise!" But within a few hours of such declarations they find out that they cannot keep that promise and are once again involved in the behavior that disgusts them. Furthermore, each time they break a promise and go back into their addiction, their shame grows even greater.

Sexual addicts know many other things that will *not* keep them from acting out. The person who is powerless over Internet pornography may have used filtering software, taken out

---

6. www.SASH.net

Thirty Days to Hope & Freedom for Sexual Addicts

their modem, or even given their computer away. But within a few hours, they discover that they can go to a public library or their office and use those computers to act out. Or they use their cell phone or other mobile device to continue their cybersex. Even if there is not another computer available, they find that their addiction will just take another turn and their acting out will be in another area.

Lies and secrecy are the constant companions of the sexual addict who is still suffering. I have heard more than one recovering sexual addict remark that while they were living in their addiction, they were "world-class liars." The nature of the disease demands that the addict learn to lie and lie well in order to keep others out of his or her secret world. As the maze of lies grows, many addicts find that lying has become such a habit that they lie about things that make no difference at all. A sexual addict will realize he or she is lying about the most trivial matters that no one else even cares about. Lying becomes a habitual way of life.

Secrets are part of the fuel that keeps sexual addiction alive. By the time a sexual addict reaches adulthood, secrets have become so numerous that it becomes difficult if not impossible to be genuine with anyone. Because of the inability to be transparent, intimate relationships become untenable. The sexual addict may go through the motions of being in a committed relationship, but in reality they are just "playing house." They are incapable of sharing on a level that promotes true intimacy.

When one begins down that road called recovery, they find the journey difficult but also rewarding. With each step, the sexual addict who is seeking recovery intuitively knows that there is reason for hope, perhaps for the first time. They begin a journey that offers promise of a better life.

Why Learn about Sexual Addiction?

If your physician told you that you had a rare disease that was going destroy your health and had the potential of ending your life, you would read everything you could about this disorder. There would be no limit to your efforts to learn all that you can about this deadly malady.

Sexual addiction is such a disorder. It threatens everything that is precious to you. Unless you are able to stay in recovery and stop your acting out forever, sexual addiction will ruin your life. Without recovery, sexual addiction will destroy your relationship with your partner or spouse. Rather than bring you happiness, it will rob you of contentment. Sexual addiction will threaten your career and perhaps end it.

Continuing to engage in dangerous sexual behaviors may put you at risk of arrest. People who would never consider themselves to be sexual offenders have been arrested for masturbating in their car or for solicitation of prostitution. Others have been incarcerated for downloading pornography of persons who are younger than eighteen, or agreeing to rendezvous with a teen they met online.

There is also the threat to your health that must be considered. Your compulsive sexual behavior may expose you to sexually transmitted diseases. In fact, you may have already contracted one.

Feelings of hopelessness from repeatedly engaging in compulsive sexual behavior may even lead to such despair that you are at risk of taking your life. Sexual addiction is not an inconvenience. It is life-threatening.[7] Failure to learn all that you can about sexual addiction puts you at risk.

What Is Sexual Addiction?

Sexual addiction is a condition whereby a person is not able to manage his sexual behavior. He will engage in behaviors that are demoralizing and find he is powerless to stop. A person who is a sexual addict may make numerous efforts to stop only to fail at each attempt.

Sexual addicts often engage in high-risk behaviors such as having anonymous sexual encounters or unprotected sex. Sex becomes so central that they are unable to continue with many of the normal pursuits of life.

For some people, their behavior grows to the point where they feel as if their life is out of control. They realize that engaging in sexual behavior, as well as thinking about it and planning it, have become the focus of their day. They lose relationships, jobs, or self-respect and cannot seem to break out of the dead-end cycle of destruction.

Sexual addicts may spend so much time chasing their compulsive sexual behaviors that they do not have time for friends or family. Some college students have lost the opportunity for an education because they spent their study time engaging in cybersex. Executives have missed business opportunities because they were too busy acting out. Physicians have lost their license to practice medicine because they pursued a sexual fantasy with a patient.

People are not diagnosed as sexual addicts simply because they like sex, have sex often, or even because they engage in sex with many different persons. For a sexual addict, there is never enough sex. Life is out-of-control because of the search for sex. They are obsessed with being sexual or with efforts to stop being sexual.

It is typical for sexual addicts to make sincere promises to those they love that they will end all of their compulsive sexual behavior. They may even be successful for a period, but ultimately sexual addicts are not able to keep such promises without a program of recovery.

A person suffering from sexual addition may seek out medical help to curb sexual desires. He may look for help from many mental health experts and clergy as he tries to end behavior that is destroying his self-esteem. A feeling of helplessness and hopelessness often accompanies the failed efforts to stop compulsive sexual behavior.

---

7. The National Suicide Prevention Lifeline is 1-800-273-TALK (8255).

Am I a Sexual Addict?

There are ten criteria that may indicate a person is a sexual addict.[8] These include:

1. **Loss of Control**—A person is involved in behaviors they have previously said were not acceptable to them. They engage in sexual behaviors even though they have promised themselves they would not.

2. **The Presence of Compulsive Behavior**—A pattern of out-of-control sexual behavior over a period of time may indicate the presence of sexual addiction.

3. **Efforts to Stop**—Repeated efforts to stop compulsive sexual behaviors are met with failure. A person may measure success in terms of days or months, such as "I have not engaged in cybersex for ten days" or "It has been three months since I have been to an adult bookstore." The key here is that the efforts always meet with failure. A variation of this is when a person makes efforts to reduce their compulsive sexual behaviors. They may believe they are doing better because rather than having unprotected sex, they have determined always to use condoms.

4. **Loss of Time**—Time somehow slips away, and they do not realize it has happened. Something I frequently hear is a person will go to their computer to answer a few e-mails. Perhaps it is late at night, and they intend to be on the computer for fifteen minutes or a half an hour at most. The next thing they know it is 3:00 in the morning and they do not know where the time went. They make a deal with themselves to stay on just a few more minutes. But the sun is coming up when they finally shut down the computer.

5. **Preoccupation**—This is about obsession. Many sexual addicts plan not just an afternoon or a single day around acting out, but their entire life. Every decision they make, from the clothes they wear to the hobbies they are involved in, has roots in their addiction. For some sexual addicts, the plan begins with the selection of articles of clothing that they consider "lucky" or seductive. This may be true for both men and women. Their pulse quickens as they dress. If their acting out behavior involves paying for sex, they have a particular pattern they follow for getting money out of the bank or out of their secret hiding place. They put the money in a particular pocket or under their floor mat in their vehicle, and they drive over a certain route. Hours may have passed, and they have still not acted out sexually, but they have been involved in the preoccupation and ritual of sexual addiction from their first thought that they were going to act out.

6. **Inability to Fulfill Obligations**—This may translate to chronic tardiness at work or school or continually calling in sick at the last moment. For some persons who struggle with sexual addiction, they continually miss their children's sporting activities or dinner dates with their partner. They frequently have to "work late," but somehow they never

---

8. *Don't Call it Love* (2000), Dr. Patrick Carnes

have any work to show for their extra hours on the job. Persons struggling with sexual addiction become experts in making excuses as to why they miss things or why they have been absent. For example, think of the excuses that can be used concerning cars: out-of-gas, flat tire, car broke down, could not remember where it was parked, it got towed, the battery was dead—and some use these excuses multiple times.

7. **Continuance (continuing the behavior in spite of negative consequences)**—How do you explain a why a person with a professional career and everything going for them would continue to cross sexual boundaries at work with fellow employees and subordinates even after being warned that any continued sexual behavior in the workplace will result in termination? Or how do you explain why a healthcare professional (nurse or physician) would continue to engage in high-risk unprotected sex, despite knowing the risks of contracting STDs better than most?

8. **Escalation**—The behavior has to be more intense, more frequent, or more risky to get the same effect. Does this remind you of a drug addict or alcoholic building a tolerance for their drug? The same thing happens with sexual addicts. We hear of persons spending hundreds of dollars—even a thousand dollars or more each week in pursuit of their drug addiction. What largely goes unnoticed is that there are sexual addicts who have out-of-control spending as they feed their habit.

9. **Losses**—Suffering loss is frequently a fact of life for sexual addicts. They may suffer the loss of relationships, health, freedom, self-respect, or reputation. Sexual addicts may give up on hobbies and other parts of life that were once significant, all so that they can pursue their addiction.

10. **Withdrawal**—As in the case with chemical dependency, for some sexual addicts, stopping their sexual behavior may cause anxiety, distress, restlessness, depression, or even physical discomfort.

Are you a sexual addict? If at least three of these criteria are present in your life, chances are the answer is *yes*. As you consider this list, remember what was said about denial earlier in this book. If you are really honest with yourself, you may find that many of these criteria fit you.

Is It Sexual Addiction or Drug Addiction?

Why would I even ask such a question? If you were a drug addict, you would be reading a book on drug addiction—right? Perhaps you have never even experimented with any drugs. You have never taken a larger than recommended dose of a prescription drug. How then is a question about drug addiction even relevant?

It is relevant because each of us has a whole symphony of naturally occurring chemicals in our brains called neurotransmitters. Many of these are familiar names to you. Some may not be as familiar. These are the chemicals that relay information from neuron to neuron, sometimes amplifying or modulating the signals. These chemicals are released periodically in the brain in response to various stimuli.

For example, serotonin is central to regulating the mood of a person. When the level of serotonin is out of balance, a person may be depressed or have some other mood disorder. Dopamine has a number of critical functions in the brain. Chief among these is the role it plays in the reward system.

Sexual addicts are addicted to the neurochemical "high" provided not only by acting out, but even by any sexual thought. You are able to trigger a release of various neurotransmitters by recalling past sexual events, engaging in sexual fantasy, and remembering pornographic images. Contemplating the possibility of engaging in sexual activity is also enough to trigger a release of these brain chemicals.

The high that a sexual addict gets from the release of these neurotransmitters is not unlike that received by drug addicts taking their drug of choice. True sexual addiction is not primarily about sex. Rather it is about generating one's own neurochemistry. You may never consider taking some illicit drug, but if you are a sexual addict, you are addicted to the drugs you produce at will in your brain. The only difference in your addiction and that of a junkie living on skid row is that you do not use a needle to inject your drugs. Just as some drug addicts get addicted from the first introduction of a drug to their system, some sexual addicts are quickly addicted to the neurochemical high that they receive from looking at pornography or engaging in sexual behavior they would consider forbidden.

As you learn more about sexual addiction, begin reading everything that you can about the subject. Read voraciously. The more you learn about your addiction, the better equipped you will be for your lifelong task of recovery.

Day 5: Stop the Affair!

If you are in a marriage or other committed relationship and you are having an affair, it must stop NOW! Often affairs are part of addictive behavior. Some may wonder why this is not an activity for the first day of recovery. Certainly this may be a step a sexual addict is able to take on the first day. If you are able to do this on the first day of recovery, then you are better off.

Trevor's Story

Trevor is an airline pilot for one of the major airlines. He regularly flies the same international routes. Through the years he had developed some long-standing relationships with several women in cities all over the world. Trevor is married and has three children. His wife felt they had a good marriage. Things began to come unraveled when Trevor decided to send all of his partners and his wife a nice flower arrangement at Christmas.

Six arrangements were ordered. He actually used the same note on each arrangement but addressed each to a different person. However, the online florist mixed the names and addresses. When his wife received an arrangement addressed to a different person, she contacted the florist. With a little detective work she was able to get the names and addresses of all of his partners. On Christmas Eve when he arrived home expecting his wife to be grateful for the beautiful arrangement he had sent her, he was confronted with the evidence of his secret life. Trevor is now trying to decide whether he wants to stay married and give up his other relationships or whether he is going to get a divorce and continue with what is left of his secret life.

There are many sexual addicts who can look back over a lifetime of serial affairs. They are constantly on the search for Mr. or Ms. Right. When they identify a person as the one they have been searching for, they may go to extraordinary efforts to attract that person. They may engage in elaborate efforts to win another person's affection. There may be one or several such relationships going on at once. Nothing in life matters except succeeding in a particular relationship. Time and energy may be expended writing letters, planning dates, doing various romantic things to establish or maintain the relationship. These activities would likely surprise their spouse who may not see evidence of much romance in their primary relationship.

For a number of sex and love addicts (or relationship addicts), once they triumph in establishing that new relationship, they find the person who looked so perfect from a distance is just another flawed individual who will not satisfy the relationship desires of the addict. So the search continues for the next "right" person who has the promise of fulfilling the addict's relationship needs. Sex may or may not be a large part of the relationship. In fact, if sex is not a big part of the relationship, that may tend to validate a false belief that this is the perfect relationship.

Since you are reading this book, you may have already concluded that you are a sexual addict. For the good of your primary relationship, all other sexual or romantic relationships must end today! Do not put this off until later. Delaying this crucial behavior will only delay your recovery, and it may prevent you from ever truly entering recovery.

Part of the powerlessness of sexual addiction comes with not being able to control or stop certain behaviors. If you are now in an affair and have found yourself powerless to end it, don't lose heart. As you begin your road to recovery, it is imperative for you to realize that one of the components of recovery will be to stop sexual relations with anyone outside of a committed relationship. Recovery begins with your drawing a line and stepping across that line. As you step across, you commit to stopping your compulsive sexual behavior just for today. When tomorrow comes, you commit to doing the same thing.

To bring relationships to an end may require an e-mail or a letter to the persons with whom you have been involved. If you typically see acting-out partners during the course of your regular activities, it would be best to use the help of a friend who is also in recovery to provide you accountability as your end the relationships. Get help from someone in recovery (in Twelve Step meetings) so as not to slide back into the relationship you are trying to end.

Think about how you have entered into relationships with anonymous people, persons you work with, and with repeat encounters with casual acquaintances. What patterns do you see emerging? Do you notice flirting behavior on your part that has become so ingrained that you engage in it without being conscious of it?

If you are in a relationship with someone on your job, you have an added level of complexity that must be dealt with for you to be successful in recovery. This may involve getting a transfer to another location or even getting a new job. Extreme? Yes. But radical change is necessary if you are to be successful in recovery.[9]

Change the Number

Much of the acting out done by sexual addicts is facilitated by cell phones. People who would never dream of giving out their home phone number do not think twice about divulging their cell phone number. The ability to receive calls in "silent mode," as well as password protected voice mail boxes, often leads sexual addicts to freely give their phone number to their acting-out partners.

One of the first actions to take upon entering recovery is to eliminate the possibility that a former sex partner can contact you. If anyone you have acted out with in the past has your cell phone number, you must change that number immediately. This is a non-negotiable step. It does not matter if you believe no one from your past will contact you. Neither does it matter if it has been weeks or even months since a former acting-out partner called you on that number. And do not let the inconvenience of a new number keep you from this critical task. I have known people whose entire career has been dependent on a particular cell phone number take the courageous step to change it regardless of the business implications.

9. More suggestions on dealing with this very difficult situation are given on Day 13.

The purpose of this change is to lessen the possibility of having your recovery ambushed in the future by a former partner. At the least, a contact from the past will disrupt your serenity. There remains the possibility that a future contact will come at a weak moment and jeopardize not just your sobriety but your whole recovery program. And if you are in a committed relationship and you have already made a shift to restoring your integrity, you will want to tell your partner about this contact and that may add stress to the relationship between you and your partner.

Get a New E-Mail Address

If any person you have acted out with has your e-mail address, you must also change it immediately. This action is not a sign of weakness. Rather it is a sign that you are taking your recovery seriously. I know what you are thinking: "But I have had the same e-mail address for years. All of my friends know how to contact me." The little bit of inconvenience you suffer in changing e-mail addresses and cell phone numbers is worth it. You can contact your friends and family members and let them know of the change. New addresses and new numbers are common with people changing phones or providers. (And while you are at it, you may want to consider changing your home phone number.)

You must also close all of the additional e-mail addresses you have used as part of your acting out. Make sure you also eliminate all of the addresses you used to order items or services you did not want your partner to discover.

Close Social Networking Accounts

Social networking sites like Facebook and MySpace can provide endless hours of entertainment. They are great ways to connect with friends and acquaintances from the past. But for sexual addicts, social networking sites are problematic.

Your social networking accounts give others access to your contact information—the very thing you want to stop. They also may lead to someone from your distant past contacting you and tempting you to begin a clandestine relationship. It may be helpful to enlist the help of a friend who is also in recovery as you close your accounts. The added accountability will help keep you safe.

This would be a good time to consider if your recovery would be stronger by not spending time on any social networking sites—even business-related sites. The benefits offered by the sites are offset by the potential of harming your recovery. Good recovery strongly suggests that you make a clean break with this activity.

Change to a New Internet Service Provider

Are you continuing to receive unsolicited pornography in your e-mail? Contact your Internet Service Provider (ISP) and ask for their help in eliminating the problem. They may be able to offer some assistance in blocking objectionable e-mails. If your ISP is unwilling to help you or if you are unsuccessful in eliminating the pornographic intrusion into your life, change providers. You do not have to continue receiving unwanted porn. You have a right to be able to check your e-mail without having to worry about being stalked by pornography.

Playing with Fire

There is a temptation to believe that a few months or even a few years of recovery will insulate one from the temptation of falling back into addiction. This is one of the subtle lies that cause some people to lower their defenses. "Since I have been sober for a couple of years, I will be safe in having casual friendships with some of my old sex partners, won't I?"

While you may easily see through the insanity of such a statement, you may not be as perceptive when it comes to maintaining any kind of a link to the past. There are addicts who wrongly believe that if they do not contact former Internet acting-out partners, there is no reason to change their e-mail address. Others believe that after a period of sobriety, it is unnecessary to change cell phone or home phone numbers because old acting-out partners have not called them. It is foolish to allow any link with the past to remain intact. If a former acting-out partner still has a phone number or address where they can contact you, cut the tie with the past and change the number immediately. Those who play with fire end up with ashes.

My Commitment

Today _____ (date), I make a commitment to end all affairs and other destructive relationship(s). I will communicate this to my affair partners by _____ (e-mail, letter, or phone call). To help ensure that I do not get drawn back into these relationship(s), I will contact (name of an accountability partner also in recovery) _____

_____ before and after every contact with these persons.

I further commit to changing my cell phone number and my e-mail address, and to close social networking accounts, in order to help ensure the relationship(s) comes to a permanent end.

Signed _____ Date _____

Thirty Days to Hope & Freedom for Sexual Addicts

Day 6: Enlist a Shaman—
Translation: Get a Sponsor

Stan's Story

Stan has looked at pornography ever since he can remember. As an adult he has habitually masturbated to pornography multiple times each week, sometimes to the point of injury. Prior to entering recovery Stan would substitute catalogs and lingerie ads for pornography. While he felt he was making progress, he realized that for him, these ads were just as harmful to him as pornography. He was using them to get a neurochemical "high" so that he could masturbate. Stan realized that if he was honest with himself that he would have to declare that lingerie ads, catalogs, swimsuit sites, and other photos that he used as masturbation aids had become his pornography. This new level of honesty is what finally got him to attend his first Twelve Step meeting. At that meeting he enlisted a sponsor.

One of the most significant things you will do early in recovery is to find a sponsor. A sponsor is someone who is further along in recovery who will act as a mentor or guide in your recovery. For someone to serve as a sponsor, they must be at a good place in their own journey so that they can assist you without endangering their recovery.

A sponsor is someone who has already worked the Twelve Steps of recovery. They have been led through the Steps by their own sponsor. A sponsor must also be living in sexual sobriety. Someone who cannot stay sober cannot model sobriety for anyone else. Finally, this is a person who has been released by his own sponsor to begin sponsoring other people.

Your sponsor is responsible to do four things

- mentor you in recovery
- guide you through the Twelve Steps
- provide you accountability
- model sobriety and good recovery habits

If you are new to recovery, it is suggested that you attend several different groups to increase your opportunity of meeting the person who will ultimately serve as your sponsor. Finding a sponsor should be seen as your most critical early recovery task. You may want to attend three, four, or more groups each week when you are just entering recovery. The more groups you attend, the more opportunities you have of coming into contact with potential sponsors.

If the meetings you attend pass a "phone list," take the names of several people who are willing to be sponsors. Call them all, and ask them the questions listed below.

Another way of finding a sponsor is to listen to the sharing that takes place at various meetings. It may be that something someone shares strikes a chord with you and you feel it may be worthwhile to explore the possibility of that person serving as your sponsor. You may also ask someone sitting near you to arrange an introduction with a potential sponsor after the meeting. Whatever approach is used, it is key to realize that this step is preliminary and should not be taken as the end of the selection process.

When speaking with a potential sponsor, tell them that you would like to visit with them for a few minutes and discuss the possibility of them becoming your sponsor. Explain to them that you want to meet with several people to find the best possible match. Sometimes members are not able to consider serving as a sponsor because they have not gotten through the Twelve Steps themselves, they are having difficulty in their own recovery, or they are already sponsoring what they consider to be the maximum number of persons.

Do not look for a perfect sponsor—there is no such thing. The person you choose as a sponsor may become a lifetime friend. However, do not base your selection on whether or not you believe the possibility for friendship exists. You are not looking for a friend—you are looking for a sponsor. Your sponsor should be of your gender and not be a person to whom you are attracted or of whom you have fantasies. Some of the best sponsors are persons who have clear boundaries around their sponsoring relationships. They keep them very business-like and do not engage in any social interactions.

The suggestions given here are not meant to supersede any direction given by a particular Twelve Step fellowship for finding a sponsor.

Questions for Potential Sponsors

The following are suggested questions to ask a potential sponsor:

1. **How long have you been in recovery?** While there is no ideal answer to this question, you will want a sponsor who has had some time in recovery and is able to share what they have gained from the process. They will be further ahead of you in their journey.

2. **How long have you been sober?** Again, there is no one right answer. If a person says they have ten years of recovery but only have a few weeks of sobriety, they are not in a position to serve as your sponsor. A sponsor should have an established record of sobriety in order to be able to guide a sponsee into a life of continuous sobriety. A good rule of thumb is to look for a sponsor who has a year or more of unbroken sobriety. There are, however, very good sponsors who may have less than a year of sobriety. Sponsors also have their own sponsor who guides them and holds them accountable.

3. **How far along are you in working the Steps?** It is best to find a sponsor who has completed all Twelve Steps so that they can guide you through the process. They should have worked the Steps with a sponsor rather than having worked through the Steps on their own. The process of sponsoring and being sponsored is behavior that is modeled and passed on from one person to another. A person who did not have a sponsor lead them through the Steps cannot model behaviors they have not had

modeled for them. You want a sponsor who has walked the road before you and can guide you as you take the journey.

4. **May I call you at any time if or when I have a recovery emergency?** Having access to your sponsor in the event of an emergency is vital for your recovery. If you are in danger of slipping, you must be able to call your sponsor and get some straight talk about your situation. Such access demands respect on the part of the sponsee to not abuse the privilege. There are some very good sponsors who cannot be available by phone because of work demands or their travel schedule. In those cases be diligent in meetings about collecting phone numbers of other recovering persons. Hopefully, you will find someone who is available to take emergency calls from you.

5. **Would you be willing to meet with me on a weekly basis as I complete my Step work?** These meetings may last thirty minutes to an hour or longer. Many sponsors have these meetings just before or just after a Twelve Step meeting that is attended by both the sponsor and sponsee. When it is not possible to have a face-to-face meeting, connecting with your sponsor by telephone or e-mail can be effective.

What to Expect of Your Sponsor

You can expect your sponsor to:

- **Take sponsorship seriously**—It is a solemn responsibility to guide a person through the Steps of recovery. You have a right to know that your sponsor is committed to sponsoring and is giving their best efforts to guiding your progress.

- **Keep in confidence what you say**—What you share with your sponsor should remain with your sponsor. You have a right to expect your sponsor to hold in confidence everything you tell them.

- **Encourage you**—It is not your sponsor's job to work your program for you but to encourage you as you work through the Steps. While your motivation for working the Steps is not to receive the praise of your sponsor, his or her regular encouragement is supportive of your recovery work.

- **Confront you**—A good sponsor may find it necessary occasionally to confront you. Since they are further along in the recovery process, they are in a good position to identify pitfalls and behavior that is not supportive of recovery, and to help you get past hurdles in working the Steps. Confrontation is done in the interest of your recovery and should be received as a gift.

- **Hold you accountable**—Working the Steps requires a great deal of work on your part. Your sponsor will make periodic assignments to you. They will want to review the work you have done between sponsorship meetings. Some sponsors require their sponsees to call them on a regular basis to check-in on how they are progressing in recovery. These check-in calls may be once a day, several times a week, or not required. Still, your sponsor will hold you accountable to do your recovery work and to not waste their time.

- **Set good boundaries**—The relationship you develop with a sponsor is primarily for your benefit. While sponsors will readily admit that working with sponsees is central to their own recovery, your sponsor will not expect you to help him through rough spots in his recovery. He will share with you his experience, strength, and hope. This sharing is to help you on your journey rather than to support your sponsor as he works through difficulties in his own life.

- **Set the pace**—There is no one right pace for working the Steps. Some people work them faster than others. No special status is gained by getting through the Steps in record time. By the same token, laboring month after month on the same Step without much progress is counter to good recovery. It is the sponsor's task to set a pace for working the Steps that takes into account various factors in your life.

- **Terminate the relationship when necessary**—During the course of recovery, you may change sponsors. Schedule conflicts sometimes necessitate such a change. There are also occasions when a sponsor finds it necessary to terminate a relationship with his sponsee because his own recovery is in jeopardy. If this happens, see it as part of the journey in finding the right sponsor for the next stage of your recovery.

If you are unable to find a person who meets the criteria to be your sponsor, you have the option of asking someone to serve as your temporary sponsor. Make a list of potential sponsors. Contact each one and ask the questions above to see whether there is a potential match.

My Potential Sponsors

1. _____

2. _____

3. _____

4. _____

5. _____

Day 7: Professional Help—
Therapists and Treatment Facilities

Willis's Story

It seemed like a peculiar place for him to hang out, but Willis could be found reading a book most afternoons while sitting on a bench in the mall near his home. Actually Willis was quite strategic in his selection of a reading place. Willis's obsession is in looking up women's skirts. His reading bench is near an escalator. He spends hours waiting for a glimpse of skin. On two occasions he has been confronted by shoppers who noticed him trying to look up skirts. Last week, the guard at the mall told him if he did not leave, the police would be called. While this was a wakeup call for him, Willis is now looking for a new "reading bench" to continue his voyeurism.

Now is the time to determine whether you are going to seek professional help for your addiction or not. Not every sexual addict works with a professional. Some people do very well in their recovery without going to a single therapy session. They attack recovery with a vengeance. They attend every Twelve Step meeting that their schedule will allow, read all that they can about sexual addiction, and work tirelessly on their Step work.

Still others in recovery do all of these things and still find that they would benefit from the help of a professional to guide their recovery. They find that the accountability of weekly therapy sessions keeps their recovery on track. Also, being able to process with a therapist the many things that happen in the recovery journey speeds and strengthens their recovery.

Individual Therapy

Individual therapy for sexual addiction recovery may include a number of things. First there may be a significant amount of family of origin work to help the client understand some of the factors that may have contributed to the addiction. The term *family of origin* refers to the family you grew up in. It includes your parents, any other major caregivers such as grandparents and perhaps neighbors who served as babysitters, and siblings. This is not a parent bashing time. The truth is, all parents make mistakes and wound their children. Every parent hopes they have not wounded their children too badly.

In sexual addiction recovery the therapist will lead the client to examine childhood experiences that may have set them up for their addiction. This is not in an effort to relieve the addict of responsibility for his actions. Rather, it is a time of trying to get to the roots of the addiction. What childhood occurrences contributed to their addiction? Were there signs of abuse or neglect? Did any of the major caregivers have addiction problems?

Therapy will also help sexual addicts identify thinking errors. Faulty thinking is part of the addictive process and should be identified so that recovery can proceed. Some thinking errors are, *If I could only get a date with that person, my life would be fine*, or *My behavior is not harming anyone but me—and it is not even hurting me that much*, or *I am a normal person who just likes sex a lot*.

Therapy is also helpful for persons who are having a problem dealing with their denial or resistance to recovery. The therapist can help sexual addicts get a clearer picture of themselves. Unlike drug or alcohol treatment, the goal of sexual addiction treatment is not lifelong celibacy, but rather a termination of compulsive, unhealthy sexual behavior. Therapy is useful in helping to identify those unhealthy sexual behaviors and then helping the client to develop a healthy attitude toward sex as well as healthy sexual behaviors.

Group Therapy

Group therapy is effective in treating sexual addiction. Some therapists will do individual therapy for a while with a goal of moving clients into group therapy, either as an adjunct to their individual therapy or as the next step in the recovery process. One significant advantage to group therapy is that it is typically less expensive than individual therapy. Group therapy sessions are usually twice as long as individual therapy sessions. Group members have the advantage of processing their recovery journey in a setting with other sexual addicts, with each person learning not only from his or her own work but from the work of the other group members.

Marty's Story

Marty was passed over for several promotions because he did not work hard enough. Repeatedly, he had managers tell him that if he would apply himself, he would be able to get the promotion that he wanted. However, with each disappointment, he became less and less motivated. Marty would look for relief from his disappointment by acting out. He spent part of each day researching places to get a massage that would turn into a sexual experience.

Each day, Marty would spend his lunch hour going to a new massage parlor. He finally realized that he was stuck in a destructive cycle. The more he tried to soothe his disappointment by acting out, the worse his job performance became. This cycle resulted in more time lost at work and poorer performance reviews, which led to more acting out to relieve his stress. After years of postponing getting help, Marty finally sought out the help of a therapist.

Selecting a Therapist

What should you look for in a therapist? The first thing you want is someone who has experience and expertise in treating sexual addiction. It is not enough that you verify that a therapist has other sexually-addicted clients. They must have training and proficiency in sexual addiction therapy.

Well-intentioned therapists who lack expertise in treating sexual addiction may cause more harm than good. For example, without an understanding of sexual addiction, a therapist may tell a client who complains of his inability to stop looking at pornography that he is normal and that "all men struggle in that area to some degree." An untrained therapist working with the partner of a sexual addict may insist that if the partner will just be more adventuresome in the bedroom that the compulsive behavior of the sexual addict will stop.

The best training program available was pioneered by Patrick Carnes, Ph.D.; a counselor in this program becomes a Certified Sexual Addiction Therapist (or CSAT). The program is administered by the International Institute for Trauma and Addiction Professionals (or IITAP).[10] The training program consists of more than 120 hours of classroom instruction, completion of individual assignments and reading, followed by thirty hours of clinical supervision. CSAT certification normally takes several years of work to complete.

Therapists may have additional training in treating multiple addictions, as well as specialized training in treating the trauma of partners. In selecting a therapist, do not be shy about asking about their training and experience. You must know that your therapist has the background necessary to help you. A list of therapists who work with sexual addiction can be found at www.sash.net and www.iitap.com.

Intensive Outpatient (IOP) Treatment

Intensive outpatient programs (or IOP) provide significantly more therapy and concentrated recovery help in a short period of time. An IOP may last for a few days or for as long as four or five weeks. Clients stay in a local hotel and attend sessions at the treatment center or counseling center during the day.

Intensive outpatient programs may include both individual and group therapy. Clients may also be required to complete assignments in the evening. In addition to therapy, it is common for IOP programs to require attendance at Twelve Step programs that are on the premises or nearby.

Intensive programs are helpful for clients who are just getting started in recovery, as well as those who have been in recovery for a while but cannot achieve long-term sobriety. IOP programs are also effective in treating persons who have experienced a slip or a relapse. Some programs, such as the Hope & Freedom program,[11] are specifically designed to assist in the restoration of relationships damaged by compulsive sexual behavior.

Bailey's Story

Bailey liked to gamble. He would routinely go to a casino that was a two-hour drive from his home. His partner did not enjoy those trips and even encouraged Bailey to go by himself. Bailey found that he enjoyed his gambling junkets more if he would "get in the mood" before he arrived at the casino. To accomplish this he would usually drink a six pack of beer during his trip.

---

10. www.iitap.com
11. www.HopeAndFreedom.com

Arriving at the casino around dark, Bailey would gamble and continue drinking throughout the night. If he was winning, he would celebrate by going to a nearby strip club to have a sexual encounter. If he was losing, he would console himself by going to the strip club, hoping it would make him feel better. Bailey knew he had a problem when he had a near accident in his car, driving home on the wrong side of the freeway. He finally sought inpatient treatment when he woke up in his car in another city with a sack containing several thousand dollars on the seat beside him. He did not know where he had been. Bailey could not remember gambling or winning or why he was in a city several hours from his home.

Inpatient Treatment

Inpatient treatment usually lasts for a month or more. Patients live at the treatment facility and have their activities and recovery progress closely monitored. The focus of treatment concentrates on group work with some individual therapy. Each week of treatment may have a different emphasis such as understanding and coping with childhood trauma or learning the basics of recovery. Some treatment centers offer a family week where family members are invited to participate in the therapeutic experience.

Inpatient treatment is useful for persons who cannot or will not control their acting out well enough to make progress in individual therapy or an IOP program. Also clients with multiple untreated addictions are able to get specialized help for each addiction.

When a person is at significant risk of harming himself, he must get inpatient treatment. This is true for anyone, not just sexual addicts. Any therapist can assess a person for the risk of self-harm and give direction on getting the appropriate treatment.

In Appendix B you will find a partial list of intensive outpatient and inpatient treatment providers. Additionally, you may check the Society for the Advancement of Sexual Health's website for a listing of individual, IOP, and inpatient treatment providers.[12]

---

12. www.SASH.net

Day 8: Triggers—What Are They and How Can I Combat Them?

A trigger is anything that has been repeatedly associated with acting out. It becomes a conditioned stimulus that then triggers a conditioned response. Initially, these things may be neutral from a psychological standpoint, but repeated exposure to them, coupled with acting-out behaviors or fantasies, can make them powerful triggers. For example, classical music would not normally be thought of as music that triggers a desire to act out sexually.

Hank's Story

Hank used to visit a particular massage parlor. Over time, the massages he received there became more and more sexual. At first, they included only a supposed accidental touch of his genitals. Then massages progressed to the point where they always ended with him engaging in sexual touching with the person giving him the massage. Finally, he was having intercourse with the massage therapist at each visit. Classical music was always playing during each massage session, as well as during each time he was sexual with the person giving the massage.

Later during psychotherapy, Hank was asked if he had any trigger associated with his acting out at massage parlors. Initially, he said the only one he was aware of was seeing signs or advertisements for massage services. However, he later became aware that every time he listened to classical music, he had memories of his sexual encounters at that particular massage parlor. So for Hank, classical music was a trigger.

Someone once said, "Be grateful for triggers because they help you with your Third Step. They give you additional opportunities to surrender."[13] Triggers evolve. They may be different over time. What might be an intense trigger early in recovery may not be as provoking after years of sobriety. As recovery progresses, you are able to more clearly see the things that have potential for sidetracking your recovery. As you get stronger, you will develop clearer boundaries and likely find there are additional things you avoid because of their triggering potential.

Triggers can be divided into internal and external triggers. A thoughtful study of triggers and potential triggers can help sexual addicts avoid the possibility of a slip or relapse. Think about the things that trigger you. After reading this section you will have an opportunity to make a list of your triggers.

---

13. More information on the Twelve Steps is given in Day 21.

External Triggers

External triggers are anything that is outside of you that causes you to think about acting out or creates a strong desire to act out sexually. Basically, any person, place, or thing can be an external trigger. Not everyone is triggered in the same way.

Something that is outside of a person such as the flashing red lights on an emergency vehicle can be an external trigger. Seeing the lights may cause your heart to speed up. And if the lights are right behind you, they may trigger a desire to move over or feelings of shame if you think you have broken the law.

When you go to a movie, prior to the feature you will see commercials of soft drinks, popcorn, and hotdogs. These are external triggers that cause people to connect with their feelings of hunger or at least a desire for some concession-stand food. So even if you are not hungry, the external trigger of the food advertisements may be largely responsible for you ordering food you did not previously intend to order.

Natalie's Story

Natalie first fantasized about kissing women when she was a teenager. Previous acting jobs had not called for her to be intimate with a woman, but she looked forward to a role that would allow her to experiment. She mentioned her fantasy to her husband when they were playing "truth or dare" in a bar with several other couples. When confronted with a dare, she kissed a woman in front of her husband and her other friends.

A few weeks later, Natalie approached her husband about including another woman in their sexual relationship, under the pretence of her wanting to do something more to satisfy her husband. After engaging in this behavior a number of times, she realized that she preferred being sexual with women rather than with her husband, but she also believed she would never leave her husband and live an openly lesbian lifestyle. As a result, Natalie engaged in a series of short-term affairs with women.

These relationships weighed heavily on her since each encounter was secret and violated her vow to be monogamous with her husband. Regardless of whether she ultimately determined to live a gay or straight lifestyle, she felt powerless to stop her compulsive secret relationships. Though she made promises to herself to stop, she felt drawn to start additional relationships soon after each secret relationship ended.

Her partners all have a similar appearance. She has noticed that their hair is about the same color and length. They are generally of the same age, and they even have similar facial features.

People

People can be very triggering. Summertime brings warm weather and also some very revealing attire. You do not have to venture to the beach to be triggered by skimpy attire.

You can also be triggered by people who remind you of other people you have acted out with or have fantasized about. A particular hair color, the way a person walks, or the sound of someone's voice may prove to be a powerful trigger.

Persons of a particular body type or with certain physical characteristics may be triggering to you. Also, obviously vulnerable people or people who either sound or look like they may be an easy target may be triggering to you. People who fit the profile of your preferred acting-out partner will be a particularly potent trigger.

Continued association with people you have acted out with in the past may prove to be a powerful and troubling trigger. Your situation may be complicated by the fact that some of the people you have acted out with are work associates, friends of your spouse, or neighbors.

What changes will you have to make to distance yourself from people who are closely associated to your addiction? Will you have to change jobs? Will it ultimately involve your moving to a new residence? While these major changes are not ones to be made quickly or without thought and consultation with your sponsor or therapist, it may be necessary for you ultimately to change jobs or move in order to stay in a healthy state of recovery.

Places

Places where you have acted out in the past may be significant triggers. This may include a particular place, such as a certain hotel, or it may include every hotel in a particular chain. Some parts of town may be more associated with acting out more than others because of the presence of sexually-oriented businesses or because they are known hangouts for prostitution.

If you travel in association with your job and you have acted out while out of town, then you might be triggered by a number of things having to do with travel. Airports may trigger you. Checking into a hotel room or just entering a hotel may prompt in you a strong desire to act out.

Things

The list of things that may trigger you is virtually endless. You may be triggered by lingerie ads, the smell of a certain perfume or cologne, or even the taste of a pizza. Anything that you take in through your senses may trigger you. Things affecting any of the senses—sight, sound, smell, taste, and touch—can be powerful triggers. You may be triggered by a sign for a legitimate massage therapist because you have a history of seeking sexual massages, as well as other sexual acts in brothels that hide behind the cover of "massage services" or "spas."

Visual triggers are in abundance. They may be more numerous at a beach, swimming pool, or health club. They are everywhere. Not only are known pornography websites triggering, but you may find it tempting as you peruse new websites because of the abundance of sidebar ads that offer the allure of skin and the promise of a moment of pleasure.

Situations

You may be triggered by certain situations. For example, if you know that you are going to be home alone in the near future, just thinking about having that time to yourself may be compelling. In the past you may have acted out many times when in that situation.

When there is stress or conflict involving your job you may feel particularly triggered. In the past, rather than deal with the conflict and stress in a productive way, you may have medicated your feelings with acting out. Any time there is stress on the job, you are tempted to act out. You look for something on your computer to take your mind off of the current situation.

Conflict with your partner may also prove to be a significant trigger. In truth, you may have engineered some of the conflict in the past so as to give you an excuse to act out. Now each time there is conflict with your partner, you are tempted to run away from the tension by pursuing some sexual outlet.

External Triggers

I struggle with the following external triggers: _____

_____

_____

_____

_____

_____

Internal Triggers

Internal triggers may include thoughts, feelings, moods, and emotions. For example, boredom may be a trigger. If you are bored, you may look for something that will lift your spirits. You may turn to some sexual behavior to temporarily relieve the boredom.

Memories of past acting out can also be triggering. Likewise, fantasy is an internal trigger. Some fantasies may actually be healthy in that they allow for a brief mental vacation. Other fantasies are destructive, as they monopolize thoughts and paralyze a person's performance.

Depression and anxiety are also powerful internal triggers. When feeling anxious or depressed, some people seek escape with compulsive sexual behavior. Other emotional states such as anger may also be triggering.

Hunter's Story

Hunter has worked hard to identify his triggers. He readily identified many of them. One of his most helpful insights came from watching his dog. He noticed that when he would get vocally enthusiastic while watching a ball game, his dog would hide in another room, just like it did when he and his wife would argue. He realized that his dog interpreted all strong behavior as anger, causing it to hide in self-defense.

Hunter realized that he often interpreted his partner's feelings the same way. When she expressed any kind of strong emotion, Hunter internalized it and assumed she was angry at him. Sometimes that was the case. Most of the time, her strong emotions did not have anything to do with him. However, Hunter still was fearful of being abandoned. Fear of not being loved or of being abandoned is a significant trigger for Hunter. He realized that in the past, when he is afraid, he would often act out to mask his fear.

Fear of abandonment often has roots in childhood. Perhaps a person was lost for a few minutes when very young. Or maybe they became very fearful after the death of a parent or after their parents divorced.

Another very powerful trigger—perhaps the most powerful of all of the internal triggers is resentment. Resentment can grow until a person seeks relief by engaging in sexual behavior. Sometimes resentment becomes a convenient excuse for acting out.

Internal Triggers

I struggle with the following internal triggers: _____

_____

_____

_____

_____

_____

With all of this emphasis on identifying triggers you may be discouraged—especially if you conclude that you can be triggered by a multiplicity of things. Truly you will be triggered by numerous things. But learning to identify triggers and recognizing situations that may be triggering are significant building blocks of successful recovery. You do not have to respond to triggers by acting out.

Positive Coping Strategies

When you are triggered, your task is to cope with the trigger. A negative way of coping is to act out sexually. That is what you have been doing. Sexual acting out is a negative coping strategy. The reason you have gone back to it repeatedly through the years is because it works, at least in the short term. Stress, anxiety, or other internal or external triggers are satisfied for a while when you act out. The down side is that the self-loathing, despair, and depression that come after the acting out leave you in worse shape than you were in previously.

Your task is to find other coping strategies that work and do not have the after effects of your negative coping behaviors. Positive coping strategies are anything that you do to take you out of the triggering situation. You may use various means of distraction, as well as numerous healthy activities, as coping strategies.

1. **Humor is a powerful coping strategy**—Go to a comedy club. Read a joke book. Watch an old Laurel and Hardy or Three Stooges movie. Look for humor in whatever situation that you are facing.

2. **Call a friend**—One of the best ways to break the power of a trigger is to tell someone about it. Other recovering people understand what it means to be triggered. You can freely talk to them about your experience, and you may find that triggers often lose their power when you break out of your isolation.

3. **Get a pet**—Whether you are a cat person, a dog person, or if you find joy in watching fish, pets often provide cheap, effective therapy. Spending time with a pet can provide relief from many internal and external triggers.

4. **Volunteer for a cause you believe in**—When you give of yourself, you get back more in return. Volunteering will get you out of your own world and help you focus on making the world a better place.

5. **Read a book**—A good novel or a biography can open your imagination and provide you an escape from your triggers. And reading a book about recovery can equip you for doing battle with your daily triggers.

6. **Go to a movie**—Better yet, call a friend in recovery, and go to a movie together. You can use the company, and a movie may be just the ticket to get you through an evening of boredom.

7. **Cook your favorite meal**—This is not about pigging out but about occupying your mind and body with some healthy activity. Once again, you can invite a friend to share your meal or take a dish to an elderly neighbor.

8. **Take a walk**—Go for a run or do something else for exercise. Remember, when used as a coping strategy, this is not about physical health. Improved physical health is a byproduct of these stress-relieving activities.[14]

9. **Write in your journal**—Putting your thoughts on paper may help you get a clearer view of the situation. It may also help defuse your triggers. Write about your feelings as well as your thoughts. And daily journaling is a powerful tool to guard against slips and relapse.

10. **Clean your living space or your work space**—Doing something productive will often give a sense of accomplishment. You can parlay that achievement into warm, positive feelings about yourself.

Avoid making major decisions when triggered. This is not the time to decide on your future. You do not want to give attention to thinking about moving, changing jobs, or solving the world's problems. All of these decisions can wait until you are in a healthier frame of mind.

Now take a few minutes and decide what coping strategies fit you best. This will not be an exhaustive list. In fact, you will probably come up with many more that will work in your situation in the coming months. So while you are not being triggered, write a list of the strategies you will use the next time you are triggered.

Coping Strategies

The next time I am triggered I will use one of the following coping strategies: _____

_____

_____

_____

_____

_____

_____

---

14. The chapter on Day 19 gives a more complete understanding of the benefits of physical exercise in treating addiction.

Day 9: Study the Past

Philosopher and poet George Santayana said, "Those who cannot remember the past are condemned to repeat it."[15] Yet even those who can remember the past may choose to forget it due to painful memories of childhood trauma. Recovery provides an occasion to look closely at your family of origin and consider how it may have contributed to your sexual addiction.

Wall of Innocence

In my therapy office I have what I call the "wall of innocence." That wall is filled with antique toys. There is an old wagon, a carousel horse, a Navajo war bonnet headdress, an antique fire engine, an old tricycle, and several other things that date back to childhood. When I have a client who has endured some childhood abuse or other trauma, I will encourage them to look at the toys along that wall. I ask them to think back to a time when they would have enjoyed playing with these and other similar toys. I then tell them this is the wall of innocence that can take them back to a time before abuse and before addiction.

For many, this is a very emotional moment. Without any additional help, clients often are able to make the connection to how their innocence was lost when abuse began. I see men who are otherwise very controlled and disciplined deeply grieve the loss of their innocence and the accompanying loss of their childhood.

For those who have been sexually abused this is a difficult moment. They may feel shame at what happened to them. They may even feel guilty because they had sexual responses toward their abuser or felt that the abuse was pleasurable. I remind them that the abuse was not their fault. If they responded sexually, that does not make them a guilty party. I point out that they are a sexual being and their physiological responses were natural. They were still the victims of abuse.

Jimmy's Story

Jimmy had worked hard on his disclosure for his wife. He was determined to stop all of his high-risk compulsive sexual behaviors. As part of his disclosure his therapist asked him if there were any shameful or traumatic sexual events from childhood he wanted to disclose. "There is one thing, but I would not call it a traumatic event. When I was five, some older boys dragged me into the bushes and made me perform oral sex on them. But I would not consider that abuse or trauma. If it was traumatic, it should hurt, right? It doesn't hurt. It was no big deal."

---

15. (Santayana, 1905) p. 284

When the time came for Jimmy to tell his wife about his childhood, he could not get any words to come out. After a long minute of silence, tears began to flow down his cheeks. He started to sob in silence, but then the inaudible weeping gave way to heart-wrenching howls and moans as he cried in his wife's lap. When he was able to compose himself he said, "Well I guess that did hurt a little. I was crying like a baby." His therapist said, "Not like a baby but like a wounded five-year-old boy."

Origin of Sexual Addiction

Did Jimmy become a sexual addict because of that one instance of abuse? No one can know for certain the impact of that abuse on Jimmy. What we are sure of is that several traumatic events contributed to Jimmy's sexual addiction. That does not lessen his responsibility for his adult behaviors. Sexual addicts are responsible for all of their decisions and actions.

Jimmy experienced a lot of guilt over the fact that he did not try to run away from the older bullies who abused him. He also felt guilty that he did not even try to resist. But what he did not take into consideration is that at five years of age he was not equipped to do either.

When faced with a threatening situation, a natural response is to fight or to flee. At the moment of danger this mechanism kicks in, allowing us to escape. This fight or flight response[16] is key to survival and is not taught but is an automatic biological reaction.

Children, however, are not equipped to fight off a threat and may not even be able to flee a dangerous situation. Instead, children often freeze or surrender in order to survive.[17] Jimmy believes he failed himself since he did not run or resist his abuse. But he did the only thing that he could as a five-year-old. He found a way to survive.

Jimmy's surrendering to his abusers is known as a dissociative response pattern.[18] He was so successful at numbing out at the moment of the abuse that even as an adult, he was still able to dissociate from the trauma, believing it had not affected him. But as he prepared to tell his wife about the event, all of the fear and pain that he suspended at age five came flooding back.

Childhood abuse and trauma are only part of the puzzle that is reconstructed when digging into the past. The family system in which you were raised dramatically shaped your life.

Ronnie's Story

Ronnie was ten when he had intercourse for the first time. Every afternoon after school he would go to a neighbor's house where a woman in her twenties would babysit him until his mother got home from work. The babysitter introduced him to some "secret games" where she told him that it was her job to educate him about sex. She got him to participate in several sexual games that culminated in them having intercourse. This abuse went on for several months. He never told anyone—until he got into recovery at age 35.

Until recovery, Ronnie always considered what happened to him as a child to be just the result of him being "lucky." He felt he "scored" early because he had sex with a grown woman when he was just

---

16. (Cannon, 1914)
17. (Perry, Pollard, Blakley, Baker, & Vigilante, 1995)
18. (Perry, Pollard, Blakley, Baker, & Vigilante, 1995)

a child. He resisted any thought that what happened to him was abuse. In his mind, Ronnie thought he was the guilty one because he thinks he enjoyed what happened and he knows he was sexually aroused by the babysitter.

Only when his therapist asked him to reverse the gender of the child and the abuser did he get it. He agreed that if a man coerced a child into sex that it was flagrant child abuse, even if the child appeared to be willing and was sexually aroused. At age ten, he was not mentally or emotionally ready for a sexual relationship.

In reviewing Ronnie's sexual history, he realized that many of his "sexual conquests" through the years were with women who were significantly older than he. Ronnie just thought that he liked older women. It never occurred to him that each time he got into another sexual relationship with an older woman that he was reenacting the trauma he experienced as a child.

History of Abuse

A study of your family of origin is not complete without also looking at a history of abuse. Often sexual addicts were the victims of sexual abuse. In many cases, there were other forms of abuse.

Stu's Story

Stu's first memory is of being held by the ankles while his father angrily beat him with a belt. He screamed in terror and remembers that his father beat him until he got too tired to continue. That early memory is just one of many physically abusive episodes with his father.

Stu recalls his father trapping him in the bathroom and beating him as he tried to hide behind the toilet. On another occasion Stu remembers his father leaning him and his younger brother over a bed, pulling down their pants and beating them until one of them confessed to some juvenile blunder. Always the beatings would be accompanied by his father loudly decrying the bad behavior.

As a teen Stu engaged in many destructive acts of vandalism that were intended to get back at his father, though he did not know that at the time. He knew that he was not big enough or brave enough to confront his father's rage head on, so he found covert ways of getting back at him until he finally escaped home by joining the army at age seventeen.

Today Stu is in recovery from sexual addiction. He has worked hard at understanding his addiction, although he has been reluctant to see any connection with the physical abuse he received as a child and the destructive ways he has acted out. Gradually through therapy he has come to understand that they are closely linked.

Stu has also been able to recall things from his childhood that have convinced him that his father was probably a sexual addict. He also remembers hearing that his grandfather was physically abusive to his grandmother. In Stu's case, addiction and abuse have been a constant throughout his life. While he cannot say that the physical abuse he suffered as a child is the cause of his addiction, he knows that it is one of several factors that provided fertile soil for addiction to germinate and grow.

Spend a few minutes thinking about your own abuse history. The abuse may have been physical, mental, or sexual. Neglect is also abuse. Allowing pornography in the house for you

Abuse History Worksheet		
Abuser	**Type of Abuse**	**What Happened?**

Thirty Days to Hope & Freedom for Sexual Addicts

to find as an adolescent is abusive. If your parents were not there for you—to provide love and discipline, to protect you from harm, to guide you through the early years of life, you may have been the victim of abuse.

After completing your abuse history worksheet, what can you conclude from the chart? How may the abusive things you endured have contributed to your sexual addiction? This can be a painful exercise. You may want to just sit down and have a good cry. It is okay for you to weep over your stolen childhood. And the tears you shed may be part of the path to your healing.

Religious Training

A significant factor that may be a contributor in the formation of sexual addiction is religious training. There are times when religion or religious teaching can be abusive. There are other times when religious teaching, though not necessarily abusive, may be so dogmatic that it stifles a person's natural desire to know and to understand. Being forced to embrace certain teachings or be rejected by God for their actions is religious abuse. And it may shift a person's natural curiosity into clandestine searching for information about things that one's religion considers "dirty."

Avery's Story

When Avery got into recovery, he felt he was fortunate. Looking back at his childhood, he realized he had not been abused sexually, physically, or verbally. His parents were still married to each other. As far as he knew they were happy and that was also his impression of them when he was a child.

While completing a family of origin questionnaire, Avery began to wonder if he had an accurate view of his parents. His parents were strict with him, but he did not think they took things too far. They were very religious and saw that he was in services every weekend. There were always lots of rules that he had to follow. When it came to sex, he knew better than to ask his parents about it. He had the distinct impression that there was something dirty about it. In fact, his mother once confided in him that what she did in the bedroom with his father was her "dirty duty."

When Avery went to college, the first thing he did was to look for answers to his sexual questions on the Internet. He was amazed at what he found. More than that, he was hooked on finding out more and more about the "dirty" world of sex that repulsed his mother. Before long his grades were suffering because he used his study time pursuing his sexual fantasies online.

Religious training can be a very good thing. But it can also be a significant risk factor in a person developing into a sexual addict. Strict, conservative religious training may result in children learning a lot about rigid walls and very little about setting healthy boundaries. The only thing some people learn about sex while growing up is that it is something to hide and is shameful to talk about.

Addiction History

Addiction rarely occurs in isolation. That is, if there is addiction in one generation, it may be found in preceding generations as well. Such information may be difficult to obtain because addictions are often part of carefully guarded family secrets.

Ethan's Story

Ethan never saw his mother take a drink. Both parents were teetotalers. But he does know there was a bottle of whiskey at the back of a top shelf in the kitchen. The only thing it was for, he was told, was when his mother came down with "one of her spells." She would mix a little of this "medicine" with honey, and it would relieve her symptoms, whatever they were.

Now more than twenty-five years since leaving home, Ethan is able to look back on his childhood and realize that his mother was a closet drinker and most likely an alcoholic. That has been a difficult admission for him to make. He never saw her drink socially and never saw her drunk, but he knows the level of liquid in the whiskey bottle fluctuated through the years.

Taylor's Story

Taylor's husband worked out of town a lot. She never intended to have sexual relationships outside of her marriage. It just happened. She said she was lonely. She had young children, but she was always discreet with her extracurricular sexual behavior.

She had a door from her bedroom directly to the side yard. Taylor would invite men to her home at night when her husband was out of town. The visitors would park down the block, walk into her yard, and slip into her bedroom. One night her seven-year-old son walked in on Mom in a sexual embrace with someone other his father. Taylor wished she had sought help for her sexual addiction before her children were injured by her behavior.

Addictions often go from generation to generation. Even if children never find out, they often sense something is wrong in the home—tension, strife, anger, and rage. They do not know why things are as they are, and they may assume it is their fault. In the dysfunctional atmosphere they may try to escape to fantasy—and then find their way to addiction. And the addiction gets passed on to another generation.

A study on smoking has shown that youth raised in a home with smoking parents are 3.3 times more likely to smoke than those raised by nonsmoking parents.[19] Other studies have shown that children of drug-addicted parents are more likely to become drug addicts.[20]

One study looked at families that were at risk of developing substance abuse problems but where no member of the family was actually addicted. They found there was a significant relationship between the executive functioning of parents and children.[21] In other words, the way children think and process information is similar to the way that their parents process information. Children owe much of the way they think and behave to their parents.

Anecdotally, I know that a number of sexual addicts have parents who have an addiction. In many cases, clients have a parent or a grandparent whose addiction is of a sexual nature. It is often difficult to get a clear picture of parent's and grandparent's addiction history. After all, addiction is something that people keep hidden. In your own case, you may have successfully

---

19. (Bantle & Haisken-DeNew, February 2002)
20. (Pathways to Addiction: Opportunities in Drug Abuse Research, 2009), p. 119
21. (Jester, Nigg, Puttler, Long, Fitzgerald, & Zucker, June 2009)

hidden your addiction from friends and family members for years. If it were not for the crisis that brought you into recovery, you would still be keeping your addiction a well-hidden secret.

Genograms

A good way of studying your family of origin is to draw a genogram[22] of your family. Developed by Monica McGoldrick and Randy Gerson for use in family therapy, genograms are useful tools for sexual addicts as they explore their family history. They take a while to develop, but they give a clear picture of how addictions are passed on from one generation to the next.

A genogram is a graphical representation of an extended family. It looks much like a family tree except that it includes a great deal more data like dates for births, deaths, marriages, occupations, education, major life events, and illnesses. It also includes information as to the closeness of relationships that exist between family members. A genogram also includes addiction and abuse histories, as well as emotional disorders like depression.

A variety of software exists that can be used to draw a genogram. But the actual drawing of the diagram is the easiest part. The time-consuming part is doing the research to find out more about family members.

Begin by interviewing each member of your family and asking questions about their parents, grandparents, and siblings. Ask direct questions about alcohol use, substance abuse, addiction history, anger issues, and any other information that presents itself during your interview. Transfer what you learn to a simple diagram of your family. Specialized software will make a cleaner presentation, but a hand-drawn genogram can be just as effective.

As you look at the data you collected, what have you learned about your family? Were you able to interview grandparents and uncles and aunts? As you put the pieces of the puzzle together, you will realize that the puzzle you are constructing may help answer the question as to the origin of your sexual addiction.

You are not doing this to place blame on someone else or to shirk responsibility for your actions. Instead you are trying to find out if there is a history of things that may have directly or indirectly contributed to your sexual addiction. You will likely find some clues that help answer the "why" questions.

---

22. (McGoldrick & Gerson, 2008)

I think the following people in my immediate and extended family may have addictions:

Family Addiction History Worksheet

Name	Relationship	Addiction	Why I Think So

Thirty Days to Hope & Freedom for Sexual Addicts

Sexual History

Your sexual history will also help as you piece together the puzzle of sexual addiction. Write out your sexual history in detail. Include any sex play you did as a child with both boys and girls. Also include the first time you saw someone nude, whether you ever saw your parent's nude or walked in on them making love. Include your age at your first masturbation and how you learned to masturbate. You will also want to include your age the first time you saw pornography and how you found it.

Continue your sexual history into your teen years. Include dating relationships and how they changed through the years. You will want to include your first intercourse and how you came in contact with that person.

As an adult, trace the history of your compulsive sexual behavior. Identify as closely as you can when various behaviors started. Notice when behaviors escalated into new or riskier behaviors.

Your written sexual history will be helpful as your sponsor guides you through your First Step. Hang on to it at least until you have completed this Step. You may or may not choose at this time to share this information with your partner or spouse. Eventually you will want to be able to talk with your partner openly about your past. A therapist skilled in working with sexual addicts and their partners will be a critical element in seeing that this sharing is done in the appropriate manner.

Even if you have chosen not to engage in therapy for your sexual addiction, you might want to consider working with a therapist at least while surfacing your family of origin issues. Take your sexual history and your genogram to a therapist who specializes in sexual addiction treatment. Invest several sessions of your time and money into delving into this most significant part of your recovery. The clarity that results from this work may be the crucial piece to understanding your sexual addiction.

In the final analysis, it doesn't matter if you can trace the exact origin of your addiction or not. You can point to many factors that have contributed to your current situation. What matters is that you can find some of the missing pieces to the puzzle. And your childhood holds the key to many of those missing pieces.

The fact remains that if you are sexually addicted, you must find relief. There has to be some way out of the pit of addiction. Good news! There is a way out. Whether or not you know the complete origin of your addiction, you do not have to live the rest of your life as a slave to your compulsive sexual behavior.

Day 10: Doctor! Doctor!
Get Healthy—Mind and Body

What does physical health ha[ve to] do with sexual addiction? Plenty. Often sexual addicts have such a low self-esteem that t[hey believe] they do not have personal worth and therefore are not interested in taking care of t[hemselves.] [One goal for] yourself in your recovery should be that you value both your physical and [mental health.]

Sleep Well

Your body m[ust have sleep. If you were] completely deprived of sleep, you would die. Ma[ny people believe] that their bodies do not require that muc[h ... with the] little sleep that they get each night.

The [experts recommend that we] get between seven and nine hours of sleep e[ach night ... The amount of] sleep required varies from individual to individua[l ...] hours of sleep each night, your mind and your body wi[ll ...] to yourself includes getting a good night's sleep every night.

If you are married, I wo[uld suggest that you] adjust your schedule so that you and your spouse can go to bed at the same tim[e ...] he same sleep schedule as your spouse may significantly reduce any tendency to act o[ut while yo]ur partner is asleep. This will take practice and patience. It is worthwhile in terms of reducin[g] nighttime acting out, improving physical health by getting more regular and hopefully more restful sleep. And it can aid in developing a healthier sexual relationship, since you and your spouse have an established time when you are physically close and have the potential of developing sexual intimacy.

Dealing with Sleep Disturbances

One of the primary factors that negatively impacts the sleep of sexual addicts is the habit of acting out at night on a computer or television. If you have had the habit of getting up when the rest of the family is sleeping so that you can act out on a computer, it will likely take you a period of time before you break your body of this bad sleeping habit. In recovery, you are no longer acting out, but it will take your body a while to get used to staying in bed and not roaming around while others are sleeping.

I need your HELP!!
Willing to write a review on Amazon?
Here's how:
1) go to amazon.com
2) search for Milton Magness
3) click on appropriate title
4) write a review
The review you write will help get the word out to others who may benefit.
— Thanks for your help, Milton Magness

---

23. (How Much Sleep Do We Really Need?, 2009)

There are many causes for sleep disturbances. This section is not intended to be exhaustive in its treatment of sleep or to take the place of sound medical care to address those sleep disturbances that have some medical root. Listed here are numerous suggestions that may work in helping you get a good night's sleep.

- **Eliminate caffeine from your diet.** Caffeine is a stimulant. It is a drug that you can do without. Often people believe they must have caffeine to get them going in the morning, but the residual stimulation often lingers until evening. Coffee, tea, soft drinks, and even chocolate are all sources of caffeine, so make sure you do not just eliminate caffeinated coffee but continue reducing or eliminating caffeine consumption from other food and beverages.

- **Eat a moderate dinner several hours before bedtime.** A heavy meal late in the evening may keep you from having the restful sleep that you desire.

- **Reduce or eliminate alcohol consumption.** While a moderate amount of alcohol may help relax a person so that sleep comes more easily, in some people the consumption of any amount of alcohol may be a detriment to a good night's sleep. And if you have had the habit of drinking larger amounts of alcohol, you may fall asleep quickly, but the alcohol may keep you from staying asleep and feeling rested in the morning.

- **Develop a bedtime routine that you do not vary.** Many of the items below will be part of that routine. You can train your body to fall asleep and to sleep throughout the night. But to do so, you will want to stick to a routine that you keep consistent each evening.

- **The heart of the routine: Go to bed each night at the same time.** Get up each morning at the same time—even on a day off. This will require practice, but it is effective.

- **Stop work several hours before bedtime.** If you are engaging your mind in problem-solving and other invigorating activities just prior to bed, it may be difficult to fall asleep when you would like. Get all of your work completed so that your mind will have time to continue processing those unfinished items before you go to bed.

- **Avoid conflict with your partner or others for several hours before bedtime.** If it appears that conflict is inevitable, negotiate for a better time to have the discussion. Suggest that you set aside time the following afternoon when you can fully explore the subject at hand.

- **Get a moderate amount of exercise before bed.** A brisk walk around the neighborhood, a few calisthenics, or an easy run may help you sleep. However, it is essential to understand that exercise before bed has the opposite effect on some people. Experiment to find out if exercise before bed helps or hinders your sleep.

Thirty Days to Hope & Freedom for Sexual Addicts

- **Practice meditation or prayer before bed in order to clear your mind of worry and concerns.**

- **Take a hot bath just before bed.** This can work wonders in helping you relax your muscles, especially the muscles in your legs. And if you have been lying awake for a long period of time trying to fall asleep, get up and take another hot bath.

- **Move the television out of the bedroom.** TV watching is responsible for many of the sleep disturbances people experience. If you want to watch television in the evening, do it in a different room than where you sleep.

- **After you get in bed, read a good novel, biography, recovery book, or addiction resource for ten to fifteen minutes, then turn out the light.** Avoid reading anything that requires much mental effort or proves to be very stimulating.

- **Keep a pad of paper and a pen on the nightstand.** If you think of something you must do the next day or if you find yourself worrying about a problem, write yourself a note that is just long enough so that you will remember the item the next day. Then mentally release that item so that you can sleep.

- **Consider wearing ear plugs and using a sleep mask (blindfold) as you sleep.** If your partner snores, the ear plugs may be essential. But even some people who always sleep alone use ear plugs so that they can block out little sounds that may disturb sleep. Another benefit from ear plugs is that when wearing them, you may even hear your own heart beating. Listening to the rhythmic beating of your heart can be very soothing and help induce sleep.

- **Turn on a fan, blower on the furnace, air conditioner, or some other "white noise" generator.** Raising the ambient noise level can help significantly in blocking out annoying noises that disrupt sleep.

- **Drink a cup of warm milk just prior to bedtime.** Milk contains tryptophan, an essential amino acid that is naturally produced in the body. Tryptophan helps induce sleep probably by raising the levels of serotonin in the brain. In moderate levels, serotonin has a calming effect.[24]

- **If all else fails, see your physician.** It may be helpful for you to have a sleep study performed. For example, if you suffer from sleep apnea—you stop breathing at night for a few seconds—your sleep may be interrupted multiple times, keeping you from ever enjoying restful sleep. If that is the case, you might be encouraged to use a CPAP (Continuous Positive Airway Pressure) machine that keeps breathing constant throughout the night. There are other sleep disturbances that can be diagnosed with a sleep study. The time and expense involved are insignificant when compared to getting more restful sleep.

---

24. (Wurtman, Hefti, & Melamed, 1981)

- **As a last resort, consider asking your physician if there is a medication that might help you for the short term.** Be careful because many sleep medications are extremely addictive. If used for a long period of time, the user develops a dependence on the medication and has to have it in order to sleep. And with other addictions, it may take more and more of the medication to induce sleep. The best course of action is to look for more natural remedies for sleep.

Eat Healthy

Healthy eating is another way of recognizing that you are a person of inestimable worth. This stands in contrast to the feelings of shame, self-loathing, and contempt that are often present when a person is acting out. And if you feel self-contempt, there is little to motivate you to take care of your body.

Healthy eating does not mean that you have to completely eliminate foods that you enjoy. But it does mean that you give consideration to which foods are healthy for you to eat and which are unhealthy. Increase those that are healthy and reduce what is unhealthy. And limit the quantity of the food that you eat.

Engaging in healthy eating does not necessarily mean that you must subscribe to a strict diet. In fact, traditional dieting may prove a greater hindrance to your mental health than any positive outcome that may result. Begin with incremental changes. And make those changes because you are a person of worth and value, and you deserve to take good care of your body.

When we were looking at sleep disturbances, I suggested you eliminate or limit caffeine and alcohol consumption. This is also a good idea from the standpoint of healthy eating. It may be that putting a strict limit on caffeine and alcohol consumption may be the single most positive dietary change that you can make.

Exercise Regularly

Is your idea of regular exercise walking to the kitchen to refill your glass of iced tea? Physical exercise often takes a vacation when sexual acting out is at its peak. Some sexual addicts may not exercise at all. Again, if self-esteem is already low from acting out, there may be little motivation to take care of one's body.

A good physical exercise routine is necessary if you are going to get the maximum longevity and quality out of life. Consider getting a good cardio workout for at least twenty minutes, three times a week. When you start out, this may be as simple as a vigorous walk in the evening. As you get adjusted to your new physical routine, you may want to add some weight training or other types of resistance workout to exercise all of the muscle groups in your body.

The focus here is only on the physical benefits of exercise. On Day 19 we will consider the mental and emotional benefits of exercise. The better you take care of your body, the healthier you will be in terms of your overall recovery.

Get a Physical Examination

How is your physical health? Do you monitor the state of your health? When is the last time you had a physical exam? Do you know for certain that you do not have any hidden health concerns?

Prior to engaging in any exercise routine, it is important to have a complete physical exam. It is also a good idea to have an annual exam just to monitor the state of your health. Some sexual addicts pay more attention to their automobiles than they do to their physical health. With a car or truck you normally have a periodic inspection or tune-up to check out the safety equipment and to ensure all systems are operating as they should. Your body deserves no less. Verify or rule out the presence of any sexually transmitted diseases. If they are present, they require treatment. And if you find out you have an STD, your relationship partner or partners must know so that they can receive treatment. Use the support of a trusted friend when contacting former sex partners. This person is preferably someone else who has been in recovery longer than you and who will guide and support you as you make these necessary contacts.

Hormone levels should to be examined. This is true for both men and women. An imbalance in this area may make recovery difficult. And if an imbalance is discovered, you may be referred to another physician such as an endocrinologist or other specialist.

Get your doctor to evaluate all of the prescription medication that you are taking. Ask if you require every prescription. They may still be important. Or your condition may have changed so that you no longer require a particular medication.

Have a Dental Check-Up

Neglecting your teeth may be an indicator that your life is out-of-control. Good recovery and good dental care go hand-in-hand. When is the last time you went to a dentist? If you cannot remember, that is probably an indication that it has been too long.

What does good dental care have to do with recovery? It is amazing how many people who struggle with sexual addiction have not had dental care in years. Infrequent dental care may be a sign of poor or nonexistent recovery.

Make a dental appointment today. Determine that you are going to take care of your teeth so that they will last throughout your lifetime. You are worth it!

Visit a Psychiatrist

"I don't need a psychiatrist. I'm not sick!" This closed attitude has kept many people who could benefit from psychiatric care from seeking the treatment they require. Addiction brings guilt and shame, which are usually accompanied by significant self-esteem problems. It is hard to feel good about yourself when you make a vow to not act out and find that you cannot keep that promise—sometimes not even for a day. The result? Addicts often end up in the pit of depression.

Guilt and shame often lead to depression. Knowledge of previous acting out and the people who have been hurt may contribute to a profound depressive state. In some cases depression can be so significant that inpatient treatment is indicated.

In addition, addicts may suffer from heightened anxiety, fear of discovery, uncontrollable anger or rage, feelings of inferiority, and any number of other things that could possibly benefit from the intervention of a psychiatrist. There may be an underlying psychiatric cause for one's inability to say no to various acting out behaviors.

An alarmingly large number of sexual addicts have been victims of various kinds of abuse as a child. These psychological wounds may be at the root of sexual addiction. Without psychiatric intervention coupled with therapy and Twelve Step recovery groups, it may be difficult to engage in successful recovery.

Psychiatrists treat mood disorders such as depression with a variety of medications. Some of these medications have the side benefit of treating insomnia, which is frequently experienced by those battling sexual addiction. Once properly regulated, medications to treat the emotional problems that sexual addicts suffer, may bring about a level of relief the addict did not think was possible. The role of psychotropic medications is to help stabilize the addict as he or she learns new behaviors and how to make better choices.

While certain disorders may require a person to remain on medication for a lifetime, some addicts only require medication for a year or two. Psychiatrists schedule frequent visits for medication checks. They will be interested in how the patient has felt since the previous visit, what kind of progress the patient is making in recovery from sexual addiction, and any possible side effects.

It is unfortunate that some in society still attach a stigma to psychiatric intervention. But as one addict put it, "I'll gladly see a psychiatrist three or four times a year for the rest of my life if it will help me remain sober."

If there are no emotional issues that require psychiatric intervention, the doctor will dismiss you with his or her best wishes. It is much better to have visited a psychiatrist and find out that you did not need their help than to dismiss the thought of making such an appointment for fear of being stigmatized. Failure to get psychiatric intervention when indicated may cause you to struggle in recovery because you do not have medication that could help ensure your successful recovery from sexual addiction.

At Hope & Freedom, we routinely screen individuals for several things including depression and other mood disorders, as well as attention deficit/hyperactivity disorder (ADHD). This is also the practice of many other psychotherapists. If one of our screenings indicates the possible presence of one or more of these disorders, we routinely refer the client to a psychiatrist. Sometimes I may get an indication from one of the screening instruments that a person may suffer from ADHD or depression or anxiety disorder. However, a thorough examination by a psychiatrist may reveal the presence of a different disorder. The reason is because several disorders may have the same symptoms. To properly diagnose what is present takes time as does eliminating other disorders that may be present with similar symptoms.

At the time of your exam, tell the doctor you struggle with sexual addiction and that you want to be evaluated for mood disorders (the most common of these is depression), ADHD, and any other disorder that may be present. A skilled psychiatrist will be able to quickly zero in on the things that may be impacting both your addiction and recovery.

If you have some underlying condition such as a mood disorder or ADHD, it must be treated and effectively managed in order for you to be successful in recovery. It is not that we would say that a mood disorder or ADHD is the cause of the sexual addiction, but we do know that leaving such underlying conditions without treatment may prevent a person from making much headway in recovery.

Some of the medications for treating depression and other disorders have a negative impact on a person's sex drive. While taking such a drug is not a cure for sexual addiction, the sexual side effects may be helpful in the early stages of recovery. As recovery progresses and you learn healthy boundaries and build a significant length of sobriety, it may be beneficial to change to other medications that do not lower your sex drive so that you can focus on developing a healthy sexual relationship with your spouse.

On another note, there has been some promising treatment over the past few years with a drug call naltrexone. Its primary use has been in treatment of alcohol dependence. It has been used experimentally with the treatment of addiction to heroin as well as with sexual addiction.

As of this writing there have only been a few studies published concerning the use of naltrexone in treating sexual addiction. These were small studies that gave individual results of case studies where naltrexone has been used. The early results indicate this medication may be useful in reducing the compulsive behavior that accompanies sexual addiction. More studies with a much larger population will have to be conducted before this drug gets wide-spread use in treating sexual addiction.

Various medications may be beneficial in treating other underlying conditions that are co-occurring with sexual addiction. However, there is no known drug or combination of drugs that will cure sexual addiction. Some people spend a lot of time and energy searching for an easier way to recovery. There is great value in medications that treat underlying mental and emotional disorders, but pharmacology alone will not restore you to healthy sexuality. There is no substitute for engaging in a strong recovery program.

Why visit a psychiatrist instead of your family doctor? Any physician can prescribe psychotropic medications. However, psychiatrists treat only mental and emotional disorders and have superior diagnostic skills when it comes to recognizing what is going on with a person's emotions, as well as understanding how various medications can help or hinder recovery efforts. Psychiatrists are more inclined to give appropriate medication check-ups to ensure the proper drug in the right dosage is being prescribed.

If you have some underlying condition such as depression, ADHD, or anxiety disorder, it will require a great deal of patience on your part for you to get to the appropriate level of the right medication for your condition. Your doctor will likely start you on a small dose of a particular medication, then adjust the dosage over the next several weeks until you are taking the appropriate amount of medication for your condition. Or, the routine will start again with a new medication and gradual increases in the dosage.

Not everyone responds the same way to various medications. Stay with it. Continue your quest. Your patience will result is getting a therapeutic dose of the right medication for you. You will discover, perhaps for the first time, what it feels like to be "normal." Keep pressing on. Your efforts will be rewarded when you find that recovery is more manageable with all of your underlying conditions receiving proper care.

Caution about Ropinirole

Ropinirole is a drug used for treating Parkinson's disease. It has also been approved to treat restless leg syndrome.[25] The drug is a dopamine agonist, meaning that it is a compound that activates dopamine receptors in the brain. Dopamine plays a key role in the pleasure and reward system.

Sexual addicts are addicted to the neurochemical high that is produced by their compulsive sexual behavior, and dopamine is one of the primary neurotransmitters that is involved in that feeling of euphoria. A common side effect of dopamine agonists is pathological addiction including gambling, shopping, Internet pornography, and hyper-sexuality.[26]

If this drug, which goes under various trade names, has been prescribed for you, be certain to tell your physician that you struggle with compulsive sexual behavior. The benefit may well outweigh the potential side effects. However, it is also true that this drug may provide fuel for your addiction.

---

25. (Lipp, 2008)
26. (Dopamine Agonist, 2009)

Thirty Days to Hope & Freedom for Sexual Addicts

Day 11: Count the Cost

What has your addiction cost you? Depending on your frame of reference you could answer this question in many ways. In this chapter I want to stretch your thinking a bit as you consider what price you have paid so far for your addiction.

Bernie's Story

Bernie was a senior executive with a Fortune 100 company. Through the years he had been sexual with several employees though he told himself that he had always been discreet. There had been an occasional threat of sexual harassment suits, but he was not concerned. Bernie felt he was untouchable, because he was such a high performer and was in a "class by himself."

He was shocked when the president of his company and a guard showed up at his desk and gave him fifteen minutes to clean out his office and exit the building. He was terminated "for cause." He received no severance pay and no recommendation. He found that his reputation had preceded him. In spite of his best efforts he could not find another job at his level in his industry. Bernie now wonders how he ever got so far off course.

Hard Costs

When asked what something costs, we may think immediately about the cost in terms of dollars and cents. And this is a good way to begin evaluating what your addiction has cost you. The most immediate costs you may think of are those where you paid for pornography or you paid someone for sexual services.

If you have paid someone for sex, break it down into categories such as escort services and unlicensed massage parlors. These are places of prostitution even if they are not called brothels. Include all of the houses of prostitution that you have frequented even if they were called spas, studios, or salons. Also include what you have spent on streetwalkers. Include any additional expenses that you incurred such as transportation, hotel costs, and any time you missed at work and were not paid for the absence.

Next, total up all that you have spent on pornography. Include all sources of pornography including print, Internet websites, pay-per-view movies at your home or in a hotel, and any videos you have rented or purchased. Since a person does not have to spend any money to see pornography online, some people will not have spent any money on pornography. If that describes you, do not be deceived into thinking that your addiction has cost you nothing.

If you have lost a marriage or perhaps even more than one marriage to your addiction, include the total cost of your legal fees. If you or your partner has filed for divorce, but you never actually ended the relationship, include all of those legal fees as well. And if you are paying child support as the result of a marriage that ended due in any way to your sexual addiction, include the total that you will have to pay.

Sometimes alcohol or other drugs are used as part of acting out. If you have pursued any other addiction as part of your sexual acting out, include all of those expenses. If you also have a gambling addiction, include all of your gambling losses and transportation costs.

If you have received therapy in the past or are currently in therapy to address sexual addiction, include all of those costs. If you have been in therapy during previous relationships and you know that you were acting out during those relationships, then include those costs as well. Include all transportation costs and any costs associated with missing work.

Any psychiatric expenses you have incurred as a result of your addiction should be included. For example, if during your treatment for sexual addiction, you have been sent to a psychiatrist for depression or ADHD or some other disorder, you will want to include those expenses. Once again, add in your transportation costs.

If you have had affairs, detail the financial cost of each of them. Include the costs of hotels, meals, entertainment, trips, and all associated transportation costs. If you have purchased gifts for your affair partner, include the cost of each of these.

For persons in committed relationships, include the cost of any guilt offerings. These are the gifts you purchased for your spouse because you were feeling guilty about your behavior. The gifts may be as simple as a bouquet of flowers to something as expensive as an automobile or perhaps something even more expensive. Just because your spouse gets some usefulness out of the gift does not eliminate the fact that it is a guilt offering.

At this point, some people who had thought their addiction has not cost them much have had their eyes opened. You may be realizing that you have spent more money on your addiction that you once thought. But monetary expenses are not the only costs of sexual addiction.

Wynn's Story

Wynn considered himself to be a cut above most people. He was successful in his career with a salary that was several times that of most of his friends. His company turned to him anytime they had a significant problem that was in his area of expertise. They knew he would solve the crisis, whatever it was. Wynn felt a bit cocky though he described himself as just being self-assured.

When he visited his first strip club, he found that he could get all sorts of sexual favors performed for anywhere from $25 to several hundred dollars. He was well able to afford whatever the charge. It was not uncommon for him to spend more than a thousand dollars at each visit as he engaged multiple partners. He was known for his large tips. His generosity made him very popular with all of the dancers in his favorite club.

Everything seemed to be going well until he was caught in a compromising position in the VIP room by an undercover police officer. To make matters worse, the city where he lives has an electronic billboard that rotates the photos and names of men who have been charged with soliciting prostitution. He lost his job not long after his photo appeared the first time on that billboard.

Time Spent

How much time have you spent acting out during your lifetime? Begin by estimating the hours you have spent per week for each year of your life beginning at age eighteen. Take the time necessary to look back at each year, and then make your best estimate as to how many hours you spent acting out. Multiply the number of hours per week times fifty-two, and then multiply that number by the number of years you have been a sexual addict.

The resulting number should be the total number of hours you have spent acting out during your adult years. Take that number and divide it by 8,760 (the number of hours in a year), and you will find how many years (or the fraction of a year) you have spent acting out if it had been done all day, every day. You can also take the total number of hours you have acted out and divide it by forty to get the number weeks you have spent if your acting out had been a full-time job.

Consider this the same as losing an equal amount of time from your life. What if at the very end of life, you could regain all the time that you spent acting out? You cannot do anything about the past, but you can keep from wasting any more time on your addiction in the future.

To drive the point closer to home, spend a few minutes thinking about what your hourly wage or salary would have been for each year of your life. If you multiply your hourly wage for that year with the number of hours spent acting out, you will find what your acting out time was worth during that year. And if you add the annual totals together, you will likely find a very shocking number that represents the value of the time you spent acting out during your lifetime. It is not unusual for this to be a very large six figure number and sometimes even much greater than that.

Opportunities Lost

Next, consider the opportunities that you have lost due to your addiction. It may be that you missed the opportunity to further your education because of your acting out. I have known many people who have either dropped out or flunked out of school because of their addiction. And I know of several cases where people were in medical school but ended up dropping out because their obsession with cybersex cut into their study time.

In addition to lost educational opportunities, what about lost business opportunities? Have you lost business, not actively pursued a potential contract, or lost customers or clients, all because you were focused on acting out? Is it possible you might have received a promotion or perhaps several promotions if you had been more focused on your job?

I have talked to people who have bankrupted their businesses due to their acting out. All they have to show for their efforts is a key to a business they no longer own. And while this may seem extreme to you, it is not beyond the realm of possibility. Could that be your future if you do not make recovery a priority?

Strained or Ruined Relationships

If you have been through a divorce or the end of another relationship, you may have already calculated the dollar cost of the break-up. But take a few minutes and consider how many lives you have negatively impacted as you pursued your addiction. My purpose here is not to make you feel bad about the past but to help you get a clear picture of the cost of your addiction.

It may be easy to forget the pain that came to others due to your acting out. This may especially be true when you move to another relationship. But the wounds you caused by your behavior may impact other people for years to come. Some of them may never get over the pain and suffering that you caused.

If you are a parent, how has your sexual addiction impacted your children? Even if your marriage is still intact, there are likely more wounds present in your children's lives than are readily apparent. How has your pursuit of addiction affected them? Just because they may not know the details of your behavior does not mean that they have not been affected. It is impossible for there to be an addiction present in a family and it not have some adverse impact on the other family members.

Cost of Addiction

When I consider the dollar value of the time I wasted in addiction as well as the money I spent on addiction and recovery, my addiction has cost me $ _____.

In addition, I have incurred the following costs due to my addiction: _____

_____

_____

_____

_____

Purpose of this Exercise

What is the purpose of this exercise? It is intended to give you a reality check. Sexual addiction has probably cost you more than you may have realized. Whatever it has cost, you do not have to continue to incur new addiction costs. Recovery costs may continue and may be significant. But regardless of the cost of therapy and/or treatment, it is often a fraction of what has been spent on the addiction.

Day 12: Pre-Planning!
Plan and Prepare When Sober

Fire departments spend a great deal of time pre-planning how they will fight fires in particular structures. They have a plan that they put into operation at each type of fire. Some of the plans are somewhat generic—single story houses, small apartment units, etc. For other buildings, they have a specific plan for that structure. If you are in a high-rise building, you can be sure there is a specific plan that has been written for that building and that the fire fighters assigned as first responders know how they will proceed, should there be any type of fire emergency. Just as fire fighters do, you must pre-plan for the next sexual trigger.

When are you the most vulnerable to acting out? Carefully consider the last time that you acted out. What were the circumstances that led to your actions? Think of all of the factors that contributed to your behavior.

Next, spend time considering each of the previous five to ten times that you acted-out. Repeat the exercise above and list all of the factors that came into play. Sit down with your sponsor and go over each of your lists. Ask your sponsor to point out anything that you may have overlooked.

Go back and consult the worksheets from Day 8 about internal and external triggers. They will help to reinforce your memory about your specific triggers. Even though circumstances may change, your triggers will likely remain constant.

For example, one person found that the circumstance where he was the most at risk was when he had to travel to a nearby city for business. He found there were several things that were going on for him that put him at risk. He went back to the last trip where he acted out and tried to remember what happened right up to his acting out. His plan is below:

Sample At-Risk Plan

The following is a plan that was developed to deal with an upcoming situation that was likely to be triggering.

Circumstance: Last similar situation
- Planning car trip to Charlotte tomorrow for business.
- Had thoughts last night about the potential for acting out in strip clubs where I am unlikely to meet anyone that I know.
- Check my wallet to make sure I have sufficient cash to cover anything that I may want to do in the strip club.

- Just before bed, I tell myself I will not go to the strip clubs this trip. As a result I am able to sleep better.
- Next day driving to Charlotte, I can't stop thinking about the strip clubs.
- My business presentation is at 9:00 a.m. I should be through by 10:30 a.m., plenty of time left to go to the strip club and still be home by mid-afternoon.
- On the way to my business meeting, I go by my favorite strip club to see whether there are many cars in the parking lot.
- I check to see whether I have my secret credit card, just in case I spend more than I have planned.
- I realize this is not going to be a brief visit, so I call my wife and tell her I am going to have to stay in Charlotte and have dinner with my client. I now have more than enough time to do whatever I want.
- As I remember this particular trip, I am reminded that I spent more than $1,800 that day. That is the most I have ever spent at a strip club. The irony is that I spent that within the first couple of hours. I got home earlier than my wife was expecting me. She was so glad to see me. To show how happy she was to see me, she cooked me a special dinner. That night she wanted to be sexual. I had to fake a headache because I knew I would not be able to get an erection. In retrospect, I would have enjoyed being sexual with my wife much more than the things I did on that trip.

Plan: Things I must do next time

- When planning my next trip out-of-town, I want a plan for how I will productively fill each moment while I am away.
- I could invite one of the male junior account managers to travel with me. That alone would prevent me from acting out because I don't want anyone to know of my secret life.
- When checking my wallet, I must leave all of my cash behind. For parking and lunch I will use my company credit card.
- I realize it is time for me to get rid of my secret credit card. I can't close the account because I owe so much on it, but I can destroy the card and call the lender and say no further charges are authorized on that card.
- I plan to leave my personal credit cards and my debit card at home.
- When I get to Charlotte, I am going to avoid going to the parts of town where I have acted out in the past. I recognize that in the past I have told myself it is not acting out just to drive by a strip club to see how many cars are in the parking lot. But that is where my addiction really gets fueled.

Accountability: My Circle of Five

- Before my trip, I am going to call my sponsor and the men in my Circle of Five[27] and tell them of my plans.
- On my way to Charlotte, I am going to call my sponsor, verify that I am not carrying cash and that the only credit card I have is my company expense card for my lunch and parking.
- When my meeting is over, I am going to call one of the men in my Circle to tell him I am on my way home. I will ask if it is all right if I call him again when I arrive at home.
- When I arrive at home, I will call again to report that I have arrived safely.
- In addition to calling the men in my Circle, I will call my wife after my meeting to let her know when I will be home.

Now it is time to make your own At-Risk Plan. When you work the plan on the next page, you may find that your "plan" is similar for each "at risk" circumstance you have identified. If that is the case, do not worry about making a separate plan for each situation. Instead make a plan that works with many of the occasions.

However, you may find that a certain situation requires a specific detailed plan that is unique to that occasion. In that case, make copies of the following chart and come up with a detailed plan for each circumstance. The greater the detail, the better your plan.

---

27. Circle of Five is five people to whom you are always accountable. For a more detailed account of the Circle of Five, see *Hope & Freedom for Sexual Addicts and Their Partners*, pp. 77-78.

At-Risk Plan Worksheet

Think back to when I have acted out in the past. What was going on in my life that put me "at risk" on those days? The circumstances may have involved my primary relationship, some other relationship, my job, finances, or some personal circumstance. What are the things that indicate that I am "at risk" on a particular day?

Circumstance	At Risk	Things I Must Do	Plan	Accountability	Circle of Five

Thirty Days to Hope & Freedom for Sexual Addicts

Commitment

My desire is to remain completely free from all acting out behavior. To that end:

1. I commit to stay aware of circumstances that indicate that I am at an increased risk of acting out.

2. I commit to implement my "At-Risk Plan" the moment I recognize I am at risk.

3. I commit to calling _____ at _____ to tell them that I am at risk and what I am going to do to address that risk.

4. If I cannot contact the person above, I will call _____ at _____.

5. If that person is not available I will continue calling my Circle of Five until I contact someone.

6. I further commit to calling the person contacted above at the end of the day to report my progress in working this plan.

Signed _____   Witness_____

Date _____

Day 13: Behavioral Inventory—
Stop, Start, or Change?

Making inventories is a key part of recovery. When you work your Fourth Step, you will be making inventories about your resentments, your character defects, your sexual history, and perhaps other inventories, such as a list of your strong character qualities. I would like to suggest that there are some more inventories that would be helpful. It might even be helpful if you would make three lists right now. First, what are the things I should *stop doing* now that I am in recovery? Second, what are the things I want to *start doing* since I am in recovery? Finally, what are the things *I need to change* to support my recovery?

Lucas's Story

The open road beckoned Lucas every time he was home for more than a couple of days. He had worked as a long-haul truck driver for more than twenty years. He made good money and loved seeing the country. Most of all, he loved truck stops.

He had placed subtle markings on his truck indicating to truck stop prostitutes that he was always looking for company. Lucas was careful to use protection. He did not let his secret life on the road intrude into his family life. He loved his family and felt he had the perfect set-up—until his wife contracted an STD. How was that possible? After all, he used protection. Lucas discovered that it was indeed possible to contract an STD even when using a condom.

Things I Need to Stop

Are there things you need to stop to support good recovery? Begin with a list of all of the things that have been associated with your acting out. What are the dangerous behaviors that have been associated with your past compulsive sexual behavior? As you identify these behaviors, think about how you can eliminate them from your life.

Next, you will also want to stop any abusive behavior toward your partner or others. On the surface it may not seem like this has anything to do with recovery. But it has everything to do with recovery. If you are not feeling good about yourself because of the secret and shameful things you have been doing, do you think it is possible that you have let your feelings toward yourself spill out in the way you speak to your spouse, your children, and your coworkers?

Think further about the way you speak to your partner. Do you respond with short, curt answers to questions? Do you think they are going out of their way to get on your nerves? Do you have a short-temper and take it out on others? Can you flip from happy to raging over little things?

Next, it is time to stop all of the behaviors that are selfish. When I am working with a married couple where the husband is the sexual addict, I am amazed at how often wives tell me they believe their husband is a narcissist. It is actually rare for me to have a client who has narcissistic personality disorder. As with the other personality disorders, narcissistic personality disorder is extremely difficult to treat. No more than one percent of the general population meets the criteria for this disorder.[28]

However, it is true that many of the behaviors of sexual addicts are very narcissistic. For sexual addicts, what matters most is how they feel, what they want, and what makes them happy. The rest of the world often revolves around them.

This is the time to expand the list of your selfish behaviors you made on Day 2 with the goal of eliminating them from your life. As you make your inventory, ask your sponsor or a trusted friend to help you see additional behaviors that are selfish. Before doing this, you will want to have an agreement with your friend that you want complete honesty so that you can become aware of your blind spots concerning your own behavior. It will require significant self-discipline to keep you from getting your feelings hurt or from dismissing the input from others as being inaccurate.

After assimilating the information you gather from your sponsor, consider having someone else you are close to review the list and give additional observations of selfish behavior they have observed in you. And if you are really brave, consider asking your spouse to look at the list and add to it. However, it is vital that you agree beforehand that you will not become angry with your spouse or later use any passive-aggressive behavior toward him or her to show your displeasure in their observations.

Your goal with this exercise is to become more self-aware. If you do not like what others are telling you, instead of being mad at them, consider what you are going to do to change your behavior. And if you do not agree with their observations, ask yourself what part of what they said is true.

If you are getting the same feedback from more than one source, this is probably a good indication that the feedback is valid and that you may be the only one who does not see the selfishness of your behavior. And if you still do not agree with others' evaluations of you, even when you have multiple sources telling you the same thing, there is another possibility. You may indeed have narcissistic personality disorder. It may be time for you to read all that you can about the disorder and then consider getting professional help to address this condition.

Things I Need to Start

What are the things you need to start now that you are in recovery? Chief on this list will be all of your recovery routines. On Day 24, you will put together a Personal Recovery Plan with a list of all of the things you will do daily, weekly, monthly, and annually for recovery. All of the things that you want to start now will be part of that Personal Recovery Plan as well.

---

28. (Diagnostic and Statistical Manual of Mental Disorders (DSM-IV-TR), 2000) pp. 714-717

Thirty Days to Hope & Freedom for Sexual Addicts

The main thing you will want to start is to begin to truly *live* your life. Rather than go through life reacting to circumstances and people, choose how you will respond. Rather than participating in the same demoralizing behavior again and again, determine that you will choose different behavior.

Volunteer your time for a cause or organization that you believe in. Take up a hobby or engage in an organized sport. Begin to participate in some religious activity. Write a book. Teach a class at a community college.

How you spend your time in recovery will help determine the level of satisfaction that you have in life. You begin by taking care of yourself, then move on to living life beyond yourself. Numerous people find a sense of fulfillment by investing themselves in the lives of others and in worthy causes.

Things to Change

What are the things you should change to support your recovery? It is helpful to think of these by categories. What do you want to change concerning your use of media? Are there changes you need to make regarding how you treat financial matters?

Concerning Relationships

As you look at your current relationships, what changes do you want to make? It may be that there are friendships that you want to end. If you have friends who do not have healthy boundaries or who participate in an unhealthy lifestyle, you might want to consider ending those relationships.

There is often a time of grieving that accompanies recovery. Ending unhealthy relationships may cause you a sense of loss. Remember, the reason you are ending them is so you can do all that is possible to support strong recovery efforts.

It should go without saying that you should end your relationships with all former sex partners. However, I realize that some people have a blind spot in this area. They may have deluded themselves into believing they can "just be good friends" with former sex partners. This is a recipe for disaster. If you have been sexual with someone, you cannot afford to maintain a friendship with that person. Sexual addicts must maintain a strong boundary in this area.

This presents difficulty when the person you have been sexual with is part of your extended family. For example, if you have been sexual with the spouse of one of your siblings, it may not be possible to completely cut off contact with that person. However, it is imperative that you set the healthiest boundaries possible when you have contact with them. For example, you should never be alone with them. You should avoid any personal conversations with them. And it is essential to refrain from any unnecessary contact with them.

You will also want to think about the changes you should make in your traffic patterns. If your normal traffic pattern takes you past the home of a former partner, you will want to vary your route so that you are spared that trigger. The same holds true for the patterns of where you walk at work. If you are triggered by someone at work, consider how you can change the way you travel in the work setting to avoid that person.

While we are thinking about traffic patterns, it would be healthy if you could alter your travel route so that you do not go to the parts of town where you have previously acted out. With some people this may not be possible since they acted out in all parts of town. At least you can take steps to minimize your exposure to the most triggering locations.

If you acted out at work, you may want to consider changing jobs. While this may seem like a drastic step, it is crucial that you do whatever is necessary to ensure that you are working in a healthy environment. If you have developed a sexual relationship with a subordinate, even if you are not that person's direct supervisor, be aware of the potential of being named in a sexual harassment lawsuit, regardless of your gender! Both men and women have been sued and found liable in such legal actions. While creating distance from a former acting-out partner, be certain not to do anything that causes this person to pay for your poor judgment, such as getting them transferred or terminated. Since you are the guilty party (even if they were the aggressor), it is up to you to make the necessary changes in your job. And do not forget that you still run the risk of being named in a future sexual harassment lawsuit.

Another change to consider concerns your use of humor. Do you tell suggestive stories or jokes? Have you ever gotten the sense that someone was uncomfortable with your jokes? Have you ever used sexual humor as a way of "testing the water" to see whether someone would be open to an advance from you? One of the best courses of action is to stop using humor completely. This may prove to be difficult. At the very least become more aware of what you say, when you say it, and to whom you are speaking.

Use of Media

A goal of your recovery is for you to become a careful consumer of media. Initially it may be easy to note which movies and television shows trigger you. Avoiding them is essential to healthy recovery.

Some people set up rules for determining which things they will watch. But humans chafe under a strict list of do's and don'ts. Rather than set up rigid rules, think instead about healthy guidelines for the programs and movies that you watch. Rigid rules are often imposed by someone else such as a spouse, teacher, parent, or law enforcement officer. Healthy boundaries are set up by you and followed in the interest of your continued recovery and not because your spouse or someone else says you must not do something.

I challenge you to establish a "media net" around you. You determine the size of the openings in the net. Early in recovery your media net may have very small openings, similar to the fine screen that is often used on windows. With that type of net, you would exclude anything that might be remotely triggering. As you move forward in recovery, you may allow more things through your media net, but you will still practice selective perception so that you ignore potentially triggering words, songs, or scenes in movies.

Would you benefit from making a change in the amount of television that you view each day? Keep a log for one week every time you turn on the television. Record how many hours it is on during the day. Would you potentially be better off if you curtailed the time you spent watching TV? Your TV viewing habits may be one of the things that are most detrimental to your recovery. If you have to limit the amount of work you do in recovery because it interferes with a particular TV show, perhaps it is time to eliminate that show. And if limited available time is the consideration, the solution is not to record the show so that you can watch it later.

Consider the subject of video games. Are there games that are not healthy for you to play? Are you spending too much time playing games that are not wise to play in the first place? It is dangerous for sexual addicts to play any video games across the Internet. Most of the game consoles now hook to the Internet and allow competition with a number of people at once.[29] Such contact may make you vulnerable to returning to your compulsive sexual behavior.

Consider the subject of surfing the Internet. It is not enough that you avoid pornography sites and sexual chat rooms.[30] The time you spend on the Internet may be negatively impacting the rest of your life. Have you missed family or work functions because you wanted to spend that time on the Internet? Would you rather spend more time with your computer than you would with people? Have you missed a deadline at work because you were spending too much time surfing the web? Has anyone close to you complained that you spend too much time on the Internet? If you answer yes to any of these questions, you probably would do well to put strict limits on the amount of time that you spend online.

Internet auctions are a fun place to shop but can also be addictive. There are sexual addicts that stop looking at porn and turn instead to auction sites to occupy their time. They bid on things they do not need and will not use. Some people spend several hours a day on auction sites but fail to see that behavior as compulsive.

One of the most troubling things involving the Internet is the explosive growth of gambling sites. While online gambling is illegal in the United States and some other countries, the illegality of the activity has not curtailed its use. It would be wise for sexual addicts to completely refrain from any Internet gambling activities because of its addictive potential.

Some sexual addicts flirt with danger and look for sites that will tantalize them but that do not actually meet the definition of pornography. They may spend their time looking at provocative sites such as underwear or lingerie sites, various modeling sites, swimsuit sites, web pages concerned with anatomy, healthy sexuality, nursing, or other subjects where the primary concern of the viewer is to feed the addiction and dance around the edges of the addiction without engaging in bottom-line addictive behavior. Such behavior is an exercise in self-deception.

---

29. More information about video games and their addictive potential is given in Day 22.
30. Additional information about safeguards concerning the Internet is found in Day 17.

Financial Changes

How you handle your finances is part of recovery. Many people who enter recovery will admit that they were secretive about their use of money. Some kept large amounts of cash that was used to facilitate acting out. For sexual addicts whose primary acting out behavior is engaging in some form of prostitution, carrying any cash is problematic, for it is possible to purchase sexual favors with very little money.

This might be a good time to think about alternatives to using cash. Using a debit card rather than cash will provide a paper trail of all of your transactions. But never make a cash withdrawal, because that will hinder the accountability.

Some sexual addicts have accumulated extremely large credit card balances. Indulging impulses to purchase things on credit may be part of a pattern of sexual acting out. Buying things you do not need may have been a medicating behavior that is more closely tied to your addiction than you realize. Do you use shopping to lift your mood? Do you buy things you cannot afford? Have you bought things on the spur of the moment only to regret your purchases later? Do you come to the end of the month and wonder where your money went?

This would be a good time to think about changing your behavior around money. But more than a behavioral change is necessary. You probably would benefit from a new attitude toward money. If you answered yes to any of the questions above, you will want to do some significant work around your finances.

The first step is to develop a budget. There are several good books that can help you. Once you make a budget, stick to it. That will likely require changes in your spending habits.

If you have a problem with spending or going into debt, there are various Twelve Step groups that can provide support for you. In Appendix B you will find contact information for Debtors Anonymous, Spenders Anonymous, and Shopaholics Anonymous. These organizations may be of great value as you seek to change your relationship with money.

Day 14: Break the Isolation

Compulsive sexual behavior carries with it a considerable amount of shame. The greater the shame, the deeper the secret. Sexual addicts are invested in keeping their secrets. There are probably some things that you have done that you do not intend to tell anyone. As your secrets have grown, you have likely isolated yourself more and more from friends, colleagues, and family members.

Cassie's Story

Cassie felt lucky to be a stay-at-home mom. Raising her children had been a rich and rewarding experience for her. When her youngest child entered first grade, she found herself wondering what she was going to do with her time. She also admitted to herself that she was lonely being at home by herself.

The first chat room that she visited seemed harmless. It catered to "bored housewives" and she knew that fit her to a tee. What she did not count on was the open sexual conversations that took place in the chat room. She was intrigued. Each morning she would spend increasingly longer periods of time moving from chat room to chat room to read of the sexual exploits of others. After a while, she engaged in the sexual conversation. Less than six months after first entering a chat room, Cassie realized her behavior had escalated when she agreed to meet in person someone she had been sexual with in a chat room.

Recovery Network

The first thing you have already done to break the isolation is to get a sponsor. You will tell your sponsor your whole story—even your most shameful secrets. Addiction lives and thrives in secret. When you tell your secrets to a trustworthy person, you break the power of shame that is associated with secrets. At this point you start making important advances in your recovery.

You can be sure that your sponsor has probably already heard of your specific behavior either from another sponsee or in a Twelve Step meeting. When you initiate this conversation with your sponsor, you find that you are no longer traveling the recovery journey alone. Your sponsor, as well as other men and women in recovery, will travel the road with you.

Verify with your sponsor that it is all right for you to call him or her frequently during the early part of recovery. Some sponsors require daily phone contact during the first weeks or months after a person starts attending meetings. Your weekly meetings with your sponsor outside of Twelve Step meetings will add the regular accountability that is of paramount importance and keep you from trying to tackle your addiction alone.

Some sexual addicts say that they do not have any true friends. That may not have been the case throughout their lives. In childhood and throughout school they may have had many friends, but as the addiction has progressed, they found themselves becoming more isolated.

Cultivating Friendships

Friendships are central to recovery. One of the best places to cultivate friendships is in recovery meetings. You already know that you have much in common with the members. You may have heard someone speak of behavior that sounds exactly like yours. Someone else who understands your struggles and desire to remain sober will know how to motivate you. They are not going to be quick to place blame but will accept you as you are.

You may have thought you do not need friends. Or perhaps you thought they were too much trouble. Truthfully, it takes time and work to cultivate friendships. It requires great effort to break through isolation. It means making a call when you might rather not talk to anyone. Instead of showing up at meetings at the last minute, get there ten to fifteen minutes early and strike up conversations with the other people arriving early. When the meeting is over, do not be the first one out the door. Instead continue conversations with others for several minutes.

Some meetings end with the members going to a nearby restaurant for coffee or a meal. Break out of your comfort zone and join the fellowship. Remember the reason you are developing the new friendships is to support your recovery. Other recovering people can be an important source of strength and encouragement as you continue your recovery.

It is sad that some of the friends you have prior to recovery may tend to be "unavailable" after they hear of your journey. Do not waste your time worrying about them. They are responsible for their behavior and obviously are not mature enough to be able to handle a completely honest relationship. Someone once said a true friend is the one who is walking toward you when others are walking away.

You cannot have too many friends or too much accountability. I encourage you to consider having a Circle of Five[31]—five people to whom you are always accountable. Keep regular contact with this Circle. Give them permission to ask you the tough questions about your behavior and how you are doing in your recovery.

One of the ways that people isolate themselves is with their computer use. If you live with others, put your computer in a public space and commit to not using it when no one else is around. Another way to break the isolation concerning computer use is to install accountability software that will send an e-mail once a week to an accountability person of the sites that you have visited. This has the same effect as having your accountability partner in the same room with you, fully aware of the sites you are visiting.[32]

One caution concerning the use of accountability software. It is not a good idea to have your spouse or partner receive that accountability e-mail. That puts them in a parental role, which is not healthy for your relationship. Instead, enlist your sponsor or someone else who is in recovery to receive this information.

---

31. For a more detailed account of the Circle of Five, see Hope & Freedom for Sexual Addicts and Their Partners, p. 77-78.
32. Day 17 contains additional suggestions for changing your Internet behaviors.

Day 15: Dump the Stash

Victor's Story

Victor nervously awaited the results of his polygraph exam. Under pressure from his wife he agreed to participate in a Three-Day Intensive[33] that he knew would include a full disclosure of his previous sexual behavior as well as a polygraph exam. Victor feigned surprise when he heard that he failed the polygraph exam. He said he could not understand why he failed because his disclosure was complete. Indeed, he had included most of his acting out on his disclosure.

What he did not reveal was that he had agreed to go to the Intensive just to buy some time so he could continue his acting out—most of which centered on his pornography use. After a difficult afternoon with his wife as well as a time of personal self-assessment, Victor made the decision to stop his acting out and commit himself to recovery. When he entered the therapist's office the next morning, he tossed a portable USB flash drive onto the coffee table and said, "There it is." "There what is?" replied his therapist. "That is my stash. That memory stick contains every video and pornographic image I have downloaded over the past few years. That is the only copy that I have." Then he hung his head and added, "That also contains photos of every person I have had sex with."

Victor initially thought he could pacify his wife by engaging in some recovery activities without really committing himself to a life of recovery. For him, his stash of pornography represented that part of his addiction that he was initially unwilling to give up. His willingness to finally relinquish his stash proved to be the pivotal event in his subsequent success in recovery.

Sexual addiction involves secrets. Often this includes secret materials or paraphernalia used as part of acting out. Chief among these is a stash of pornography.

When Internet pornography is involved, long hours are often spent looking for just the "right" image or video. Searches may occupy many hours sitting in front of a computer hoping to find the image that will provide the neurochemical high that will satisfy the craving. But the cravings are only satisfied for a few moments, and then the search continues.

People may download thousands of images and store them for later use. At this point the addiction is concerned with the hunt and the chase rather than enjoying the pornography in the moment. These downloaded images may be hidden in multiple locations at home or the office. Much like the alcoholic who hides booze so that he will never be without, some sexual addicts have multiple stashes of pornography so that a fix is always at hand.

---

33. More information in Appendix A, page 211.

Clean Up—Clear Out

When entering recovery it is crucial that you eliminate all of your stash. When you do this, enlist the help of your sponsor or someone else in recovery. That added measure of accountability will help keep you from acting out while you clean up and clear out all of the things that are not healthy. Carefully think about all of the places where you may have hidden images. Collect them all and destroy them.

Get rid of any computer bookmarks that mark the places where you have acted out. Carefully go through your favorites list and cull out all of the places that may be triggering later on. Do not forget to eliminate bookmarks of places that may not have been pornographic or explicit but that were used by you to fuel your addictive behavior.

Jarrod's Story

Jarrod received a webcam as a gift from his daughter. When she got married and moved to England a few months earlier, she wanted to be able to have frequent face-to-face conversations with her parents. Soon after Jarrod installed the webcam, he received an instant message from someone inviting him to join a webcam community. It sounded like fun.

What he did not realize is that the community he joined was devoted to sexual acting out using webcams. After a few weeks he was frequently engaging in mutual masturbation with both men and women via webcam. Imagine the shock when his wife walked in on him when he was engaged in a sexual webcam conversation with a total stranger!

If your acting out involves a webcam, you may want to consider getting rid of it. If you do require a webcam for work, it is time to consider what kinds of boundaries you are going to have around your webcam behavior.

You may want to consider getting your computer hard drive professionally cleaned. However, use caution. If you have ever accessed child porn—even once—then you would be better off destroying your hard drive and getting a new one. If even one child pornography photo is discovered by a technician, it may be reported to the authorities and could result in severe penalties that may include arrest and a prison sentence.

If you have used any sexual paraphernalia for your acting out, destroy that stash completely. For example, if you engaged in any cross-dressing behavior, get rid of all of your dress up clothes, as well as anything else that was used. Get rid of all sex toys.

Anthony's Story

Anthony has been going to strip clubs on and off for more than twenty years. He remembers the first time he went to a club and was shocked that women he did not know would walk around in front of him not wearing any clothes. On one of his early visits he received his first lap dance. A point of pride with Anthony is that he has not engaged in any other sexual behavior at the clubs, other than paying for a dance.

Thirty Days to Hope & Freedom for Sexual Addicts

After Anthony shared in a meeting that he did not do "anything" sexual in strip clubs, he was confronted by other members of the Twelve Step group. He talked openly about receiving lap dances. As the discussion went further, he admitted that he always kept a pair of nylon workout pants in the trunk of his car. Before going to a strip club he would change into those pants and wear them without underwear so that he would get more sensation when the dancers rubbed against him.

Anthony's stash included not just the nylon pants that he wore to strip clubs but other items of clothing that he kept in his car. He routinely changed his clothes so that his wife would not smell smoke or beer on him when he got home. After entering recovery he cleaned out his car as well as his office and threw away the clothing items he used in acting out.

If you have ever acted out with people, you must get rid of all contact information of former sex partners. Erase all phone numbers, e-mail addresses, and any other contact information. Again, do this with the help of others who are in recovery.

Day 16: Close All Secret Accounts

Christopher's Story

Christopher did not spend a lot of money acting out. At least not at first. There were a number of purchases he made through the years for his addiction including pornographic videos, sex toys, and an occasional hotel room. He took care of the family finances and he found that he could hide his purchases rather easily. One of the ways he did this was to make cash withdrawals at ATMs.

After his wife found the receipt for a large cash withdrawal, he knew he had to come up with another system. His job required a lot of travel, so he incurred significant expenses that he charged on his own credit card and submitted for reimbursement to his company. Since his wife did not check the credit card statement closely, he could successfully hide some of his purchases on that card.

As his sexual behavior increased and the money he spent related to his addiction grew larger, Christopher asked for his company expense reimbursement in a separate check. Ostensibly this was to make it easier to keep track of in his personal finances. The real reason for the separate check was so that he could have the cash he wanted to fund his rapidly escalating addiction. When he finally got into recovery, he calculated that he had spent over $25,000 in the previous year to pay for prostitutes and hotel rooms—all funded with his secret company reimbursement checks.

Recovery means putting an end to secrets, which are the stock-in-trade of sexual addicts. If you are in a committed relationship and you have opened any credit card or checking accounts that your partner does not know about, close all of them now. It is also time to eliminate any secret stash of cash. Secret stashes may start out as a way to save money for a gift for your partner, but for sexual addicts, a secret stash of cash is an invitation to act out.

Brandon's Story

Brandon got a secret post office box when he was planning his first divorce. He got it so he would be able to receive correspondence from his attorney without his wife knowing he was planning on a divorce. After he remarried, Brandon found a new use for the secret post office box. He ordered a number of sexual items and had them delivered secretly.

One of his areas of attraction was to teenage boys. He was careful not to access any websites with underage photos because he knew there was a risk of him getting arrested. It seemed safe to order photos and videos and have them delivered to his post office box in a plain brown wrapper. That is, it seemed safe until the day he opened his mailbox and was met by postal inspectors and FBI agents.

Secrets must to come to an end. Regardless of the reason you think justifies having a secret account or secret post office box, it is critical to your recovery that you close them immediately. Recovery means living life in the light. Put an end to all secret behavior today.

My Commitment

In recovery, I want to live my life in the light. Today, _____,
I commit myself to closing all secret accounts and secret post office boxes. As a point of accountability, I will tell my sponsor or other recovering person about my commitment and let them know when this action is completed.

Signed _____

Day 17: Make Peace with the Internet

The Internet has changed the way we live. We can find information about any subject in a matter of seconds. Some people have been able to work from home or in other remote locations thanks to the flexibility afforded by the Internet. But the Internet has also brought a number of problems to society.

Alicia's Story

When Alicia first browsed an international dating site, she was hoping to meet someone who was different and perhaps exotic. Soon she was getting replies from all over the world as men expressed their affection for her. When one of them wanted to meet her, she agreed to meet him in Europe for a romantic weekend.

Since she had lots of airline miles, she was able to make the trip very economically. Alicia did indeed meet her mystery lover, only to find out that he was just interested in having sex with her and did not want a lasting relationship. By the time Alicia began therapy for her sexual addiction, she had repeated variations of this scenario dozens of times. Each time it ended in heartbreak.

How Much of a Problem Is Cybersex Behavior?

It has been shown that sexual acting out on the Internet is of a progressive nature. The husband who begins a "harmless" cyber affair rationalizes that his activity will lead to nothing more, especially if his cyber partner lives far away. A wife may rationalize that her online sexual activities are not really infidelity and besides, she craves the attention her cyber lover gives her. However, the power of the cyber affair once unleashed, can lead people who would otherwise be faithful to their mates to become obsessed with the intrigue offered by cybersex.[34]

Data indicate those involved in cyber relationships are prone to either stretch the truth about themselves or to invent a completely false identity in order to lure potential victims. The most common misrepresentation is age, with 48 percent of subjects in a survey indicating they changed their age "occasionally" and 23 percent reporting they change their age "often" to "very often." The same survey found that 38 percent reported changing their race when online. Five percent of respondents reported changing their gender, a phenomenon known as "gender bending."[35]

Two models have been proposed to explain the phenomenon of cybersex addiction. The ACE model, developed by Kimberly Young[36] has sought to explain the addictive nature of the

---

34. (Young, Griffin-Shelley, & Cooper, 2000)
35. (Cooper & Delmonico, 2000)
36. (Young, Griffin-Shelley, & Cooper, 2000)

Internet with the words *anonymity*, *convenience*, and *escape*. The anonymity of the medium, combined with the convenience of its use, allows persons to escape into a fantasy world that has few, if any, restraints.

Young's model is a variant of an earlier model developed by Al Cooper, known as the Triple-A Engine.[37] Cooper suggested that access and affordability, combined with anonymity, account for the Internet's power to attract people into a cycle of addiction. The anonymity of the medium lures unsuspecting people into secret virtual sexual encounters. In chat rooms, users communicate with "screen names" or "handles" and live out fantasies without leaving the privacy of their home or office. That anonymity encourages users to communicate in a more open and frank manner than would be their norm.[38]

Raymond's Story

Pornography has taken over Raymond's life. He is obsessed with finding the perfect image for his fantasies. The problem is that his wife and children use the same computer, and it has parental controls to block pornography. Raymond discovered proxy servers that will allow him to use other computers to do his searches for him without having to disable the parental controls. Things were going well until he discovered that his thirteen-year-old was also using a proxy server to circumvent the pornography blocker. Both Raymond and his son are now seeing therapists for their compulsive sexual behavior.

A study was conducted to determine the role of the Internet in sexual addiction. Of 133 self-identified sexual addicts surveyed, 29 percent said they spent twenty hours or move engaging in cybersex behavior prior to entering recovery. Forty-nine percent of respondents said they engaged in cybersex between ten and twenty-nine hours each week. Only 11 percent indicated that their addiction did not include cybersex behavior.[39]

That same study asked where they engaged in their cybersex behaviors. Sixty-five percent indicated they restricted their activity to their home. Twenty percent of the respondents said they engaged in their cybersex behavior at work. In 2002 a study was conducted with a random sample of the population. Eleven percent said they split their cybersex activity between work and home. A study with a random sample showed most adult sites are accessed between 9:00 a.m. and 5:00 p.m.[40] While neither study asked about what hours the respondents spent at work, the implication is clear that when considering the population as a whole, most cybersex behavior happens at work. But for sexual addicts, most cybersex behavior takes place at home.

How big a problem is Internet acting out? In a survey that was conducted by Dr. Al Cooper on MSNBC.com, 32 percent of the nearly 10,000 respondents identified at least one major area of their life that has been affected negatively by their online sexual behavior. Many of the survey participants reported they had jeopardized or lost their job or family while others have lost their freedom for engaging in illegal activities that were associated with their compulsive

---

37. (Cooper A. S., 1999)
38. (Cooper & Sportolari, 1997)
39. (Magness M. , 2004)
40. (Kent-Ferraro, 2002)

online sexual behavior.[41] Thirty-four percent of self-identified sexual addicts in a survey said that discovering the availability of online sexual behavior was the worst thing that has ever happened in their life.[42]

Consequences of Acting Out

There is much a person can lose as the result of online sexual addiction. There have been several instances of people who have begun what they believed would be an innocent e-mail cyber relationship that progressed to injury or death when they went to a face-to-face meeting with their cyber-lover. In the survey of self-identified sexual addicts, the respondents were given an opportunity to indicate the consequences they suffered because of their cybersex activity.

- 36 percent said they experienced at least one marital separation,
- 21 percent got divorced,
- 38 percent became estranged from one or more members of their family,
- 26 percent experienced serious financial problems,
- 26 percent contracted at least one STD (one indicated contracting STDs ten times),
- 15 percent lost their job,
- 12 percent got arrested,
- 5 percent were incarcerated, and
- 25 percent said they endured some additional consequence as the direct result of their cybersex behavior including severe depression, losing sleep, worrying over having potentially contracted an STD, practicing unsafe sex, becoming a registered sex offender, missing promotions at work, losing friends, suffering embarrassment from being caught at work, having to move, and becoming suicidal.[43]

Abigail's Story

When Abigail was first introduced to the Internet, she was amazed at the information it contained. Within days of first logging on she was spending hours searching for anything and everything. One secret she had never told her husband is that she enjoyed looking at pornography. She carried great shame about this behavior, especially since people seemed to think this was a behavior relegated to men.

With the advent of the Internet, she did not have to make up stories at video stores about buying movies for her husband. Abigail developed the daily habit of looking at pornography on the Internet. Most of this behavior was done on company computers while she was at work. Once she was almost caught. The fear of being confronted by her boss or a human resources representative kept her away from pornography for a few days, but eventually she resumed her clandestine searches. Recently, while sitting in a closed office during lunch, the door opened and her worst fears were realized. Her

---

41. (Cooper & Delmonico, 2000)
42. (Magness M. , 2004)
43. (Magness M. , 2004)

supervisor and the vice president of human resources entered the office and caught her in the act of viewing pornography and then confronted her with additional evidence of her acting out.

How Much Time Is Lost?

Prior to recovery, most of the participants in our study admitted to engaging in cybersex behavior from ten to twenty-nine hours a week. Eight percent of the respondents spent between thirty and forty-four hours a week in cybersex behaviors. A complete breakdown of the time spent on cybersex behavior is below.

Hours per Week of Cybersex Before Recovery (Graph)[44]

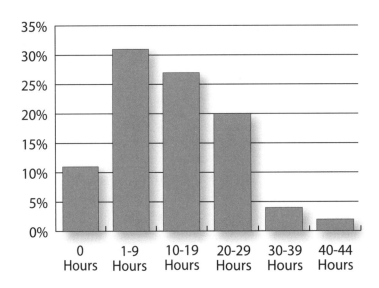

Behavioral Change in Recovery

The same group of people was asked to give details about their cybersex behavior after entering recovery. More than 68 percent had stopped all cybersex behavior completely. Another 25 percent admitted to continuing to act out on the Internet but spending less than ten hours a week. Any acting out on the Internet is unacceptable, but some of this group reported a drastic reduction in their cybersex behavior during the first several months of recovery. A complete breakdown of the time spent in cybersex behavior after recovery follows.

---

44. (Magness M. , 2004)

Thirty Days to Hope & Freedom for Sexual Addicts

Hours per Week in Cybersex After Beginning Recovery (Graph)[45]

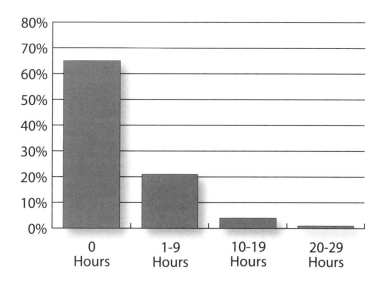

It is time to determine what boundaries should be in place concerning your Internet use. Even if you have not had a past problem with cybersex behavior, it is vital that you follow some safeguards. For example, even if you have never had an automobile accident, you still take precautions like making sure all of the safety equipment is operating and that your seatbelt is fastened. In the same way, prudence demands that you approach the Internet with the full knowledge that it could cause great harm if misused.

I have found it helpful to encourage clients to think about the Internet like a cobra inside the basket of a snake charmer. The cobra has great destructive power. As long as the reptile remains sealed in the basket, you are safe. But you can never forget that the Internet, like the venom of the snake, is deadly and has already taken the sobriety and even the lives of many other sexual addicts.

The first step in putting a lid on the Internet is to consider installing a good filter. However, all filters (at least as of this writing) are less than 100 percent effective. They do not filter out everything, and they sometimes make it difficult to use the Internet. However, even with those limitations, filters have their place.

If you have children in your home, you will certainly want to have all the computers they can access filtered. This includes providing filtered access to cell phones. Because of the limitations of filters, I am not able to give you a recommendation here, but I do try to keep a link on my website of the filter that I believe is currently the best available. You can find that link at www. HopeAndFreedom.com.

I know of some sexual addicts who rely on filters in an unhealthy way. They treat filters like a cyber parent. If they can get around the filter or if a filter does not deny access to all problematic

---

45. (Magness M. , 2004)

websites, they do not have enough resolve to keep from acting out. But as long as you recognize the role of a filter is to keep you from inadvertently going to a problem website and to keep you from receiving spam that is dangerous, then a filter can be helpful.

Since I believe the job of a filter is not to take on a parental role, it does not really matter if you have access to the administrative password or not. If you feel safer not knowing the password, then ask your sponsor or another friend in recovery to set up the password. Do not place that burden on your spouse or partner. For them to be the administrator puts them in a supervisory role, and that is not healthy for the relationship.

There are several software packages that provide a tracking option. They will send an e-mail to your sponsor or accountability partner (again, this should not be to your spouse) of all of the websites you have visited or attempted to visit. If you are using one of these packages, then you should not have access to the administrative password.

Do not put too much trust in these programs. I know of sexual addicts who can get around all of them—and these are not necessarily the computer geeks! Motivated sexual addicts can often find ways to get around these programs. That being said, it is still a good idea to install filters and accountability software on all computers.

If the Internet is a problem for a sexual addict, it might seem like the solution is to not use the Internet. However, that is not a realistic solution for most people. Instead you must to learn new behaviors concerning healthy Internet use.

One of the first behavioral changes is to move your computer at home and at work so that anyone entering the room or even passing your door can see what is on the screen. And while you are at it, always have a practice of using the computer with your door open and when other people are around. Yes, it will be inconvenient and may require that you rearrange your office or other work area. But your integrity and recovery are at stake.

Consider putting boundaries on what hours you will work on a computer. Some sexual addicts have determined that they are at greater risk of acting out on the computer after 9:00 p.m. So by setting a boundary of not working on a computer after 8:30 p.m., they have established a new behavior that can be useful in their recovery.

Another behavioral change to consider is to think about "bookending" computer sessions with someone else who is in recovery. If you have to work on the computer late one evening, call a friend who is in recovery before you begin work. Then call them again when you stop working and report on your success in staying sober and focused on your work.

The bottom line is that your behaviors around your computer use should to be carefully thought out and communicated to your sponsor, your Circle of Five, and your spouse. Ask yourself what boundaries could be instituted to make it safe for you to use the Internet. Remember to treat all mobile devices with the same care and concern you do your home or office computer.

Day 18: Tools—
Dealing with Intrusive Thoughts (Part 1)

A tool is anything that you use to challenge an intrusive thought or avoid a problematic behavior. What you fantasize about today, you may well be doing six to twelve months from today. For this reason you will need tools for dealing with intrusive thoughts. There is considerable evidence that trying to suppress thoughts may lead to obsession with those thoughts.[46] The harder some people try not to think of something, the more likely they are to be troubled by those thoughts. Rather than suppress negative thoughts, it is better to have another thought to substitute for the intrusive thought.

Phillip's Story

Phillip would never consider being sexual with someone from work even though he had frequent fantasies about several of the people he worked with. He knew of the risks of a sexual harassment lawsuit. Besides he did not want to risk his job. A couple of years ago, he was stunned when a customer of his made an overt pass at him. After he recovered from the shock, he decided that it would be all right to respond to the advances and that no one would find out. That opened a whole new world to Phillip.

He found that many of his customers held him in high esteem because of his expertise in his field. He also discovered that several were willing to be sexual with him. Things began to fall apart for him when one of his customers believed she was in an exclusive relationship with Phillip but found out he was being sexual with other customers. She wrote a letter to the CEO complaining that he had taken unfair sexual advantage of her. In the investigation that followed, several other customers admitted to sexual relationships with Phillip. After thirty-four years with his company, he was fired.

Why is it crucial to deal with intrusive thoughts? This is important because the battle that you fight is not the battle between your legs but the battle between your ears! Soldiers study battle strategy and learn the importance of determining the position from which one fights. Choose the wrong battlefront, and the battle may be lost. But when the right battlefront is established, the war is winnable.

If you are fighting the battle between your legs, you have already lost. But if you change the battle lines and fight the battle between your ears, there is no other battle. The primary focus must be on changing the way you think. If you are successful with this, you can then be successful with changing your problematic behaviors.

---

46. (Wegner, Schneider, Carter III, & White, 1987)

Terrence's Story

Terrence had been with more sex partners than he can count. At one point in his life that was a badge of honor for him. But by the time he got into recovery he truly wanted to be free of all of his old memories. Not only did Terrence have the memory of innumerable previous partners, he had been a frequent user of pornography.

Upon entering recovery, Terrence found out that he was finally able to live free from all of these behaviors. However, he was tormented by his memories. There were times that he felt that he had lost total control of his thoughts as he was flooded with past memories. Finally, his sponsor suggested that he see whether a therapist could provide help. Beginning in his first session, Terrence started learning tools that allowed him some relief from old intrusive memories.

Thought Replacement

One of the basic tools for dealing with intrusive thoughts is to engage in thought replacement. The essence of thought replacement is to first identify the unwanted thought and then to substitute a positive thought to replace it. For example, if the intrusive thought has to do with some previous sexual experience, replace it with thoughts of a positive experience you have had that is both pleasurable and healthy.

A key to being successful with thought replacement is practice. The new thought has to be repeated over and over again until it becomes embedded in your mind. The more times you repeat this new information, the more likely it will be that the new thought will take root. New thoughts have to be rehearsed repeatedly until they become dominant.

If you are struggling with the belief that you will never achieve lasting sobriety from compulsive sexual behaviors, instead picture yourself sexually sober, and think about the joy you will experience when you are living that way. Envision a future without acting out, where people trust you and you live in integrity in every part of your life.

For thought replacement to be effective, the replacement thoughts should be relevant to the situations that trigger the unwanted thoughts. For example, if your negative thought is that you are a bad person, the positive thought you use to replace it might be of something you did that was particularly noteworthy. The more detail you have in the replacement thought, the better.

Double P (Pop and Pray)

Intrusive thoughts are often subtle. They may come on slowly but gain traction as they continue unchallenged. The longer an intrusive thought remains, the greater the effort needed to redirect thoughts to what is more welcomed and appropriate.

The Double P employs a rubber band and a memorized prayer or meditation. The two "Ps" stand for "Pop" and "Pray."

Place a rubber band on your wrist. When you have an intrusive thought, pop it over the inside of the wrist and then recite this memorized prayer to yourself: *Give me a new mind and a new heart and renew a right spirit within me.*

If someone asks you about the rubber band on your wrist, you simply reply, "It is a reminder to pray." If they are spiritual or religious, they will typically have good thoughts about you for attending to the spiritual dimension of life. And if they are not spiritual or religious, they will likely not ask anything else for fear of what you might say. So telling them the rubber band is a reminder to pray is a good way of maintaining your privacy.

The rubber band stings a bit when popped. But the object is not to create pain. When the focus is on pain, it is called aversion therapy which, while having its place, is often not effective over the long term. Instead, the rubber band is used to break through the fog of the intrusive thought so a person can put a different thought in its place. So this is a variation on thought replacement with the thought that is offered as a replacement being the memorized prayer.

For background, it is helpful to review a story from Jewish history about the greatest king of Israel, King David.[47] The king was at his palace at a time when he should have been with his army in battle. While walking on the roof of his palace, he saw a woman bathing. He sent for her and had sex with her, leaving her pregnant with his child. Discovering that her husband was away at war and knowing that his-less-than honorable deed would be found out, David thought up a plan to cover his actions.

He sent for her husband, Uriah the Hittite, a soldier, and asked that he be sent back to the palace to report on the battle's progress. Upon hearing the news, the king told Uriah to "go home and relax."

However, Uriah did not go home, but slept on the porch of the palace instead. When the king questioned Uriah's decision not to go to his wife, he replied that it would not have been right for him to enjoy the comforts of home and his wife when the rest of the men were still engaged in battle. The bottom line here is that Uriah had too much integrity to take advantage of his situation when the rest of the army could not have a similar opportunity. He even resisted a second time when the king resorted to getting him drunk.

Integrity is the key word here. Recovery is all about helping you return to being a person of integrity. You may be a person of great integrity in every area of life except the sexual area. This lack of integrity, however, permeates everything you do, denying you the privilege of claiming this positive character trait.

Back to our story. The next day, the king sent sealed orders to the general which were carried by Uriah. The orders read, "Put Uriah on the front lines in the heart of the battle and then withdraw the army from him so he will be killed." So, in the heat of battle Uriah was abandoned on the front line and died just as surely as if the king himself had run him though with a sword.

The king, once confronted with his treachery, had a change of heart. In fact, King David had a real encounter with God. Among other things during this time, he wrote the Fifty-First Psalm. The prayer used in the Double P is a paraphrase of what King David said in that psalm: *Dear God, give me a new mind and a new heart and renew a right spirit within me.* This prayer is especially fitting for a sexual addict because it was first said by someone who also had poor sexual boundaries.

---

47. 2 Samuel 11. The chapter is paraphrased here.

The moment that you recognize you are having an unwanted thought, pop the rubber band and say, "Dear God, give me a new mind and a new heart and renew a right spirit within me." If the intrusive thought is still there, continue reciting the prayer.

Scripture tells us that King David was a man who had a heart like that of God. This is remarkable considering his checkered past. But it is also a reminder of how a person can change and be restored to being a person of integrity.

Thought Stoppage

Thought stoppage is a simple tool but a powerful one. It is so simple that I often tell people that its simplicity may cause them to dismiss it without giving it a chance. Yet this tool may prove to be the most effective of all of your tools for dealing with intrusive thoughts.

There are three basic components of thought stoppage: verbal, physical, and mental. These three combine to provide a powerful psychological tool for dispelling problematic thoughts. The verbal ingredient is to say the word *stop*. The physical component is to hold up your hand like a policeman stopping traffic. Finally, the mental element is to imagine and visualize a huge stop sign.

All three of these elements should occur simultaneously along with a loud shout and an exaggerated physical gesture. However, use some caution. This is a tool that you should practice and learn to use when you are alone. Otherwise you may find yourself the target of distressed family members who think you may be losing contact with reality.

Once again, practice is essential to making this tool effective. Practice the use of it continually when you are alone. An interesting aspect of this tool is that it is not just for dealing with intrusive sexual thoughts but with any thought that is problematic for you.

After learning about this tool, one man told of how his son has used this tool. His son has bipolar disorder. His manic episodes are so extreme that he becomes a threat to himself and to others and often requires hospitalization. In the midst of one of these manic episodes this gentleman watched his son stand before a mirror and shout "stop" at himself at the top of his lungs. He continued the shouting at a rapid pace and at significant volume. Within a few minutes, the boy's father noticed the pitch of his voice had dropped, the volume had decreased, and the pace of repeating the word "stop" had diminished. He reported that his son basically used the tool to lift himself out of his manic episode.

After you gain practice with thought stoppage, you can use it when you are around people. You simply do all three things mentally: imagine yourself shouting the word "stop;" visualize your hand stabbing through the air declaring your thoughts to halt; get a mental image of the huge stop sign. It may be helpful to tense up your arm and close your eyes for a moment as you imagine the sound of your voice and the physical sensation of your hand thrusting upward.

Feelings Check

How do you feel? This may seem to be an irrelevant question, but it is fundamental to sound recovery. When asked how we feel, we may respond by saying that we are "good," "fine," or "well." Yet, none of those words describe feelings.

Perhaps you are afraid of your feelings. Maybe you were raised in a home where you were taught "real men don't cry" or that "good girls don't do that." If it was not safe to express your feelings, you may have gotten good at stuffing them and denying that you have feelings. You may be reasonably successful with this technique until your emotions build to the point where they come out in inappropriate ways.

Sexual acting out can be a way of medicating feelings of despair, loneliness, sadness, or shame. In order to keep from experiencing one's feelings, sexual addicts often act out in inappropriate ways. Learning to identify your feelings can help you recognize when you are at risk of a slip, so you can learn to avoid it.

You may find it helpful to check the Internet for a feelings chart. Some of these have accompanying drawings of faces that correspond to various moods. Keep this chart handy and use it multiple times a day to ask yourself how you are feeling. You might find it beneficial to keep notes in your journal of how you are feeling on a given day or multiple times a day.

Prayer and Meditation

Prayer and meditation are powerful tools for combating intrusive thoughts. Whether you use a book to guide the process or use your own individual practice, concentrating on positive thoughts in prayer and meditation is helpful in recovery. Even for a person who does not particularly value prayer and meditation, going through spiritual exercises has value in that they help focus one's thoughts on the positive behavior desired. More attention will be given to the subject of spirituality in Day 21.

Schedule Intrusive Thoughts

Another way of dealing with intrusive thoughts is to schedule a time for them. If you find you are routinely plagued by thoughts of low self-worth or worrying about various things, set aside time each day when you can indulge all of those thoughts. For example, you might decide that your time for worrying and ruminating is from 7:00 p.m. until 7:15 p.m. each evening. If you have an intrusive thought at some other time, you tell yourself that you cannot entertain it then, but that you have to wait for your appointed time in the evening.

Then when it is your time to worry and ruminate, write in a journal all of the things you can remember obsessing about during the day. Write as quickly as you can. Include all of the things you have worried about for that day or that you dread about tomorrow. When your time is up, stop writing and return to other activities.

Reframing

Reframing is a psychological technique that can be useful in dealing with situations that may otherwise lead to acting out. To understand reframing it is useful to think of how a picture frame provides borders and boundaries that help to experience the picture. If you had an interior designer change the décor of your home or office and gave instruction that you wanted to keep a certain picture, most likely the frame would have to be changed in order for it to fit in the new decorating scheme.

One of the simplest reframes to make in recovery is changing how you look at time when you are alone. Being alone can be especially triggering. If you have a weekend alone when you do not have any activities planned and you do not anticipate any interactions with friends or family, you might feel vulnerable. *Lonely* is the word that best describes your frame of reference.

Now consider the same situation for a person in recovery who will spend the weekend alone without any interactions with family or friends. Rather than seeing the situation as one of loneliness, they choose to see it as a time of *solitude*. Solitude can be useful for planning the future, studying, learning more about recovery, and just getting comfortable in one's own skin.

Consider another reframe. Your boss gives you a project that is new to you. You do not have any experience on that type of project. One way of thinking about that project would be to see it as a *challenge*. Reframing it, you can look at the same project as an *opportunity*.

When a person is acting out, the numerous visual triggers one sees may be considered opportunities. But when a person is in recovery, the same visual triggers should be viewed as *threats*. The trigger is the same. But by reframing, it is possible to use the same trigger as a recovery tool.

Another simple reframe expands on the previous tool. Change the word you use for your triggers. The word *trigger* may carry the connotation that you are on a precipice ready to fall. Instead of a *trigger*, consider the same situation and think of it as a *threat*.

Even things that are not necessarily triggers that would cause you to want to act out may benefit from reframing. For example, the next time you are tempted to complain about your long day at work, how about pausing and giving thanks for your job? While it may not appear this has much to do with recovery, it certainly does. The reason it relates to recovery is because for some, the next move after complaining about a long hard day at work is to consider how they are justified to act out to relieve tension.

The next time you go out of town on a business trip, how will you view your situation of being away from friends and family and living temporarily in a hotel? Before entering recovery, perhaps you would view the situation with fear. In recovery, rather than being fearful you will act out, you can reframe the situation so that you are cautious and on guard to avoid acting out.

Attitude Shift

Closely associated with reframing is making an attitude shift. Rather than focusing on the negative, ask what is positive about a situation. For example, going to the beach with family may be a special concern in the summer. As a sexual addict, your initial thought may be to focus on the visual threats or, more accurately on trying to avoid them. A shift in attitude would be to think about the many positive things you can get from going to the beach. The trip will offer the opportunity to have time with your family. You will have a chance to enjoy the sunshine, seashells at your feet, the sensation of the wind, and the sound of the waves.

The problem is not the thoughts in themselves but your attitude toward them. Rather than being anxious for having intrusive thoughts, remind yourself that you do not have to act out on them. They are just thoughts, and you can change how you view them.

Think back to a list of victories you have had in the recent past. Focus on the last day of sobriety you had and remember the feeling of contentment you experienced. Recall a compliment that you received for a job well done. Think about to the last time you received a word of praise from your employer, spouse, or a friend. Relive those positive thoughts.

One benefit from intrusive thoughts is they may provide a good indication of the level of stress or anxiety you are experiencing. With that in mind, they may serve as a warning to you that mentally you are in a dangerous place. They are not an indicator of what is going to happen in the future. Rather, they are a flashing neon sign that tells you to engage in other recovery activities such as attending a Twelve Step meeting and talking to other recovering individuals.

Spend a few minutes reviewing the eight tools in this chapter. Which of these tools are you already using? Which tools do you believe will be the most effective in helping you combat your addiction?

During the next week, make a conscious effort to focus on one or more of these tools each day. Practice using them until they becomes second nature to you. After you have gained expertise with these tools you will find that you will select the appropriate tool for the situation without giving it much thought.

The next chapter will give you eight more tools for your arsenal in your battle for recovery.

Day 19: Tools—
Dealing with Intrusive Thoughts (Part 2)

Jonathan's Story

Jonathan's job always keeps him busy. Well, almost always. He runs from meeting to meeting, handling multiple tasks at once. He is the "go-to guy" at his company. When something really has to be done and done right, Jonathan is the one who is called upon.

Occasionally Jonathan will be not have anything that requires his immediate attention. He instantly gets bored when he does not have several things that are all competing for his attention. When he is bored, Jonathan will often aimlessly wander around the Internet. He is not looking for pornography, but it seems that pornography always finds him.

During his eighteen months of recovery, the longest Jonathan has been sober is two weeks. He has a sponsor and is attending several meetings each week. He does everything that his sponsor asks him to do, but still he continues to slip. All of his slips happen when he is bored.

Bored List

What Jonathan needs is a Bored List. His therapist suggested that he plan ahead for the next time he is bored. He started by making a list of things that should be done but had been neglected. To his amazement, he has a long list.

In constructing a Bored List, start as Jonathan did and list all of the projects that you have intended to do but have not done because life is just too busy. Next, add to it a list of things that you enjoy doing in your spare time. Finally, add projects that you dread and about which you may tend to procrastinate. The following is a sample Bored List.

Bored List

- Plan your next vacation
- Plan a weekend away for you and your partner
- Plan birthday celebrations for family and friends
- Work on your taxes
- Plan your next home improvement project
- Play a video game (this should be time-limited)
- Organize a closet or drawer at work or at home
- Take a walk
- Phone your sponsor
- Call prospective clients or customers

When your list is completed, figure out where you are going to keep it. You might decide to keep it in your wallet, in a planner, or as a file on the desktop of your computer. Or you might consider adding your list to a smart phone so that you always have your list at hand.

Find the Distortion

Some of the most destructive intrusive thoughts are negative thoughts about self. For example, if you have failed at a task at work, you may be tempted to say, "I always mess up." The distortion here is the word *always*. Words like *always* and *never* are often distortions of thought because these are absolute words. Another distortion would be to reflect on a weekend spent alone and say, "I don't have any friends." What is true is that you are alone. What is not true is that you do not have any friends. If you, in fact, have few friends, you can identify that reality and choose to make a change in that area of your life.

Problem Solving

Another tool for dealing with intrusive thoughts is to engage your brain in problem solving. Solving a crossword puzzle or engaging in some other mental challenge can distract you from interfering thoughts. With this in mind, you might want to keep a book of brain-teasers or other puzzles on hand. Keeping your mind occupied can be of significant value in helping you out of a precarious situation.

Imagine the Worst

What is the worst that could happen? The next time you find yourself worrying about something or obsessing about how something will work out, ask yourself, what is the absolute worst-case scenario for that circumstance? Will you lose your relationship? Lose your job? The worst case usually does not happen, but even if it does, what does that mean to you? It will mean that life will be different, but life will still go on. You will have a new opportunity to live life differently.

Physical Exercise

On Day 10, we looked at the physical benefits of exercise. Now we will consider the mental and emotional benefits. Strenuous physical exercise is a powerful tool for countering intrusive thoughts. Lacing on your running shoes and taking a jog around the neighborhood will give you a remarkable mental lift. You can accomplish the same thing with a brisk walk or even dropping to the floor and doing several sets of push-ups or sit-ups.

Dr. John Ratey, a professor of psychiatry at Harvard University, has found a strong relationship between exercise and the mind.[48] Physical exercise not only improves the way we feel physically, but it can drastically improve mental well being. A variety of mental disorders includ-

---

48. (Ratey, 2008)

ing depression and attention deficit hyperactivity disorder can be improved through vigorous exercise. That is not to say that exercise is a substitute for pharmacological interventions, but rather that a regular program of vigorous exercise may help you better cope with the stresses of life. Additionally, such exercise may allow your physician to reduce your medications.

Dr. Ratey also advocates strenuous exercise as a way of dealing with addiction.[49] Rather than engaging in addictive behavior, try exercise instead. For a person who has used drinking as a coping mechanism, try jumping rope when stress builds.

Dr. Bess Marcus of Brown University conducted a study that looked at the value of exercise on persons who were trying to quit smoking. She found that smokers who exercised three times a week while trying to quit smoking were twice as likely to succeed as smokers who did not exercise.[50] Could it be that the same holds true for sexual addicts who want permanently to stop all acting out?

Stay Present

Are you worried about what is going to happen tomorrow, next week or next year? Are you sad about the mistakes of yesterday? There is nothing you can do that will change a single thing that happened yesterday. And until tomorrow comes, you do not have a stake in that day. You can anticipate what will happen, but you have no way of knowing exactly what the new day will bring. In addiction, you have one foot in yesterday and the other in tomorrow.

Yesterday and tomorrow are two awful eternities. You may look at one with regret and the other with dread. The only day you can do anything about is today. Live in today. Embrace each of the opportunities that today brings. When you find your mind drifting to the past or the future, remind yourself that you have to live in the present.

God Box

The God Box has been around recovery circles for years. It is an old tool but an effective one. Tape the lid on a shoe box and then cover the box in plain white paper. Cut a slit in the top that is about a half of an inch wide and about five inches long. When you have thoughts that are troubling that you cannot seem to shake, write the thoughts on a slip of paper and put them in your God Box. And as you place them in your God Box, simply say, "I'm giving this problem (or concern or situation) back to you, God." Let this be the point where you give up trying to control that obsessive thought and release it to God alone.

Texas Three Step

The Texas Three Step is a tool for dealing with visual threats. Some people in recovery are encouraged to use the so-called "three second rule" to deal with visual threats. However, I believe three seconds is too long for a sexual addict to drink in a visual threat. (The only thing I believe

---

49. (Ratey, 2008) pp. 167-190
50. (Marcus, et al., 1995)

the three-second rule is good for is if you drop food on the floor; you can eat it if you retrieve it in less than three seconds.) The three-second rule is dangerous in that it may provide a false sense of security because it allows a person to ogle a visual threat, even if just for a short time.

It is much safer to employ the Texas Three Step as a way of dealing with visual threats:

- Step One: Break visual contact. At the moment you recognize that you have gone beyond simply looking at a person but are, in fact, checking out body parts or thinking of them as an object for your pleasure, simply look away. Find something else to be the center of your focus.

- Step Two: Humanize the person. You simply say to yourself any one of the following statements that you believe fit the situation:
  - She (or he) is somebody's daughter (or son).
  - She (or he) is somebody's wife (or husband).
  - She (or he) is somebody's sister (or brother).
  - She (or he) is somebody's mother (or father).
  - She (or he) is a precious child of God.

- Step Three: Pray for them as you go on your way. Say to yourself just a brief prayer in passing, "Help him (or her) to have a good day," or "Help him (or her) to be a good dad (or mom)." If you would rather, you can just say an affirmation about that person to yourself, "She (or he) is a person of worth and value and not an object for my pleasure."

This tool, like all of the tools suggested here, requires practice in order to gain expertise in use. As is the case with a person who is learning to cook or someone who is learning the art of cabinet making, practice in using tools leads to skilled use without having to give much thought as to which tool is appropriate for a particular task. As you practice each of these tools, you will become accomplished at selecting the right tool for the right task.

Now you have sixteen tools that you can use in your battle for continuous sexual sobriety. Unless you review the tools daily, you will not gain proficiency in their use. Spend a bit of time at the beginning of each day reviewing one of the tools from these past two chapters. Get so familiar with them that you can name them and identify situations in which you might use each of them. Continue the review process daily for the next six months of recovery.

Day 20: Learn to Have Fun Again!

Do you know how to have fun or has acting out become your only "recreational" outlet? Many will probably answer that life is too serious for them to have fun. You may have been led to believe that once you became an adult, you needed to banish fun to the realm of activities reserved for children. Nothing could be further from the truth. The lack of activities that you consider fun may be a factor that has led to your acting out.

The dump truck carefully backed into the empty lot. It unloaded a huge pile of sand that was going to be used for foundation work on a new building. Since it was a Saturday, there were lots of children playing in the neighborhood. The kids on the block spotted the sand pile before it was completely unloaded. When the truck pulled out, boys swarmed the pile of sand and spent the next hour playing "King on the Mountain" where challengers would try to push the champion from the top of the hill. They laughed and caused such a ruckus that several of their fathers came out to watch what they were doing.

As the men gathered, they laughed at the fun their children were having. They told their own stories of when they played the same game. As they watched, their kids changed games and were having a contest to see who could run up and down the sand hill the fastest. After that they tunneled in the sand, went home for their Tonka trucks for yet more fun, and when they were done, most of the day had passed and the pile of sand had been spread throughout the empty lot.

Several remarks by the fathers who watched the delight of their children were overheard. One said, "I had forgotten how much fun a pile of sand can be." Another said, "I think I had just forgotten how to really have fun."

Lighten Up

Taking life too seriously may be one of the core components that create an environment where sexual addiction can grow. Could it be that you have forgotten how to have fun? Has life gotten so serious for you that you feel guilty if you enjoy a lighter moment? Perhaps it is time to ask yourself if you should return to the healthier aspects of childhood.

When you stop acting out, you will have to do something else to take up the time you once spent on dysfunctional behaviors. Look for a hobby, sport, or other avocation that you can enjoy in your unused time. Take care not to exchange your sexual addiction for some compulsive behavior that may also be harmful.

Healthy Ways to Have Fun

What can you do to have fun? The following list is not exhaustive, but it is a good place to start as you think about how to have fun. These are things you can participate in or just watch. And your fun can be even greater if you find someone to enjoy these things with you. If you are in a committed relationship, see whether there are things that you and your partner can enjoy together.

Some of what passes for fun is so competitive that it is more like work. Competition may indeed be fun. But once something becomes so consuming that it is no longer fun, perhaps that is an indication that you may benefit from a new hobby.

Archery

Art

Auto racing

Backgammon

Badminton

Baseball

Basketball

Bicycling

Billiards

Bird watching

Board games

Bow hunting

Bowling

Boxing

Car trip using back roads

Cards

Canoeing

Checkers

Chess

Coaching

Collecting anything

Computer games
(within healthy limits)

Cooking

Cricket

Croquet

Cross country skiing

Crossword puzzles

Cycling

Dancing

Dog sledding

Drawing

Entertaining

Fencing

Fishing

Flying

Football

Frisbee throwing

Garage sale scavenging

Go carting

Going to the beach

Golf

Gymnastics

Handball

Hang gliding

Hiking

Hockey

Horseback riding

Hot air ballooning

Humor: jokes, riddles, anecdotes

Hunting

Ice fishing

Ice skating

Jogging

Judo

Jujitsu

Karate

Kayaking

Kendo

Kite flying

Knitting
(for women and men)

Kung fu

Lacrosse

Lawn darts

Marathoning

Marbles

Model building

Motorcycle touring

Mountain climbing

Movie watching
(within healthy limits)

Music: playing, singing, or
listening

Netball (popular in England
and Australia)

Painting

Pet ownership

Photography

Ping Pong

Polo

Quilting
(for women and men)

Racquetball

Raise a pet

Reading a book

Rock climbing

Roller skating

Rugby

Sailing

Scuba diving

Shooting

Shopping
(within healthy limits)

Singing

Skateboarding

Skiing

Skipping rope

Skydiving

Sledding

Snorkeling

Snowboarding

Soaring

Soccer

Spelunking

Spending time with friends
and family

Squash

Surfing

Swimming

Taekwondo

Tai chi

Tennis

Trampoline jumping

Travel and tourism

Tree climbing
(you are not too old!)

Underwater games

Visiting an amusement park

Volunteering

Walking for fitness and for
sightseeing

Weight lifting

Wind surfing

Wrestling

Writing

Woodworking

Working out

X-Box or other systems
for video games
(within healthy limits)

Xylophone or some other
musical instrument

Yodeling

Yoga

Zoo trip

Fun Worksheet

One of the factors that may contribute to acting out is the absence of fun. Life gets serious, career and family demands consume time once used for recreation, and stress increases. Unfortunately, some turn to acting out as a stress reliever.

What are activities you once enjoyed but no longer practice?

1._____

2._____

3._____

4._____

5._____

What factors keep you from enjoying these past activities today?

1._____

2._____

3._____

What are the activities that you might enjoy in the future?

1._____

2._____

3._____

4._____

5._____

What prevents you from participating in these new activities now?

1. _____

2. _____

3. _____

What planning or preparation is required for you to begin to enjoy these new activities?

1. _____

2. _____

3. _____

Commitment

In the next seven days I will commit to doing at least one of the things on this list solely for the purpose of having fun. Further, I commit to doing something for fun every week.

Signed _____ Date _____

Day 21: Do Not Neglect the Spiritual Dimension

You may feel like the last thing that you want to read about in a book on sexual addiction is anything spiritual. There is a growing body of evidence that says it is vital for people to believe there is a power greater than themselves, not only to find recovery from sexual addiction, but to live a full and balanced life. A number of secular therapists and psychologists, while staunchly rejecting religion, state the importance of spirituality for their clients and for themselves.

Sheri's Story

Sheri has struggled with her compulsive sexual behavior since she was twelve. After being fondled by her uncle, she came to believe that the way to make men happy was to be sexual with them. She reenacted her past trauma throughout her teenage years as she sought to be accepted by men.

As an adult, her behavior escalated into numerous clandestine relationships, even though she considered herself happily married. Most of the relationships were brief, but some of them grew into such deep attachments that she has been tempted to end her marriage. What makes Sheri's story significant is that she has wanted to get help for years but has been fearful that seeking treatment would mean a public scandal. Sheri is a news anchor for a television station in a major city. Each time she has considered getting help for her sexual addiction she has hesitated, certain that therapy would make her the lead story on her own newscast.

When she finally did get into recovery, she worried about the repercussions to her career if the story got out. In a Twelve Step meeting she heard someone use the slogan, Let go and let God. She was not sure what that meant, but it was the beginning of a spiritual quest for her. She found that one of the keys to her recovery was discovering that true recovery was a spiritual experience. This was also one of the most challenging parts of Sheri's recovery. Sheri continues her recovery today, attending online and telephone-based Twelve Step meetings.

Is there a difference between religion and spirituality? There are good arguments both ways. For those who see religion and spirituality as separate, they draw a sharp distinction between organized religion and spirituality. All Twelve Step groups speak of a Higher Power and universally state that it is essential for a person to believe there is a power beyond themselves. Little or no effort is made to identify that Higher Power. There is even the thought that if a person is an atheist or agnostic, that the Higher Power can be the Twelve Step group itself.

On the other side of the coin, there are those who teach that the only way to find recovery is to have a profound religious experience. They will say things like, "The key to deliverance from sexual addiction is God," or "Just pray and God will deliver you from your addiction." Numerous people will "testify" to having prayed and then being immediately set free from their addiction. But what about the many people of faith who have prayed repeatedly to be delivered from addiction, only to find that their addiction is alive and well and unchecked by their most fervent prayers?

Somewhere between believing in some nebulous Higher Power and the other extreme of believing all one must do is pray to God for deliverance, the rest of people in recovery find a comfortable place for expressions of faith. Regardless of a person's religious background, or lack thereof, sexual addicts must look beyond themselves and believe there is a power that can bring them out of their addiction.

The Spiritual Journey

Recovery has always had spiritual roots. From the beginning of Alcoholics Anonymous there has been an understanding that recovery must engage body, mind, and soul. Regardless of your belief system, you likely see value in giving attention to the spiritual side of your life.

Embracing spirituality is a significant challenge for many in recovery. You may have been coerced as a child to accept certain beliefs. You may have been forced to adopt particular religious practices. Regrettably, you may even have suffered sexual abuse at the hands of a religious leader.

At this point in your recovery, strive to have an open mind about spiritual matters. Be willing to study the possibility that there is a spiritual dimension to life, and be willing to embrace it when you are able. Remember, spirituality is not synonymous with religion. You may or may not choose to be involved in organized religion.

In the Big Book of *AA*,[51] the word *God* is used seventy-six times. A *Power Greater than* ourselves, himself, or myself is used thirteen times. *Creator* is used twelve times. The term *Higher Power* is used twice.

Throughout the Twelve Steps, there are references to God. In the Twelve Steps of SAA,[52] the word *God* is used eight times and the term *Power Greater than* is used once. As you continue your recovery within Twelve Step groups, you will continually be reminded of the spiritual nature of recovery.

The following discussion takes the Twelve Steps and examines the spiritual dimension of each. For the sake of continuity, I have chosen to use the Twelve Steps of Sex Addicts Anonymous. The wording of the Steps is similar in other "S" fellowships. They all come from the Twelve Steps of Alcoholics Anonymous.

You will notice that even on the Steps that do not overtly mention God, there is a decidedly spiritual dimension. All of the Twelve Step fellowships adapt the Twelve Steps of Alcoholics Anonymous[53] to their own fellowship.

---

51. (*Alcoholics Anonymous*, Fourth Edition)
52. See Appendix B
53. (*Alcoholics Anonymous*, Fourth Edition)

Step One: Surrender

Step One: "We admitted we were powerless over addictive sexual behavior—that our lives had become unmanageable."[54] The First Step is about surrender. Surrender is about letting go of the process and the outcome. It involves a giving in to the sense of hopelessness that a person feels in the midst of their addiction.

How do you know you have surrendered? The book, *Sex Addicts Anonymous*, or what's known as the Green Book says, "We...raise the white flag, and accept that the battle is over."[55] The indispensable element that is necessary for surrender is honesty. That means an end to denial. It means to stop lying to self. "As long as we can be honest, even a little bit, we can move forward in our recovery."[56]

The second part of Step One, admitting "our lives have become unmanageable," involves a willingness to examine the painful consequences of your behavior. When was that moment you recognized life had "become unmanageable?" If you could use some help recognizing the unmanageability of your addiction, spend a few minutes making an inventory of your losses. What have you lost in terms of:

- Time?
- Money?
- Job/career?
- Business losses?
- Trust?
- Health?
- Freedom?
- Relationships?

Lonnie's Story

Lonnie worked for a large oil company. His assignments often took him to Third World countries for several months at a time. He found that there were many sexual opportunities in his travels. The poverty of these countries caused prostitution to be out of control. For a few dollars Lonnie could have his choice of many sex partners.

He was shocked to find that teens and younger children were working in the sex trade. On one recent trip to Africa, he was approached by a teen, and this time he did not resist. This began a pattern of sexual contact with minors.

Lonnie felt as long as he did not do anything with minors in the United States that he would be able to escape the scrutiny of the law. However, Lonnie was recently arrested for child trafficking and is being prosecuted. The Department of Homeland Security took the lead in the case, and he was charged with violation of the Protect Act of 2003, which is intended to keep children from being exploited and to prosecute

---

54. (*Sex Addicts Anonymous*, 2005) p.22
55. (*Sex Addicts Anonymous*, 2005) p.22
56. (*Sex Addicts Anonymous*, 2005) p.22

sex traffickers. At his trial, Lonnie said he never intended to be sexual with a minor. While this behavior is not typical of sexual addicts, some have allowed their behavior to escalate into various illegal behaviors.

Make a detailed list of your losses in each of the preceding categories. Keep this list in your journal or someplace where you are likely to see it daily. Periodically review the list to remind yourself of the great cost of your addiction.

I have suffered the following losses as a result of my compulsive sexual behavior:

_____

_____

_____

_____

_____

_____

_____

_____

_____

_____

_____

_____

_____

Step Two: Hope

Step Two: "Came to believe that a Power greater than ourselves could restore us to sanity."[57] Step Two is about hope. There are two parts of "coming to believe." The first part is the existence of that power. The second is the belief that the power can restore you to sanity.

Actually, there is a third part to this Step—believing that life is not just unmanageable, but that it is insane. The only reason you must be restored to sanity is if you have lost it. And if you look carefully, you will find ample evidence that your life is insane.

This involves a personal quest that may lead you to exploring various religious systems, churches, synagogues, or mosques. That search may involve lots of reading. It will certainly involve some personal soul-searching. You may or may not be able to identify that power. You may give that power the name of Jesus, Buddha, Mohammed, God, or Allah. Or you may simply refer to that power as a force, the universe, or by some other term. For the purposes of sexual addiction recovery it is less significant what you call that power than it is that you recognize the existence of that power.

As you continue your quest and see evidence of that power at work, you will likely gain a greater understanding and appreciation for that power. For some, this may be returning to the faith of one's childhood. For others, it may include embracing a belief system and faith that is new to them.

There are hindrances to Step Two. If you were physically or sexually abused by a religious leader, you may have trouble with this Step. Also if you suffered covert religious abuse as a child you may have difficulty embracing this Step. That covert religious abuse may have involved inundating you with phrases like, "God won't love you if you _____." Or, "Good _____ (Jews/Christians/Buddhists, etc.) don't _____." The implication for both of these is that you may not be a good person and that if you do something that is perceived to be bad by religious leaders or even a religious parent, then God will reject you.

Another thing that may hinder a person in trying to work the Second Step is personal success. The more successful a person, the greater the possibility that they will believe they alone are responsible for their lives and any success that they have achieved. Perhaps this is the reason so many sacred texts have parables and proverbs about the perils of riches and success.

What else is there that hinders you as you continue your recovery journey? Are you able to accept the existence of a power greater than yourself? Are you willing to continue that quest? You do not have to have a full understanding of that power in order to complete this Step.

Step Three: Commitment

Step Three: "Made a decision to turn our will and our lives over to the care of God as we understood God."[58] This Step is about commitment and surrender. This Step involves surrendering to the idea that you are not able to take care of sexual addiction on your own. It involves let-

---

57. (*Sex Addicts Anonymous*, 2005) p.25
58. (*Sex Addicts Anonymous*, 2005) p.28

ting go of habits and behaviors that have not served you well. This also means you must release some old thoughts, like, *If there is a God, He doesn't care about me,* or *I may be so bad that I have gone beyond God's ability to forgive.*

"Made a decision" is the action expressed in Step Two. The "coming to believe" that is talked about in Step Two is a gradual process. Making a decision is something that is done at a point in time. Once a person makes that decision, they have appropriated the power of Step Two for themselves.

The Green Book says, "We come to believe that it is God's will that we not act out. In this way, we give up debating about how to handle our addiction and simply do what is right according to our program.... We may also begin to practice opening ourselves up to the guidance of a Higher Power. For many of us, these are our first rudimentary attempts at prayer."[59]

In working Step Three, sexual addicts begin to see changes in their lives. You will become more honest with yourself and others, and you will not isolate yourself as much as in the past. You will notice that you are attending Twelve Step meetings more consistently and even experiencing sustained sexual sobriety.

Someone has suggested that a good summary of the first three Steps is:

- Step One: "I can't"
- Step Two: "He can"
- Step Three: "I think I'll let Him"

Step Four: Honesty

Step Four: "Made a searching and fearless moral inventory of ourselves."[60] This Step is about honesty and builds on the work done in the first three Steps. It involves taking a number of inventories on subjects like character defects, positive character traits, sexual conduct, fears, and resentments. Though this Step does not appear to be overtly spiritual, getting to a level of true personal honesty is a spiritual experience.

Step Five: Truth

Step Five: "Admitted to God, to ourselves, and to another human being the exact nature of our wrongs."[61] This Step is about truth. With this Step you come out of hiding. You build on the personal honesty gained in the previous Step and get honest with "another human being" and with God. This Step involves taking complete responsibility for your behavior and not trying to blame your partner, your parents, your sponsor, your therapist, God, or fate for your actions.

For some people this Step includes reading the inventories of Step Four to a sponsor, a religious leader, or to a Twelve Step group. Exactly how you work the Step is up to you and your sponsor.

---

59. (*Sex Addicts Anonymous*, 2005) p. 30
60. (*Sex Addicts Anonymous*, 2005) p. 31
61. (*Sex Addicts Anonymous*, 2005) p. 37

Step Six: Acceptance

Step Six: "Were entirely ready to have God remove all these defects of character."[62] This Step is about acceptance and the practical result of working Step Three. In working this Step you are willing to allow God to make changes in your life. To do this Step, you must have a deep commitment to recovery.

Working this Step means you are ready to leave all of your compulsive sexual behavior behind. You give up the thought that you will be "good for a while" and then return to your old behavior on occasion. This Step will involve taking your list of character defects in Step Four and being willing to part with all of them.

Are you still holding on to some character defects? Which ones are you reluctant to release? Which ones do you still enjoy?

Step Seven: Humility

Step Seven: "Humbly asked God to remove our shortcomings."[63] This Step is about humility and is often worked through prayer. In working this Step, your understanding of your Higher Power will grow. You ask God to remove your character defects and recognize that He will do so in His timing.

With humility comes gratitude. If you are able to ignore your own shortcomings, there is no need for humility or gratitude. Instead you will just stay in the self-centered world that has been a hallmark of your addiction.

In this Step, you might want to refer to your list of character defects or shortcomings. How many on that list have already been removed? How many are in the process of being removed? Which shortcomings are still struggles for you? This Step may be one that you continue working throughout your lifetime.

Step Eight: Willingness

Step Eight: "Made a list of all persons we had harmed and became willing to make amends to them all."[64] This Step is about willingness. It does not require you to make the amends but only to become willing to make them.

Perhaps you have dreaded this Step from the moment you entered recovery. As you make the list of persons you have harmed, try to resist the urge to determine how you will make an amends to them. Making amends is something that will happen later in consultation with your sponsor.

Your list may be daunting and lead you to feeling depressed. It is helpful to remember that at this point you are no longer engaging (hopefully) in those behaviors that have harmed others. If that is the case, then it is appropriate to take a moment and embrace a spirit of gratitude for your progress in recovery.

---

62. (*Sex Addicts Anonymous*, 2005) p. 40
63. (*Sex Addicts Anonymous*, 2005) p. 43
64. (*Sex Addicts Anonymous*, 2005) p. 45

The harm you have caused others may include being dishonest to them, exposing them to disease, destroying their trust in you, breaking promises to them, being financially irresponsible, or being unfaithful. You may have used others. Perhaps you led them to think that you really cared for them, but you were just using them. Maybe you have been critical of them.

This is the Step where you begin the process of repairing damage you caused by your addiction. When you can mend the past, you have the opportunity to leave it behind and move into the future. Not that you will ever forget what you have done, but this Step will lead to you finally being able to forgive yourself as you embrace a future that does not include acting out. That forgiveness of self takes place in the next Step.

Step Nine: Forgiveness

Step Nine: "Made direct amends to such people wherever possible, except when to do so would injure them or others."[65] This Step is about forgiveness, especially to oneself. Many sexual addicts have great difficulty forgiving themselves. They may even think that if they forgive themselves that they are not taking their addiction seriously.

Some sexual addicts wallow in the shame of the past as if doing so is a form of penance. They may also be fearful that if they forgive themselves that their partner may believe they have not suffered enough, or that they are treating the addiction in a cavalier manner. But forgiveness of self is crucial to recovery. Failure to forgive oneself may condemn a person to repeatedly return to the demoralizing compulsive sexual behaviors.

An exercise that is helpful is to write a letter of forgiveness to yourself. This is not a letter that minimizes the impact of your addiction on others or its consequences to yourself. Instead it is a letter that affords a bit of grace to yourself. In this letter, you treat yourself the way you would treat any other person who is on a road of recovery and is truly remorseful about their past behavior. When you complete the letter, read it to your sponsor, an accountability partner, or a spiritual advisor. And once you have forgiven yourself, do not go back and pick up that same burden of shame again.

One of the ways you forgive yourself is by making amends to others you have harmed. The amends process is often expressed as "cleaning your side of the street." This truth became very clear to me when I visited Kyoto, Japan a few years ago. Each morning at sunrise, I would go out for a morning run along an alley that paralleled the main street through the city. There were numerous shops that lined both sides of this tiny street. Every morning each shopkeeper would clean the street in front of their store. Some of them would use a bucket and a brush and carefully scrub the street up to the center line. The shopkeepers on the opposite side of the street then cleaned their side of the street right up to the center dividing line.

Making an amends is making your best effort to clean up the mess that you made in your addiction. You boldly tell those you harmed of your deep regret for your actions and of your resolve to live a different lifestyle.

---

65. (*Sex Addicts Anonymous*, 2005) p. 48

What if that person does not accept your effort at making an amends? What they do with the amends is "their side of the street." Your responsibility is to make the amends. And that effort is valid regardless of how the other person responds.

Shawn's Story

When Shawn began making his amends, he knew he would have a difficult time. He became convinced that he should make an amends to many of his wife's friends who knew of his actions. He reasoned that when he hurt his wife, he also hurt them since they cared about her.

Shawn made the first few amends to his friends and found that they were gracious and wished him well. One person even expressed the belief that no amends were necessary. But then Shawn called another of his wife's friends and confidently went through the rehearsed amends speech he had already given several times. To his horror, this person reacted negatively to the amends. She called him several choice names and told him he should be ashamed for the way he had hurt his wife.

Ashamed is just what he felt. His shame was so great that he thought he might abandon the rest of his Ninth Step. But when he talked to his sponsor, he gained some insight that allowed him to continue his amends process. His sponsor pointed out that he had done his part and that he was not in charge of the other person's response. He had indeed "cleaned his side of the street." What that person did with their side of the street was not his responsibility.

In making amends, it is imperative that you seek the direction of your sponsor. Your sponsor will most likely believe there is too much risk to you in making direct amends to former acting-out partners. For those people, a living amends—living just the opposite from how you lived when you hurt them—is the best approach.

It is also essential that you rely on the power of God to direct you in your amends. Wisdom is necessary in making this Step. You can find that wisdom from God. "Our faith in our Higher Power increases when we realize that we've squarely faced the wrongs in our past."[66]

Step Ten: Maintenance

Step Ten: "Continued to take personal inventory and when we were wrong promptly admitted it."[67] This Step is about maintenance. Daily you are to reflect on how you have lived. You do not have to wait for a particular time to do this ongoing inventory. Instead you take stock each day of how you have lived and then correct your missteps. "We ask God's help with the challenges that face us, while thanking God for the blessings of life and recovery."[68]

---

66. (*Sex Addicts Anonymous*, 2005) p. 52
67. (*Sex Addicts Anonymous*, 2005) p. 52
68. (*Sex Addicts Anonymous*, 2005) p. 53

Step Eleven: Gratitude

Step Eleven: "Sought through prayer and meditation to improve our conscious contact with God as we understood God, praying only for knowledge of God's will for us and the power to carry that out."[69] This Step is about gratitude. Notice that prayer and meditation are the means for improving our contact with God.

Prayer has been characterized as asking God for what we want. Meditation has been described as listening to God. Daily we seek God's will. And when we know His will, we ask for the power to do His will.

Step Twelve: Service

Step Twelve: "Having had a spiritual awakening as the result of these Steps, we tried to carry this message to other sex addicts and to practice these principles in our lives."[70] This Step is about service. Service results from the spiritual awakening that comes from working the steps.

Together these Steps say there is hope for the sexual addict. You do not have to live a defeated life. Not only is there hope but as you live out the Steps in your daily life, you will find freedom!

Spiritual Retreats

It is possible to go on a spiritual retreat by yourself. There are numerous retreat centers around the country that offer various opportunities throughout the year, many of which are open to the public. Some of these centers provide opportunities for individuals to participate in a private retreat with or without intervention by a resident religious leader.

It is not necessary to go to a retreat center to have a spiritual experience. You can plan your own retreat incorporating the elements of prayer, study, meditation, and contemplation, as well as some physical activity. You may have access to a cabin in a secluded place or know of a hotel that is a bit off of the beaten path. For that matter, you can have a spiritual retreat at your own home.

Location is not a critical factor, though some locations are more conducive to reflection and contemplation. Instead of location, the focus should be on getting away from the many distractions of everyday life and devoting time and effort to getting in touch with God.

Distractions like television, recorded music, and telephones must be eliminated from the retreat setting. Interactions with other people should be kept to a minimum unless they are part of the retreat experience, such as on a Twelve Step retreat.

The following are some of the elements that are helpful during retreats:

- **Simple food.** The focus of the retreat must not be diverted to food. Keep your meals simple.

---

69. (*Sex Addicts Anonymous*, 2005) p. 55
70. (*Sex Addicts Anonymous*, 2005) p. 58

- **Music.** Let the music come from you. If you play an instrument, take it with you. If you enjoy singing, you will have an opportunity to lose yourself in your songs. But what about those of us who cannot carry a tune? It doesn't matter what you sound like. No one will hear you but yourself. Music is a pathway to your soul. Use that pathway as you explore your relationship with God.

- **Study.** If you identify with a particular religion or belief system, you can use the retreat to study selected passages of scripture or other sacred texts. Read a book on spirituality or meditation during the retreat.

- **Physical exercise.** There is something about a brisk walk, a hike, or doing some other moderate to active exercise that helps one get in touch with thoughts and feelings. Exercise can be conducive to your spiritual quest.

One caution should be voiced. Care should be taken to ensure that you do not use the seclusion of the retreat setting as an opportunity to act out. For this reason, there may be wisdom in joining an organized retreat, going with an accountability partner who is having his or her own retreat but is available several times a day for mutual accountability, or having some kind of check-in with your spouse or partner. A spiritual retreat can be a significant component in your recovery. Many recovering sexual addicts make such retreats an annual or even semi-annual event.[71]

---

71. Hope & Freedom Counseling Services offers spiritual retreats for men three times each year. More information can be found at www.HopeAndFreedom.com.

Day 22: Be Aware of Other Addictions

Caleb's Story

Caleb is an alcoholic. He knows that for certain. As far back as he can recall he remembers having a love affair with alcohol. He was obsessed with drinking his favorite beverage out of the proper glass in the perfect environment. Nevertheless, the end result was always the same: He could not control his drinking, and once he started he always drank to get drunk.

After ruining his marriage with his out-of-control drinking behavior, Caleb stopped cold turkey. He congratulated himself that he did not have to go to AA meetings like other people who were not as strong as he was. He did not engage in any recovery program. Caleb reasoned that since drinking was the problem, the solution was simply to stop drinking. He thought that would fix everything.

When he started dating again, he discovered Internet dating sites and felt like a child who had been released in a candy store. After a brief period he realized that he was engaging in numerous behaviors that he found detestable. With every effort to stop, he found he was marginally successful and often new compulsive sexual behaviors would take the place of the ones he was trying to stop.

Caleb made an appointment with a therapist to seek help in stopping the behaviors that he loathed. His therapist diagnosed him as a sexual addict. After getting a full history, the therapist suggested that when he stopped drinking, instead of truly getting into recovery he had just traded one addiction for another. Much like the Whac-A-Mole[72] game found in arcades, one addiction is pummeled into submission only to be replaced by another addiction that is equally out-of-control.

We have already talked about limiting television viewing, the playing of video games, and alcohol consumption. At this point, it is time to see whether there are other addictions present. In some of his early research on sexual addiction, Dr. Patrick Carnes found that a significant percentage of sexual addicts also had other addictions present.[73]

Not only are other addictions often present, but so is a lack of awareness of the tendency of addictions to morph into new areas of compulsive behavior with equally devastating results. Focusing solely on stopping bad behavior in one addiction may only result in shifting the addiction to a new area. Recovery must encompass all of life.

Alcohol Addiction

Alcoholism is a condition where a person continues to consume alcoholic beverages in spite of negative social or health consequences. Seven hundred thousand Americans are treated

---

72. Game rights owned by Bob's Space Racers www.bobsspaceracers.com
73. (P. Carnes, *Don't Call it Love* 1992) pp. 225-226.

daily for alcoholism, and many more remain untreated. Professor David Zaridze has calculated that alcohol has killed three million Russians.[74] This is truly a worldwide epidemic.

For those who consume alcohol in any quantities, take a careful look at your drinking behavior. When is the last time you drank so much that you became impaired? Some people have a hard time admitting that they are ever impaired. Perhaps a better question is, when is the last time you drank so much that you were over the legal limit to operate a motor vehicle?

When you drink, how much do you drink? Do you drink "just to take the edge off"? If that is your practice, how much does it take before you get relaxed and are feeling you can face the world? Even if your habit is only to have one or two drinks, is this a daily pattern or something that happens almost every day?

Even moderate drinking may be problematic if it is something that is a daily occurrence. If you are willing to scrutinize this area of your life, consider asking those closest to you if they believe you have a drinking problem. You may also want to ask them if they ever wished you drank less.

The CAGE questionnaire[75] is a quick way of assessing whether a person has a problem with alcohol. Its name is an acronym of its four questions. Two yes responses indicate this is something that should be investigated further.

CAGE Questionnaire

1. Have you ever felt you needed to **Cut** down on your drinking?

    _____

2. Have people **Annoyed** you by criticizing your drinking?

    _____

3. Have you ever felt **Guilty** about drinking?

    _____

4. Have you ever felt you needed a drink first thing in the morning (**Eye opener**) to steady your nerves or to get rid of a hangover?

    _____

---

74. (Parfitt, June 2009)
75. (Ewing, 1984)

Have you gotten into fights or arguments while drinking? Has anyone close to you ever indicated they were concerned about your drinking? Do you ever take secret drinks? Do you hide alcohol so you will always have access to it? Have you lied to cover your alcohol use? Take an inventory of losses you have suffered due to your drinking behavior. Have you lost friends, a job, a marriage or other committed relationship due to your drinking?

If you have a parent or grandparent who is an alcoholic, you are at greater risk of developing an addiction to alcohol. Perhaps when you were growing up you were embarrassed by the behavior of your parents and you swore that you would never be an embarrassment to your family and friends. Have you kept that promise? Has anyone close to you been embarrassed by your behavior while you were drinking?

If you are serious about examining your drinking behavior, consider keeping a log of your alcohol consumption. Be honest with yourself as you keep this log. If you are pouring your drinks from a bottle, accurately measure the amount that you drink rather than estimate it. One of the things therapists do to get a more accurate picture of what a client drinks is to take the client's estimate and double or triple it.

Take a clear look at your drinking behavior. You are not trying to please your spouse or convince your therapist you do not have a problem. Rather you are carefully looking at your life with a goal of uncovering anything that has the potential of taking you back to a place of despair and hopelessness.

Drug Abuse

If you are currently using recreational drugs, the time to stop is now! Can you really claim to be in recovery if you continue using drugs? I am frequently challenged by people who suggest that there is nothing wrong with smoking marijuana or in using a "limited amount" of cocaine. My purpose here is not to debate whether drug use is right or wrong from a moral or social standpoint but to encourage you to consider that you may have a problem with drug use.

Recreational drugs have but one purpose and that is to alter a person's reality. They are for disconnecting from life. Whether a person takes them to escape reality or to "make life more manageable," they are used as a coping mechanism and to run away from something.

Recovery is about getting in touch with life. You are not really serious about recovery unless you are willing to stop all recreational drug use. Such drug use is incompatible with recovery.

In addition to examining your life with regard to recreational drugs, consider how you use prescription drugs. Do you ever take medication that is prescribed for someone else? Have you ever taken a higher dosage of a medication than is prescribed? Have you ever searched for another physician who would be more willing to prescribe you the drug that you believe you require or in the quantity that you believe is necessary?

Abuse of prescription drugs is at epidemic proportions today. Just because you would never think of making a drug buy on a street corner in a seedy part of town is no guarantee that you do not have a drug problem. Common drugs that are misused and abused include pain killers, sleep medications, and anti-anxiety drugs.

An often misused drug is OxyContin™.[76] OxyContin is a time-released formulation of oxycodone. By 2001, it was the best-selling non-generic narcotic pain-reliever in the United States.[77] Like all narcotics it is highly addictive. While the drug is a controlled substance, it is widely available through illegitimate sources.

Hydrocodone is another narcotic pain-reliever that is often abused. It is sold under various trademarks including Vicodin™ and Percocet™—both of which have been listed by an advisory panel of the Food and Drug Administration advising that the drugs be removed from the US market.[78] Some abusers use hydrocodone and OxyContin in combination to produce even greater high.

Benzodiazepines are a class of drugs commonly referred to as tranquilizers that are often prescribed for panic attacks and other social anxiety disorders. They include drugs with the trade names Valium™, Xanax™, Versed™, Halcion™, Ativan™, Librium™, Klonopin™, and numerous others.

These drugs are effective in controlling anxiety but are also frequently abused and are highly addictive. If you have been given a prescription for any of these drugs, it is crucial that you be carefully monitored by a physician for signs of dependency as well as misuse. Psychiatrists typically monitor the use of these drugs more closely than family physicians. Regardless of who prescribes them, make sure you are not content just to have a prescription refilled repeatedly without being evaluated face-to-face by a physician. The best course is not to take prescriptions of any kind unless there is a medical necessity accompanied by close medical supervision.

Compulsive Gambling

Compulsive gambling, also referred to as pathological gambling or ludomania, is having a strong urge to gamble in spite of negative consequences and a desire to stop. Persons who struggle with compulsive gambling are prone to place bets and lie to cover up their gambling behaviors. Additionally, compulsive gamblers may resort to fraud or theft to get the funds to pursue their addiction.

Some gamblers try to fool themselves by limiting their gambling to risky behavior involving the stock market. They are continually buying and selling in search of a big win or unrealistic returns. Some will gamble with their retirement accounts or take out second mortgages on their homes to cover bets on a particular stock or to purchase a stock they consider to be a sure winner.

Some of the signs of problem gambling may include:

- Always thinking about gambling
- Lying about gambling
- Spending work or family time gambling

---

76. Produced by the pharmaceutical company Purdue Pharma
77. Prescription drugs: OxyContin abuse. Washington, DC: U.S. Government Accounting Office. 2003 December. http://www.gao.gov/new.items/d04110.pdf
78. June 29-30, 2009: Joint Meeting of the Drug Safety and Risk Management Advisory Committee with the Anesthetic and Life Support Drugs Advisory Committee and the Nonprescription Drugs Advisory Committee: Meeting Announcement, http://www.fda.gov/AdvisoryCommittees/Calendar/ucm143083.htm

- Feeling bad after you gamble, but not quitting
- Gambling with money you should use for other things

Compulsive gambling parallels drug and alcohol addiction in several ways. It is often used to escape reality. Compulsive gamblers develop a tolerance in that they have to engage in more gambling activity to get the same effects as before.

It is estimated that 2.5 percent of the population has some problem with gambling.[79] Compulsive gamblers may have had an early big win that they are trying to replicate. They enjoy the excitement that gambling gives whether they win or lose. And if they lose, compulsive gamblers often have the feeling that they will win it all back tomorrow.

Compulsive gamblers are quick to talk about their wins and often hide their losses. The biggest difference between social gamblers and compulsive gamblers is the amount of time devoted to gambling. Compulsive gamblers are five times more likely than social gamblers to spend at least one quarter of their leisure time gambling or preparing to gamble.[80]

The Internet has made gambling much more accessible. Though there are a variety of laws that are intended to limit Internet gambling, it continues to grow rapidly. Gambling on the Internet for some may be an extension of video gaming addiction.

Nicotine Addiction

Nicotine is an addictive drug. Historically nicotine addiction has been one of the hardest addictions to break. According to the National Institute on Drug Abuse (NIDA), tobacco kills 440,000 Americans each year.[81] Symptoms of nicotine withdrawal include:

- Irritability
- Impatience
- Hostility
- Anxiety
- Depressed mood
- Difficulty concentrating
- Restlessness
- Decreased heart rate
- Increased appetite or weight gain[82]

For a person to be in full recovery from sexual addiction, they must give attention to all other addictions. Can a person really consider themselves in recovery if they continue to use tobacco habitually? Whether one smokes, chews, dips, or in some other way ingests nicotine, nicotine addiction must be dealt with if a person is going to be serious about adopting recovery as a lifestyle.

---

80. (Lieberman, 1988)
81. (Tobacco Addiction: Letter from the Director)
82. (Nicotine Addiction)

Zach's Story

Zach started smoking when he was in junior high school. He smoked until he was in his twenties but gave it up because of the health risks. Since giving up smoking, Zach has had a wide variety of other addictions.

Sexual addiction was the hardest for him to control. In fact, he found he had no control over it. Each time he would try to stop acting out sexually, he found his craving for nicotine became almost more than he could resist. He finally started using chewing tobacco as a way to help him curb his sexual behavior. When Zach got into recovery for his sexual addiction, he was reluctant to give up tobacco. He knew he was just trading one addiction for another.

Video Gaming Addiction

Video games can be great fun. From the time the first video game, Pong, was released in the early 1970s, these games have offered not only amusement but escape. Unfortunately, the sensory experience afforded can be so engrossing that addiction is possible.

When comparing compulsive video gaming to drug addiction, some might be tempted to dismiss video game addiction as a nuisance. However, this addiction has the ability to ruin lives. Some video game addicts have lost relationships, jobs, and educational opportunities due to their addiction.

Dr. Kimberly Young,[83] the director of the Center for On-Line Addiction, has said that the warning signs of video game addiction include:

- Playing for increasing amounts of time
- Thinking about gaming during other activities
- Gaming to escape from real-life problems, anxiety, or depression
- Lying to friends and family to conceal gaming
- Feeling irritable when trying to cut down on gaming

As the addiction progresses, video game addicts become isolated, living in a solitary world that includes only a video screen and the virtual game-playing community. As the isolation deepens, some video game addicts completely disconnect from social activities. If forced to leave their gaming console for a meal or some other activity, they may experience withdrawal symptoms that include restlessness, irritability, and an inability to concentrate.

Video games have several "hooks" that draw players in. These hooks are purposely built into games to make them more addictive.

- **The Immediate Gratification Hook:** Video games give immediate rewards for success. As gamers develop more proficient gaming skills, they are rewarded with graphics and sound that recognize their accomplishment. This is especially appeal-

---

83. (Young K.)

Thirty Days to Hope & Freedom for Sexual Addicts

ing to younger players who chafe under parents' admonitions that there is value in delayed gratification.

- **The High Score Hook:** Video games are designed to both challenge players and give them small wins to keep them playing. The lure of beating the previous high score can keep players gaming for long periods of time and compel them to come back to beat their previous high score.

- **The Beating the Game Hook:** Similar to the High Score Hook, this lure allows players to achieve one level of success and then graduate to a more difficult level of the game. Achieving mastery of a game to the tenth, twentieth, or higher level is a badge of honor for addicted gamers.

- **The Friendship Hook:** Online friendships are fostered through the ability of video game consoles to link players from across the world. These friendships often seem more real than face-to-face friendships. Some gamers see their virtual friends as their only true friends. This is an especially dangerous hook for a sexual addict. The anonymity of the gaming community coupled with the fantasy involved during the games creates an atmosphere that is fertile for a potential descent into virtual sexual relationships. In fact, several of the games have a virtual sex component built in which encourages participants to indulge sexual fantasies and then to communicate about them with their virtual friends.

- **The Master of the Universe Hook:** Addicted game players may find a sense of accomplishment in video games that has eluded them in real life. They can achieve levels of recognition either from the game graphics or from virtual friends that allow them to retreat into a world of make-believe where they will never experience failure. While pursuing this hook, a gamer's life may be falling apart.

Treatment for gaming addiction is similar to other addiction recovery. Several treatment facilities now have specialized treatment programs for video game addiction. There is even a dedicated detox center for video gaming addiction in Amsterdam. As of this writing, there is not yet a formal Twelve Step fellowship with a broad geographical base for video game addiction, though there are some locations that have a few scattered meetings that focus on this addiction.

Eating Disorders

Eating disorders include a variety of pathologies. A broad definition for an eating disorder is eating or avoiding eating in a way that is unhealthy physically and mentally. Previously, eating disorders were thought to be limited primarily to women and girls, but men and boys also suffer from them. Only the major eating disorders, those that are most likely to be present with sexual addiction, are examined here.

Anorexia Nervosa

Anorexia nervosa is a serious and potentially life-threatening psychiatric illness characterized by a fear of gaining weight and an extreme but distorted view of body image. The term *anorexia* is of Greek origin and means "loss of appetite." It was first described by Richard Morton in 1689.[84]

A person with anorexia nervosa may look at their emaciated body in the mirror and believe they are fat. They are constantly at odds with family and friends who voice concern. They may feel that these loved ones are actually in a conspiracy with a goal of making them fat.

This disease may start with dieting in an attempt to lose weight. Over time, the dieting becomes compulsive and weight loss becomes a sign of control. A person who begins losing weight may feel such a sense of accomplishment (especially after hearing compliments about her improved appearance) that she may take dieting to the extreme. The resulting obsession with weight begins a cycle that is similar to that of sexual or drug addiction.

There is not a single cause for anorexia nervosa. We do know that cultural pressures, personality differences, family expectations, and heredity may play a role. Women who have a mother or sister with this disorder are at greater risk of developing it.

Treatment for anorexia nervosa is specialized and often necessitates inpatient care. Ongoing treatment may include psychotherapy, medications such as antidepressants to help prevent relapse, and continued aftercare to reinforce new behaviors.

Bulimia Nervosa

Bulimia nervosa is an eating disorder that is marked by compulsive overeating and some compensating behavior to counter the overeating. This compensatory behavior may include self-induced vomiting, use of laxatives, compulsive exercise or fasting, as well as the use of diuretics and enemas. This eating disorder may be difficult to recognize because an affected person may have normal body weight.

The term *bulimia* comes from a Latin word that means "ravenous." This condition was first described in 1979 by Gerald Russell, a British psychiatrist.[85] Since that time, it has been diagnosed in both males and females. Like anorexia nervosa, the overwhelming number of persons affected by bulimia nervosa are female.

It is unclear how many people are affected by this disorder. One study of college students found that more than 5 percent of female students met the criteria for bulimia nervosa.[86] Another study found more than 9 percent of girls ages fifteen to seventeen showed some symptoms of bulimia nervosa.[87] In all of the studies the number of males with this disorder was 1.5 percent or less.

As with anorexia nervosa, a variety of treatment modalities are used for this condition. Inpatient or intensive outpatient treatment programs are most effective. Psychotherapy along

---

84. (Argente, 1997, Vol. 82, No. 7)
85. (Russell, 1979)
86. (Heatherton, Nichols, Mahamedi, & Keel, 1995)
87. (Patton & Coffey, 2008)

with the use of some prescription medications have been found to be helpful. As with all eating disorders care must be taken to avoid relapses.

Compulsive Overeating

Compulsive overeating, also known as food addiction or binge eating, is marked by eating large amounts of food in a relatively brief period. This condition can develop at any age and is often linked to obsessive-compulsive disorder. People who suffer from this condition struggle with feelings of shame and disgust. They may experience extreme self-loathing and have depression to such a level they become at risk of harming themselves.

It is believed that about two percent of adults in the United States are affected by compulsive overeating. Men who binge eat may also suffer from exercise addiction in order to counter the effects of overeating. Women who are compulsive overeaters may fill the spaces between binges with dieting and feel that they are always on a diet.

Signs of compulsive overeating include:

- Binge eating
- Fear of not being able to stop eating voluntarily
- Eating more rapidly than normal
- Depression
- Self-deprecating thoughts following binges
- Withdrawing from activities because of embarrassment about weight
- A history of going on many different but ultimately unsuccessful diets
- Eating little in public, while maintaining a high weight
- A history of weight fluctuations
- Believing they will be a better person when thin
- Feelings of self-worth based on weight
- Social and professional failures attributed to weight
- Feeling tormented by eating habits
- Weight is the focus of life

People with a food addiction are differentiated from those with bulimia nervosa in that they do not purge their bodies with vomiting or laxatives. A variety of related health risks accompany compulsive overeating, including heart disease, high blood pressure, high cholesterol, and diabetes. The physical risks combined with mental risk factors make this seemingly innocuous disorder life-threatening.

Overeaters Anonymous offers Twelve Step groups, patterned after Alcoholics Anonymous, that have proven to be effective as part of a treatment program that may include individual and group psychotherapy. This program does not focus on weight loss or gains but rather the physical, emotional, and spiritual aspects of overeating. The goal is for members to develop a healthy relationship with food.

Exercise Addiction

When is exercise not a good thing? When it becomes compulsive and is a threat to a person's health. Exercise addiction is not to be confused with a positive addiction, which was popularized by Dr. William Glasser.[88] Glasser studied long-distance runners and found that their pursuit of running, otherwise thought to be boring, becomes an addiction that has beneficial side effects.

Instead, exercise addiction goes far beyond an endorphin-induced "runner's high." Some persons become so obsessed with working out that they routinely exercise to the point of injury. They may take various health-threatening drugs such as human growth hormone (HGH) and steroids. When exercise goes to such extremes and can be called exercise addiction, a person's health and perhaps even their life are at risk.

Dr. Sharon Stoliaroff[89] developed a checklist to help identify whether exercise is out of balance with the rest of life. Rate yourself as honestly as you can.

- I have missed social obligations and family events in order to exercise.
- I have given up other interests, including time with friends, in order to make more time to work out.
- Missing a workout makes me irritable and depressed.
- I only feel content when I am exercising or within the hour after exercising.
- I like exercise better than sex, good food, or a movie—in fact there's almost nothing I'd rather do.
- I work out even if I'm sick, injured, or exhausted. I'll feel better when I get moving anyway.
- In addition to my regular schedule, I'll exercise more if I find extra time.
- Family and friends have told me I'm too involved in exercise.
- I have a history (or a family history) of anxiety or depression.

Endorsing three or more of these items may be an indication you are losing your perspective on running or working out. This is also an indication that you should seek help.

Recovery from All Addictions

There are numerous other behaviors that in moderation are not harmful and may be beneficial. But taken to extremes they can become addictions. Things like watching television, spending time on Internet auction sites and shopping sites, and even reading can reach such unhealthy levels that they impact your life.

If you believe there is the possibility that you have another addiction that is present with your sexual addiction, it is imperative that you get evaluated by a health care professional who is

---

88. (Glasser, 1976)
89. (Stoliaroff, 2003)

Thirty Days to Hope & Freedom for Sexual Addicts

skilled at diagnosing and treating addictions. A good place to start the evaluation process is with a sexual addiction therapist. Many of them are trained to recognize and treat multiple addictions.

Leaving other addictions untreated puts you at risk of losing your sexual sobriety. Addictions interact with each other. While they are all used to escape, they may also feed one another. For example, a person who is both a sexual addict and an alcoholic cannot afford to let the alcohol addiction go untreated because the lowered inhibitions that come from drinking may put that person at risk of returning to destructive and compulsive sexual behaviors.

In the same way, the presence of an untreated gambling addiction may also put a person at risk of acting out sexually. If a compulsive gambler is on a winning streak, there is a risk they may want to bend their sexual boundaries in celebration. If they are losing, they may be tempted to turn back to their compulsive sexual behavior to medicate their pain.

Recovery from any addiction will follow a similar path as recovery from sexual addiction. The journey begins with the recognition that you might have a problem. An open mind and willingness to examine every area of your life are necessary if you are to be successful in recovery.

In Appendix B of this book you will find a list of Twelve Step organizations that are specific to other addictions. Get a list of meetings in your area for each of the addictions that you think may be present. Make a commitment today to attend your first meeting.

As with sexual addiction recovery, just attending meetings is not enough to get you sober and keep you sober. You need to get a sponsor in each fellowship and work the Steps of recovery in each program.

That may seem like a daunting task. You may protest and think that working the Twelve Steps in a sexual addiction program is enough, but if you have another addiction, it is imperative that you work the Steps in that program. You also need the guidance of a sponsor in each program. While the Step work will be similar, there are many specific applications that are made in each addiction.

Carefully looking at every part of your life is a necessary ingredient in your recovery. While you may have started on this journey with the thought of strictly focusing on your compulsive sexual behavior, addressing other addictions is necessary for you to be successful in recovery. Be as diligent in your search for understanding of other addictions as you have been in your pursuit of sexual addiction recovery.

Other Addictions Worksheet

In addition to sexual addiction, I believe I am addicted or may be susceptible to becoming addicted to the following things: _____

_____

_____

_____

_____

_____

_____

I plan to take the following action in response to this realization: _____

_____

_____

_____

_____

_____

_____

_____

Thirty Days to Hope & Freedom for Sexual Addicts

Day 23: A Talk with Myself

Talk to myself? Who, me? Actually, everybody talks to themselves. We may carry on full conversations in our heads. And when we are alone, or think we are, we may even talk to ourselves out loud. If anyone overhears us, we are sure they will think we are deranged. But everybody does this to one degree or another.

Nancy's Story

Nancy did not feel attractive. She wanted desperately to fit in. In her senior year of high school, she was sexual for the first time. Her date told his friends. Within a few days, she had another date. When word got out that she was "easy," she never again had a problem getting a date. Several of those she dated were younger than her. She enjoyed feeling like she was the more experienced one.

In college she never really connected with anyone her own age. She still had plenty of contacts from high school. Nancy is now in her 50s and still finds it difficult to connect with anyone her own age. Several times a year she will find young men, some as young as twenty, with whom she can be sexual. These encounters never turn into relationships. She wishes she could have a real relationship with someone her own age, but she has conceded that will not be likely. Nancy first used sex to fit in with others. During the past thirty years, she has used it to feel less lonely. She called herself many names. One of the things she said to herself most often was that she was a loser, and she was sure there was no one who was in as bad shape as she.

The question is, *What do you say when you talk to yourself?* The answer to that question may have a lot to do with your family of origin, messages you received from teachers and coaches, as well as the presence of addictive behavior. The better you feel about yourself, the more positive the messages you give to yourself. Conversely, the greater your shame, sense of defeat, and feelings of self-loathing, the more likely you are to give yourself negative messages.

Thoughts of Self-Harm

One sexual addict said, "Sexual addiction scares the **** out of me. It has driven me places I never thought I would go. It has driven me to put a gun in my mouth." Fortunately, he got help, and his suicidal thoughts did not persist.

It is crucial that any thoughts of self-harm be seen as serious. While it is true that not everyone who has ever threatened suicide has committed suicide, nearly everyone who has committed suicide has made some cry for help. If your addiction causes you to have thoughts of self-harm, immediately contact a therapist for this very serious condition.

You are worth the effort. As you seek help for your addiction, you will find that you are indeed a person of worth and value. You do count and can have a full and meaningful life. Do not let the addiction win. If you are having thoughts about harming yourself, tell someone now. Seek help with a mental health professional. Call the Suicide Prevention Lifeline at 1-800-273-TALK (8255). This is a 24-hour hotline available to anyone in suicidal crisis or emotional distress.[90]

Shame: Will It Always Affect My Life?

In order to change the way you talk to yourself, first examine the role of shame in your life. If compulsive sexual behavior has defined your life, then you are well acquainted with shame. Shame is a powerful force that comes from the memory of doing things that are inconsistent with the person you really are. As a sexual addict, there are probably many things that you have done that not only had a negative impact on your life but also hurt others. Shame is intensified when you realize how out of control your behavior has been. Even though you want to stop, you feel powerless to do so.

If you can trace the origin of your addiction back to childhood, the messages of shame may be so predominant that they color everything else in life. Every decision is made against the backdrop of thinking, *If people only knew how I really am, they would run the other way.*

For a person who is locked in a cycle of sexual addiction, shame is a constant companion. Shame flourishes in an environment of secrecy. Isolation results from the climate of secrecy, and this compounds shame.

Another factor in developing a shame-based life is a sense of loss. The loss may be the loss of innocence as with a child who was sexually abused. In this case, the loss is not just of innocence but of childhood itself. The loss may be in the form of a divorce or the loss of a job. Sometimes a sense of loss comes from the death of a parent, spouse, or perhaps the most devastating of all, the death of a child.

The profound sadness that accompanies an event of loss may be so painful that a person may seek to cope with the pain through some form of self-medication. For some, this means leaning on drink or drugs; for others it means bingeing on food. But for the sexual addict, the self-medication escape is sex. The power of sexual addiction is found in the fact that sex does indeed relieve pain, at least temporarily, replacing the hurt with pleasure. However, the relief is short-lived. Subsequent attempts to relieve pain with sex reveal that more sex is required to take away the pain, the experiences need to be more varied, or you need to have more partners or greater intensity in your sexual experiences, or perhaps you need to have all of these things in order to banish the pain.

As these factors combine with each other, shame grows. The greater your shame, the greater your sense of isolation. The more necessary it is to keep your behavior secret, the louder your inner voice shouts negative messages about your self-worth.

---

90. Additional information is available at their website: www.suicidepreventionlifeline.org

The Difference between Shame and Guilt

It is often shame that drives a person into recovery. But it is also true that shame may motivate a person to act out. Soon after entering recovery it is imperative that you separate yourself from shame and, instead, focus on guilt.

A recovery definition of guilt is, *I have done some bad things*, whereas a recovery definition of shame is, *I am a bad person*. You must break the hold that shame has on you. You are not a bad person. Instead, you are a good person who has done some bad things.

How do you see yourself? Do you think you are a good person or a bad person? Throw off the desire to beat up yourself. Resist the belief that you are not taking your addiction seriously if you are not feeling badly about yourself.

When I am working with couples, the spouse of a sexual addict often believes they are finally getting to know the real person after a disclosure of acting-out behavior. However, I think that the person they fell in love with is the real person, and the sexual addiction manifests behaviors that are incongruent with the real person. This requires a fundamental shift in thinking.

A Bargain with Yourself

When you break something, what do you say to yourself? If you lock your keys in your car, what do you say under your breath? When you say something that hurts someone's feelings, what words do you say to yourself? Do you call yourself names? Perhaps you hear a voice from long ago saying, "You're stupid." "You will never amount to anything." "You idiot."

As a youngster you may not have had any choice but to listen to caregivers, coaches, or teachers say things to you that were unkind. But as an adult, if someone were to say something unkind to you or call you names, you would not spend time with that person.

It is time to make a fundamental agreement with yourself. Decide today never to say anything to yourself that you would not want someone else to say. This is a key point in your recovery. Change the way you talk to yourself. Only you can decide to stop giving yourself negative messages.

Filter What You Let into Your Mind

You can determine not to feed your mind with bad news. This is not the same as adopting an ostrich's head-in-the-sand mentality. It is not that you deny that bad things happen in the world; it is just that you choose not to dwell on them. One of the ways of doing this is to stay away from news programs and newspapers that focus on the negative. For example, the televised national news will have facts about what has happened that day in the world. And some of it is about negative things that have happened, but there is also a sense that there is balance to what is reported. But local news will be more likely to focus on sensational items like wrecks, fires, crimes, and other items meant to grab attention and evoke an emotional response. In television journalism there is a saying, "If it bleeds, it leads" to identify which stories get the greatest focus.

You do not have to listen to a daily litany of negative stories. You are not going to be hopelessly out-of-touch if you miss the news for a day or more. When you give your mental health priority, you can find ways to keep up with what is going on in the world without resorting to crawling around in the dregs of society. Perhaps you will choose to limit your news gathering to watching a national news program a couple of times a week or reading a newspaper with a national focus.

My wife and I have a home in the Canadian Rockies. Every few months we retreat to the mountains for a couple of weeks to relax and recharge our batteries. When friends come to visit, they are amazed to find that we do not have television and do not receive a newspaper. We remain contentedly unplugged from the world. We do pick up the weekly local paper occasionally where the headlines are likely to be of a bear sighting or the movement of the local elk herd. That is about all of the "hard news" I care for during our get-aways. (As I write this I am looking out at the mountains, looking forward to an afternoon hike.)

Will your life be less rich if you do not hear about violent behavior that is taking place? Are you going to be deprived if you decide not to watch violent movies or read violent novels? Instead, select which positive sources of information you will allow into your mind. Be intentional about what you let in and what you keep out of your mind.

The Place of Affirmations

Affirmations are positive things that you know to be true about yourself. Think of them as receiving a compliment from yourself. Everyone likes hearing a compliment. You may even be able to remember a compliment or two that was especially impactful either because it came from someone you hold in high esteem or because it called attention to a trait, attribute, or action for which you are grateful.

Perhaps you have gotten few compliments through the years. The messages that were given to you when you were a child may have been harsh and critical, and the internal messages that you continue to hear may be in the voice of a critical parent, teacher, or coach. Even though it has been years since any of those persons has been critical of you, you continue to inundate yourself with those hurtful and destructive messages.

If you grew up in an abusive environment, you probably listened to messages that questioned your ability or told you outright that you were of no worth. If you have listened to years of verbal abuse, you must counter those negative messages with positive ones.

Isn't it time you receive some positive messages about yourself? How do you begin? Start off by making a list of positive character traits that you possess. Because of your addiction you may be so focused on the negative character traits that you do not think about positive ones.

There is no one better to receive a compliment from you than yourself. Many things you know about yourself are noteworthy. Even though your positive character traits may have been overshadowed by your sexual addiction, those traits are still present.

Next make a list of your personal accomplishments. Go back as far in your history as necessary so as to make this list as complete as possible. Then make a list of compliments you have

Thirty Days to Hope & Freedom for Sexual Addicts

received from others, beginning with the most recent and working backward. Write as many as you can, whether or not you believe them to be true.

With your lists completed it is time to write your affirmations. Many of these statements will include the word "I." Do not try to balance them with a negative statement. You have had enough negative messages to last a lifetime.

It is easier to come up with affirmations when we think of them as countering a specific negative message. Let's consider some of the negative messages that you have heard or that you have said to yourself.

You may have been told, "You are a disappointment to me!" Depending on your psychological makeup, this can be a most devastating message. To counter this message, you must search within your being and find the message that you would like to have heard from your parents or teachers.

Consider the simple affirmation, "I am proud of you!" Does this adequately counter the negative message that you are a disappointment? Tell a child you are proud of him or her, and watch how they respond. They stand a little taller and may smile at your words. And if the child is your own or is a child who has special meaning to you, the response is even more pronounced.

Now say the same message to yourself. Go to a mirror, look yourself in the eye and say softly, "I am proud of you!" You may feel a bit foolish, and you will make sure no one overhears you. Repeat the affirmation again. "I am proud of you!" Smile at yourself. Point to yourself as you speak. Say it again: "I am proud of you!"

In spite of the temptation to dismiss the exercise as a simple but misguided self-help effort, you begin to feel empowered. Continue repeating the phrase, varying your inflection and intensity. Move closer to the mirror and keep repeating, "I am proud of you!" Can you feel the difference in the way you think about yourself?

Now try writing some affirmations. Did you ever have a teacher make you write a sentence repeatedly, perhaps even filling up an entire page of paper? That is basically what you are doing with this exercise. Pick an affirmation that counters a particularly hurtful message you have received. Perhaps the negative message was, "You always make the wrong choices." A good affirmation would be to remind yourself, "I make good choices."

Spend five minutes writing the same sentence over and over again. Resist the urge to stop because you feel like a child in school. Continue writing the sentence. Fill up the page. "I make good choices. I make good choices." Some people may never have heard anyone else commend them on the choices they make. How does it feel? You may have heard negative messages for so long that it seems unnatural to hear a positive message.

How do you respond when someone pays you a compliment? Do you listen to what is said and take it to heart? Do you believe that person? Or do you dismiss their positive words? Do you try to shrug off what is being said, believing the person is either insincere or trying to butter you up?

If you have a history of listening to negative messages, you may have a difficult time listening to, believing, or accepting compliments. Couple these negative messages from the past with the messages you may give yourself because of your past acting-out behavior, and you have a particularly lethal combination.

I say it is lethal because it kills your self-esteem. Any sense of self-worth, any feeling of personal value is so foreign that you will either ignore the message or counter it with your own message of worthlessness. It is hard to feel good about oneself when faced with the inability to stop sexually compulsive behavior.

Take another negative message you may have heard from parents, friends, or coworkers. Have you ever been told that you are not smart enough, big enough, funny enough, successful enough, or some other variation of this theme? How can you counter the message that you are not enough? With the simple sentence, "I am enough!" Think about it. Those three words have power. If you can take them to heart and then let them shape your behavior, you will live differently. "I am enough! I am enough! I am enough! I am enough!"

You cannot say those words too many times. The simple message of that short sentence is one that you will benefit from repeating to yourself each day. I am enough!

Write affirmations in a journal. Add to the list each time you think of something positive about yourself. Each evening select an affirmation that will be yours for the next day. Write that affirmation on a sticky note and leave it in the middle of your dressing mirror. The next morning when you see that note, repeat the affirmation out loud. Continue repeating it several times with an emphasis on a different word each time.

Transfer that note to the dash of your vehicle and continue repeating it out loud as you drive. When you arrive at work or school, transfer that note to your computer screen, and each time you look at it, repeat the affirmation to yourself. When your workday is over, transfer it again to the dash of your vehicle, and repeat it out loud on your way home.

Throughout the day, any time you feel stressed, repeat your daily affirmation. If you have a negative thought, replace that thought with your affirmation. And if your boss takes you to task for less-than-optimal job performance, counter that negative message with your daily affirmation as you again repeat it to yourself.

During the course of the day, make it your goal to repeat your affirmation at least one hundred times. Let this be your practice every day. And as often as your environment will allow, repeat your affirmation out loud.

Examples of Affirmations

The following list of affirmations is not meant to take the place of affirmations that you develop. They are intended to be thought starters as you cultivate the habit of focusing on your positive attributes. Take the ones that fit and use them as your own. Adapt others to more closely fit who you are. Then make your own list of affirmations.

- I am a precious child of God.
- I have all of the gifts and abilities that I need to be successful in every area of life.
- When I concentrate, I can do just about anything that I need to do.

- I am enough.
- I am a beautiful person who makes the world a better place.
- I am a loving companion and wonderful parent.
- I live in the present and embrace joy.
- I always have enough money for what I really need.
- I do not have to repeat the mistakes of the past.
- Today I choose to live in sobriety and to receive the good gifts the world has for me.
- I release the old messages that were given to me and instead, embrace the positive.
- I don't do *that* anymore!
- I am a good friend.
- Today I will befriend someone without any expectation of getting something in return.
- I am a good (man, woman).
- I am smart.
- I am capable of change. For that reason today will be better than yesterday.
- I will give my best on my job and know that my best is good enough.
- I can and will control my temper.
- Just for today I choose not to get impatient with anyone.
- I am a wise money manager.
- Today I will be prudent with every financial decision that I make.
- I acknowledge all of my feelings because I am in touch with my feelings.
- Today I will make good decisions with regard to my health.
- I forgive those who have hurt me.
- Today I chose to forgive myself.
- Others do not determine my reality. I create my own reality.
- I am going to make it.
- I am a brave person who does not fear the present or future.

Focus on One Thing at a Time

Are there days when it seems that you just cannot move forward due to the many things that you have on your mind? You may have multiple projects due at work, as well as numerous things that require your attention at home. Perhaps you have always considered yourself good at multitasking. You may even thrive on being busy, especially since people often remark about how well you are able to juggle multiple things at a time.

However, there are those times when things just seem to pile up more than usual. Rather than being motivated by having many projects in front of you, you may seem overwhelmed by the load. These are the times when you are vulnerable to acting out.

Instead of seeking relief from the pressure by acting out sexually, it is time to have a talk with yourself about expectations. Even if others are expecting you to perform at a level you are currently not able to, learn to recognize this and repeat, "I am going to work on one thing at a time. When that task is done I will work on another."

Make a list of your tasks that have to be done. This may seem like you are spending valuable time that could be better spent on those tasks. However, take a few minutes and collect your thoughts. Determine what has to be done. Write down each of the tasks at hand. Then prioritize them with the most important tasks first.

Next, begin working the list reminding yourself, "I am going to work on one task at a time." If you are at the beginning of the day, you may find you are more productive by first tackling the item that is the most daunting. But if you are having trouble getting traction, choose an easy task and complete it. Then take another easy task finish it.

Others may have unrealistic expectations of you. Your boss may not fully appreciate the work that is involved in the many things that you have in front of you. It is necessary that you recognize that you are a capable person and that you can move forward productively if you will work on one thing at a time.

Use your power of concentration to make you more productive. Allow your total focus to be on one task. You will find that you are not only more productive, but that you are less at risk of acting out.

Daily Spiritual Renewal

The way you talk to yourself also has spiritual implications. Set aside a daily time for spiritual renewal. You deserve to have some time to refresh your mind with positive messages. During this time you may find it beneficial to pray, meditate, or read from a book that gives positive thoughts to contemplate during the day. This does not have to be a long period of time. But keep this time sacred on your calendar. Do not let other seemingly more urgent things crowd out your time of spiritual renewal.

The Value of Positive People

Many of the messages that we give ourselves come from other people. Surround yourself with positive people. Negative people not only are contagious but they can be toxic. Each morning while out for morning exercise, I pass the same gentleman who always has something negative to say. When the weather has been warm and dry, he will remark about how unbearable he finds the heat. (Since I live in Houston, comments about the heat are common.) But if we have a day of rain, he will complain about how he was not able to go outside. It has become a bit of a game with me. I will see whether I can say something positive to him each morning and see whether he will find some sinister or negative side to the same situation. So far, he has succeeded in finding something wrong with just about everything.

Make a list of your friends, family members, acquaintances, and work associates. Divide them into two groups: positive people and negative people. You may not be able to completely cut yourself off from negative people. You have to work with some and perhaps have some of them in your family. But you can choose to spend more time with positive people.

List of Friends Worksheet

The most negative people I know are: _____

_____

_____

_____

_____

The most positive people I know are: _____

_____

_____

_____

_____

Gratitude

Gratitude is a powerful force. In spite of the losses you may have incurred with your addiction, there are probably many things for which you can be grateful. If you are employed, you can be grateful for your job. Even if it is not the job you aspire to or if you find it boring, you can be grateful you are employed.

If you have a friend, a family member, or any personal possessions, then you have reason to be grateful. You can be grateful for your health. Even if you have significant health problems, you can be grateful that you have lived another day.

The fact that you are reading this book means that you have come to realize that you are probably a sexual addict. This discovery can lead you into a lifetime quest toward integrity and wholeness, and that can be cause for gratitude.

There may even be a day when you can be grateful for your sexual addiction. How is that possible? Because of your addiction you are being led to make changes in your life that you otherwise might never make. Even if you have already suffered significant negative consequences because of your addiction, you can be grateful that you have been given the opportunity to change. You have been given a chance to change the rest of your life starting today.

Complete a gratitude list. Include every cause for gratitude. Even in the most negative circumstances look for something for which you can be grateful.

After completing your list, spend time meditating and reflecting on each of the items. Supplement your list as you remember more things for which you can be grateful.

My Gratitude List

I am grateful for the following things: _____

_____

_____

_____

_____

_____

_____

_____

_____

_____

I commit to meditating on each item on this list every day for the next month.

Signed _____

Thirty Days to Hope & Freedom for Sexual Addicts

Day 24: Personal Recovery Plan

Recovery can never take a holiday. You never get a day off. You cannot afford to stop recovery and hope you have enough momentum to coast.

Nathan's Story

Life in the closet was not easy for Nathan. In spite of encouragement by one of his few gay friends, he could not conceive of coming out to his family or at work. Most of his friends thought he was heterosexual. He even had occasional dates with women to strengthen the façade.

Nathan was afraid of frequenting the places that gay men hung out on the chance that he might be recognized. Instead, he hoped for chance encounters in public restrooms or rest areas. That high-risk behavior finally got him into recovery. However, after a couple of years, Nathan thought he was cured, so he stopped attending meetings.

Soon his reckless sexual behavior returned. He seldom passed a rest area without stopping. Some of the time he would "get lucky." Most of the time he was too timid to even respond to the advances of others, much less to make an advance himself.

One evening after dark, two men at a rest stop signaled him to walk with them out to the edge of the woods. One of the men smiled at Nathan and asked him, "What's your pleasure?" As Nathan stepped forward to touch him, the other man stepped forward with handcuffs and said, "You are being arrested for public lewdness."

Nathan's life changed that day. He found that no amount of past recovery could prevent a return to his addiction. And with his return to acting out, he descended to a new bottom.

Some treat recovery like a bank account believing that as long as they make regular deposits, they can take time out of recovery as they make withdrawals on their recovery account. When you are not moving forward in recovery, you are not standing still but are actually moving backward. It is dangerous to think you can take time off of recovery without adverse consequences. Such behavior puts you at risk of a slip or a relapse.

Your recovery must continue daily. Several activities will become routine for you as you continue your recovery. Each week there will be multiple recovery activities that you perform. Some activities may not happen daily or even weekly but will be performed monthly. All of these activities are clearly identified in your Personal Recovery Plan.

A Personal Recovery Plan is something that you devise as a blueprint for your recovery. This plan contains things that you commit to do on a continual basis in order to remain in recovery. A successful Personal Recovery Plan is drafted after you have spent some time in recovery. After you learn from others, get ideas from your sponsor, and listen to your therapist, you develop a plan that you believe works for you.

Recovery Principles

As you develop your own Personal Recovery Plan, it is important to follow sound recovery principles. Incorporate the following principles into your plan.

A Sense of Hope

Hope creates an environment in which recovery can take place. An ancient proverb says, "Where there is no hope, the people perish." A sense of hopefulness invites growth as an alternative to despair. It lays a foundation upon which recovery can thrive.

Jacobson and Greenly said, "The hope that leads to recovery is, at its most basic level, the individual's belief that recovery is possible."[91] Believing that it is possible for you to live in recovery is fundamental to experiencing recovery. One of the ways to find hope is to listen to the stories of people in Twelve Step meetings who are living sober lives. This will take practice because you may be inclined to focus on the stories of those who have relapsed or who have never gotten sober. Both viewpoints are helpful to your recovery.

Honesty Must Permeate Your Life

With the secrecy and shame surrounding sexual addiction, honesty is often illusive during early recovery. Getting honest with your partner and your therapist are basic to your recovery. It may take a bit of time before you are ready to tell all to your therapist, and it may be a bit longer before you are ready to consider disclosing your past to your partner.

The most critical aspect of honesty is getting completely honest with yourself. A number of things initially may work against such honesty. A significant factor is the permissiveness of society that accepts and embraces much of the behavior from which sexual addicts want to break free. Television and movies use sex as comic relief.

Do not be lulled into minimizing your behavior by thinking cybersex is acceptable. The fact that pornography use is widespread does not lessen the negative impact it has had on you and your relationship. Anonymous sexual encounters, one-night stands, and affairs are prevalent, but that does not diminish the fact that your life has been rocked by that behavior.

You do not have a "little problem." Sexual addiction is not a nuisance; it is a serious issue that can destroy everything that is precious to you. Get honest with yourself. You are not struggling with bad behavior, innocent flirting, wandering eyes, or a high sex drive. You are caught in the grip of sexual addiction. Admitting this to yourself is a significant step toward getting better.

Strive to Be Transparent

Do you ever let anyone see the real you? Have you so insulated yourself that no one ever gets inside? When you hurt, does anyone know it?

---

91. (Jacobson & Greenly, 2001)

Thirty Days to Hope & Freedom for Sexual Addicts

As an addict, it is easy to cut yourself off from those who love you. You have learned that it is not safe to share yourself with others. Somewhere along the line you may have been told that it is wrong to cry, show anger, show affection, or any number of other feelings and emotions.

Be real. You are not perfect. However, you are in recovery. Stay the course!

No One Else Can Do Your Recovery for You

If you are in a committed relationship, your partner may have encouraged you to get help. He or she may have even bought you this book to read in the hope that you would get help for your addiction. Perhaps he or she researched various treatment options. He or she may have even made calls to therapists or Twelve Step organizations on your behalf. If your spouse could do recovery for you, he or she would have already done it.

Similarly, your therapist, sponsor, Twelve Step group, or treatment program cannot recover for you. Each can impact your recovery. But your recovery is up to you.

When I am working with a client in therapy, the client must be working harder on his recovery than I am. That means I do not chase him to make sure he keeps appointments. It is not my responsibility to try to keep a client motivated. Certainly I will do what I can to encourage clients. I will be supportive in every way that I can. But when I recognize that I am working harder than the client on his recovery, then we need to reevaluate our roles. It is time for the client to step forward and for me to step backward a bit.

Until you are ready to take the initiative and do the work yourself, you will not make significant progress in recovery. You must supply the motivation for your recovery.

You Can Benefit from the Journey of Others and from Recovery Professionals

How willing are you to listen to help from others in addressing your sexual addiction? When given direction by your sponsor or your therapist, are you open to that direction or do you think you know a better way? While you are free to determine what you are willing to do for recovery, does it make sense to choose a direction that is counter to what has been given you by mental health professionals who are skilled in working with sexual addiction? If you could have cured yourself, you would have done it by now.

Recovery Must Become the Most Important Thing in Your Life

Make a list of the things that are dear to you. If you are in a relationship, perhaps you will put that high on your priority list. If you are a parent, certainly your children are treasured. Your job and career are of great significance. Perhaps you will list your physical health or your spiritual well being.

Where is recovery on your priority list? Unless it is the most important thing in your life, your success in recovery will likely be limited. If you have already been in recovery for a while but have not been able to maintain sobriety, perhaps recovery has not yet received adequate priority.

Making recovery your number one priority does not mean that you do not spend time with your partner and children, or that you are not taking care of your job or your health. Instead it means that you have recognized that unless recovery is of paramount importance, you are putting everything else on your priority list at risk.

You Must Be Willing to Pay the Price for Recovery

Recovery can be time consuming and costly. In order to make time for attending Twelve Step meetings and therapy, you will have to make some changes in your schedule. How you spend leisure time will change. Entering recovery may mean giving up sporting events, a favorite television show, or relaxed evenings at home.

How willing are you to change? To be successful in recovery numerous things must change in your life. That may include changes in the way you spend your money. Perhaps you should sell your boat to be able to afford the treatment necessary. It might mean you need to get a smaller house or apartment to afford inpatient treatment.

Recovery Is Most Effective When It Is Done in Community

Isolation is deadly to recovery. In fact, isolation is one of the hallmarks of sexual addiction. Most acting out is done in secret or at least without the knowledge of friends or family. Upon entering recovery, you may feel that you must keep secret the journey to reclaim your life. Recovery may or may not be something that you ever share with your close friends. You maintain the right to keep recovery private from friends, but that does not mean that your recovery remains a secret.

Others who have entered recovery before you have a lot to contribute to your journey. Learn from them. Profit from their missteps, and try to avoid the same ones. Ask them questions to help you determine how to focus your efforts. Other recovering people can also offer you a level of accountability. Go back and review the section on accountability in the chapter for Day 12.

The Twelve Step Process Has Proven Effective for Millions of People

In Day 3, we looked at the importance of Twelve Step meetings. Now in putting together your Personal Recovery Plan, it is time to see how these meetings fit into your overall recovery. The Twelve Step model works. It has been proven over the decades and has worked effectively for many people. Still some people look for a better way. It is best to stick with what works.

I routinely tell clients that as a minimum in recovery, they should attend two Twelve Step meetings a week and get a sponsor who will show them how to work the Steps of recovery. The question I frequently get is, "Do I have to go to two meetings every week?" Certainly each person is free to do what they choose in their recovery, but if they go to fewer meetings they are unlikely to get positive results.

Are you free to choose your own way in recovery? Certainly, but you cannot do this without experiencing the consequences of your actions. Similarly, you are free to string a tennis racket with wet spaghetti, but you will not advance to Wimbledon. You are free to pummel the keys of a piano with a hammer, but you will not produce a classical sonata. (These helpful comparisons come from Dr. Jack McGorman of Fort Worth, Texas.) You can choose to follow wise counsel resulting in a predictable path of recovery, or you can choose your own way and risk less-than-ideal results. Which path will you choose?

There is one other thought to consider. Persons who are living in their addiction are often somewhat delusional. They think they know of a better way for doing just about everything. When they approach recovery, they may embark on a path to develop a superior recovery program. Before you develop a new recovery program, follow what has already been proven. Get free from all acting-out behaviors for at least five years. Then if you think you know some things that might improve recovery, begin implementing them one at a time and see how that works for you.

No One Does Recovery Perfectly

Let go of the desire to do recovery perfectly. It is likely that your desire and drive for perfection have contributed to your addiction. One of the sayings in Twelve Step meetings is, "We are perfectly imperfect." You will never do recovery perfectly. But you can do it well. Give yourself some latitude for your humanity and recognize that if you give recovery your best efforts, that you will do it well enough.

My Personal Recovery Plan

Your Personal Recovery Plan will include things that you do daily, weekly, monthly, and annually for your recovery. While your plan may not be the same as any other person's plan, there will be many similarities. Your plan must fit your schedule and your personality. The suggestions made here may be followed exactly, modified to fit your particular needs, or serve as a guideline in preparing your plan. Remember to check your final plan against the recovery principles to see whether it embraces them. It is also a good idea to review your plan with your sponsor and ask for suggestions to strengthen it.

Daily Activities

A good way to begin your day is with a time of prayer or meditation. There are numerous recovery meditation books, as well as books that embrace the tenets of various religions. A morning prayer for recovery can be as simple as, "Thank you for a day of sobriety yesterday. Help me to live soberly today." A similar prayer in the evening is, "Thank you for a day of sobriety today, help me to live soberly tomorrow." These prayers let you bookend the day, concentrating your thoughts on your desire to remain solidly in recovery.

Develop a daily plan of reading recovery-related materials. Learning about your addiction and recovery must be a daily pursuit for the first several years of recovery. Even setting aside ten minutes a day to learn about sexual addiction and about recovery will be helpful. Do not neglect the literature that is produced by the various Twelve Step fellowships.

Keeping a daily recovery journal is one of the more significant activities to cultivate in early recovery. Spend ten to fifteen minutes at the end of the day recording your thoughts, your feelings, recovery activities of that day, and relationship issues or concerns. Journaling can serve as an early warning system if used daily. You can track your progress or lack of progress. Journaling will force you to slow down and contemplate your recovery.

Spend some time each day doing Step work. Your sponsor will make assignments for you as you progress through the Steps. While there is no reason to hurry through the Steps, it is essential that you make regular progress and not get bogged down. Daily work on the Steps, especially during the first year of recovery helps to keep you in a recovery mindset.

Include affirmations as a daily activity. Add to this anything you identify as a daily recovery activity. The more routine you can develop into your daily activity, the stronger your recovery will be. Be particularly scrupulous during the first months of recovery to establish a daily routine and stick to it. This will pay dividends in the future.

Weekly Activities

The first thing you will list as a weekly recovery activity is attending Twelve Step meetings. How many you attend is up to you. I believe a minimum of two meetings a week is best. Three is better. You may even choose to attend one meeting a day for the first three months of recovery.[92]

By now you should have a sponsor. If you do not, make getting a sponsor your top priority. Schedule a face-to-face meeting with your sponsor each week. Even if your sponsor only has a few minutes before or after a meeting, this time will provide accountability for you as you continue your Step work.

If you live in an area that does not have Twelve Step meetings or if the only meeting in your area does not have anyone who is able to be a sponsor, you will have to locate a sponsor in an electronic meeting. While long-distance sponsorship is not ideal, it can be very effective. I know a number of people who meet with their sponsors by telephone or e-mail. And if you are already used to carrying on part of your job duties virtually, a virtual relationship with a sponsor will seem very natural.

Each week you must have contact with other recovering people outside of meetings. These are called "program calls." Make at least two program calls a week where the conversation is centered on recovery. One significant purpose of these calls is to develop a habit of seeking telephone support, so that during a recovery emergency it will be natural to call someone for help.

If you have access to a sexual addiction therapist and can afford to do individual therapy, then weekly individual therapy sessions will be a significant part of your recovery program. Group therapy can also be very helpful to your recovery. Group therapy costs less than individual therapy and has the added benefit of your being able to get feedback from others who are in recovery.

Read all your journal entries from the previous week. Look for trends in your recovery. How are you progressing? What concerns have surfaced? Are you headed toward a slip? Slips and

---

92. Review the chapter for Day 2 for a reminder about the benefit of doing a "90/90."

Thirty Days to Hope & Freedom for Sexual Addicts

relapses do not just happen. If you are journaling every day, you can spot trends before they become a problem. You will be able to spot deficiencies before they become significant concerns.

Physical exercise several times a week is a vital part of your recovery. Not only does it have physical benefits, but your attitude and outlook on life will improve with exercise. The better you feel about yourself, the less likely you will be to act out.

Remember to plan something fun during the week.[93] Life is solemn enough. And recovery is very serious. You also need time to refresh yourself. Planning a fun activity every week will help bring your life back into balance. That may mean that you want to cut back on the number of hours you work in order to be able to schedule a fun event.

If you are in a committed relationship, plan a date night for your partner. Let your partner know you cherish them. We will spend more time on giving priority to your relationship in the chapter on Day 29.

Monthly Activities

Monthly activities may include a joint therapy session with your partner. Early in the recovery process it is not beneficial to make couple's therapy the focus of your work. If you do have a monthly couple's session, it would not be aimed at working through the thorny problems that have resulted from your addiction. Instead it would focus on managing crises.

If you have not been able to afford to do weekly individual therapy, you might consider having an individual session once a month or even once every other month. If your sexual addiction therapist is aware of your limited resources and you are willing to stay self-motivated, it is possible to make significant progress in therapy with occasional sessions.

Quarterly Activities

At least once a quarter, it would be good to sit down with your sponsor to review your progress in recovery. Your sponsor will be able to help you gauge whether your recovery is on track. If you have gotten stuck on a particular Step, this would be a good time to ask your sponsor for direction in getting unstuck.

If you are in therapy, it would be helpful to ask your therapist to give you an evaluation of your progress. Therapy is not something that will be a permanent part of your life. You should be making regular progress with a goal of discontinuing therapy when your goals have been accomplished.

It is commonly accepted among sexual addiction therapists that recovery is a three- to five-year process. That does not mean that you will remain in therapy for that entire time. As you progress in therapy, you may go from weekly sessions to monthly sessions.

After reaching your therapy goals and being released from regular ongoing individual therapy sessions, quarterly checkups are a good way of ensuring that your recovery is staying on course.

---

93. See the chapter on Day 7.

Annual Activities

Annual recovery activities will include a physical exam. You will also want to include dental checkups twice annually. An annual recovery retreat and perhaps an annual spiritually-focused retreat would also be good additions to this plan.

If you are married, you might want to consider attending a marriage conference, seminar, or workshop once a year. These conferences should not be viewed as something to attend only if you are having marriage problems. They are beneficial for all marriages. Once a year make an investment in your marriage by attending one. You may even want to purposely choose a workshop that will cause you to travel to another city. You can turn your weekend out-of-town into a romantic getaway.

The Next Move

Write out your Personal Recovery Plan in detail. Clearly identify what you will do daily, weekly, monthly, and annually. Then schedule a time with your sponsor when you can carefully review your plan. Ask for suggestions as to how you can improve your plan.

On Day 28, we will take this plan a step further. For right now, start working your plan. Develop a routine of going to meetings, as well as engaging in numerous daily recovery activities.

My Commitment

I commit to discussing my Personal Recovery Plan with my sponsor and to follow it faithfully. I further commit to revisiting this plan monthly to see whether there are things I should add to make my recovery more effective.

Signed _____ Date_____

Day 25: Traveling—
How Do You Support Your Recovery?

Evan's Story

Evan has been in recovery for four years. He has generally done pretty well, though he said he has not made recovery quite the priority he knows it should be, but he had achieved more than twenty-four months of sobriety. When he got his two-year chip, he told himself that he had finally gotten recovery figured out. Only one other man in the Twelve Step meeting he considered his "home group" had more sobriety. Evan was also sponsoring a couple of other men and enjoyed his status in the group as "someone who had made it."

To add to his overall feeling of success, Evan had just been promoted to vice president in his company. To start his new position he had to travel to the company headquarters in Chicago for a week of orientation and a meeting with the CEO. To his delight, he found that his company had booked him into one of the apartments the company keeps in downtown Chicago that is kept exclusively for their senior executives and special guests.

His first day in Chicago was a whirlwind of activity, including a reception in his honor at company headquarters. That night he settled into his apartment and found it had the biggest flat screen HD television he had ever seen. For the next several hours he watched a football game and was amazed at how he felt as though he were at the game in person.

When the game was over, he started channel surfing and found there were several pornography channels that were completely unfiltered. Initially, he turned off the TV but then turned it back on just to see whether the picture quality was as good as on the football game. That was the beginning of a week-long relapse. He stayed up most of the night watching pornography and masturbating. For the rest of the week his evening routine was the same. Each morning he would regret his actions and pledge not to repeat it but the evenings were all the same.

In retrospect, he realized he had been living on the edge of a slip for some time. And he would have been less likely to have had a relapse if he had made recovery part of his travel plans. Evan knew he could have found Twelve Step meetings to attend, he could have called several of his close friends who are in recovery, and he could have called his sponsor. In fact, Evan readily identified a lengthy list of things he could have been doing that would have resulted in him staying in solid recovery.

A major hole in Evan's program was that he had always put recovery "on hold" when he traveled. When he first entered recovery, Evan traveled very little, but his business travel continued to increase until he was making two or three overnight trips each month, and most of these involved multiple nights away from home. His promotion will require him to travel in the United States, London, and Singapore each month.

Before You Leave Town

Whether your travel schedule is as busy as Evan's or if you rarely travel for business, you will want to have a travel plan that will ensure that you can continue recovery while you are away from home. Each trip requires that you write a travel plan. If you travel frequently, you will have specific travel plans drafted for each city you visit.

If you are in therapy, schedule an appointment with your therapist to talk about your recovery and your travel plans. Try to identify the things that you know will be triggering for you when you are out of town. Ask your therapist to help you identify any deficits in your recovery routine. Set up a therapy session by phone for each week you are out of town.

Plan a meeting with your sponsor. Enlist your sponsor's help in drafting your travel recovery plan. Set up a time when you can call your sponsor while you are on your trip. And if you are going to be away for an extended period, make plans for contact with your sponsor for a more lengthy conversation when you can review any assignments you have been given.

While on your trip, plan on spending time each evening doing Step work. Continue just as if you were at home. Set aside a few minutes each day to complete assignments your sponsor has given you.

Get a list of Twelve Step meetings for the cities that you plan to visit. Use the phone numbers and websites in Appendix B to assemble this list. Do not forget to check on meetings in fellowships other than those you normally attend. You may find there are meetings available in other fellowships that are closer to your location or are at a more convenient time. And if you cannot find a Twelve Step meeting in a particular city, make plans to attend an online or telephone meeting.[94]

Write a daily plan for your recovery while you are out-of-town. This plan should include which meeting you are going to attend on a particular day. You should include all the things that are part of your daily recovery.[95] Or if you believe your schedule is going to be particularly full, you might, for example, want to commit to doing three things for your recovery every day that you are out-of-town.

Pack your Travel Toolkit (next page). You will also want to pack whichever recovery book you are currently reading. Fortunately there are many good books on sexual addiction recovery. When you finish one, start another. Always keep a recovery-related book at your bedside and spend a few minutes reading each evening. This routine will help keep you immersed in recovery.

Call your hotel and have them block all adult channels or have the TV removed prior to your arrival. Yes, many hotels will remove your television upon request. Or consider booking a hotel through www.CleanHotels.com. This is a network of lodging places that do not offer in-room, "adult," pay-per-view movies. You can search by city and even book your room on this site. However, you will still have to use your boundaries to stay off the cable movie channels for they often have some questionable programming.

---

94. Check your fellowship to see whether they offer electronic meetings. Or you can go to www.saatalk.org for a list of SAA telephone meetings.
95. See Day 24: Personal Recovery Plan.

Once your travel plan is completed, contact your sponsor and review this plan together. Your sponsor's experience in recovery will be valuable in helping you identify any areas of deficit. Rework the plan incorporating your sponsor's suggestions.

Schedule the first Twelve Step meeting you are going to attend when you return from your trip. For accountability, tell your sponsor when you will attend that meeting. Also, plan your first face-to-face meeting with your sponsor as soon after your return as possible.

You may find it helpful to leave encouraging messages for yourself on your own voice mail. It might even be helpful to leave a series of messages including one that is a stern warning to yourself in the event you are struggling. You could also ask some friends to call you throughout the days you are gone and leave voice mail messages for you with additional words of encouragement.

Travel Toolkit

People who work in construction or some related field make sure they have their tools with them when they go on a job. Their tools are always in good working order and are close at hand. The following items comprise a Travel Toolkit that you can assemble. Pack this kit with you every time you are out-of-town.

- List of Twelve Step meetings and contact phone numbers for cities you are planning to visit.[96] Get a list from each of the "S" fellowships.
- Recovery audio MP3s (available at www.RecoveryOnTheGo.com).
- Recovery reading material
- Big book of the "S" fellowship you attend
- Journal
- *Thirty Days to Hope & Freedom from Sexual Addiction* (With Days 18 and 19 on tools well marked)
- *Facing the Shadow*[97] workbook
- Daily meditation book
- Circle of Five list[98]
- List of additional phone numbers of friends in recovery you can call for daily encouragement

You may also want to include things like a family photo and a piece of art work from your children. A sobriety chip would be a good addition. And you might want to include a book of crossword puzzles or some other games designed to be a mental challenge.

---

96. See Appendix B. If you cannot find a meeting that is specifically for recovery from sexual addiction, attend an Alcoholics Anonymous meeting and introduce yourself as "an addict that is visiting from out-of-town" or "from another fellowship."
97. (Carnes, *Facing the Shadow: Starting Sexual and Relationship Recovery*, 2005)
98. See Day 14. For a more detailed account, see *Hope & Freedom for Sexual Addicts and Their Partners*, pp. 77-78.

Sample Travel Plan

The following is an actual travel plan developed by a man who had a business trip to Tampa. He has been in recovery for about five years and has had unbroken sobriety since entering recovery. Prior to leaving town, he met with his therapist and worked out the basics of this plan. He then did additional research so that he knew which meetings he was going to attend.

Travel Plan for Tampa

I plan to leave for Tampa on Monday morning and will not return until Friday afternoon.

1. Pack Travel Toolkit.
2. Write a letter before I leave town on the subject: "How fragile life is…"
3. Download iRecovery app for iPhone and add the Serenity Prayer as a screensaver.
4. Plan to read some recovery-related material on the airplane.
5. Meeting schedule:
   a. SLAA meeting Tuesday at noon.
   b. SAA telephone meeting Thursday evening at 7:30 pm (Eastern)
6. When I check into the hotel, request movie access be disabled.
7. Take family picture in frame. Place it on the bedside table in the hotel.
8. Pray daily, multiple times.
9. Work on assignment given by sponsor.
10. If the desire to relax and be entertained arises, watch G-rated movie I packed in my computer case.
11. Call family each evening. Find out about my sons' day in school and have a quality conversation with my wife.
12. Review this plan with my sponsor before leaving town.

Your recovery must not be put on hold when you are out-of-town. You can use the additional time alone as an opportunity to work on your Steps or to read that recovery book you have wanted to read. Good planning before you leave town will help ensure that your recovery continues without interruption.

Day 26: Slips and Relapses

One of the most discouraging things that can happen in recovery is to experience a slip or a relapse. In many Twelve Step meetings, someone will talk about losing their sobriety—sometimes after several years of solid recovery. Not only is this discouraging to the one who has slipped or relapsed, but it can dampen the spirits of the entire group.

Maddie's Story

Maddie got into recovery after being caught by her husband in yet another affair. In her clinical disclosure[99] to her husband, she admitted that during their fifteen-year marriage, she had been involved with three or four different men each year. Recovery brought her a new sense of self-worth. For the first time, she realized that it was possible to live a monogamous life.

Early in her recovery, she was attending four Twelve Step meetings a week. She worked with her sponsor every week and was proud of herself when she completed her Step work in less than a year. When she picked up her one-year chip, she was certain that she would never go back to her former life. She thanked her sponsor for her work and told her that she was going to stop attending meetings. Maddie's sponsor pled with her to continue her recovery routines, but Maddie was sure that she was cured.

Just shy of two years of sobriety, Maddie started flirting with a coworker at an office Christmas party. She was not going to be sexual with him, but it felt good to have his attention and to feel attractive. Before the night was over she was in a dark office being groped by her coworker. Maddie stopped short of intercourse and called her sponsor on her way home.

She asked her sponsor how she could have slipped and blown nearly two years of sobriety. Maddie thought she was doing so well in recovery. Later as she reviewed the events of the previous year with her sponsor, Maddie realized that she had set herself up for a slip when she stopped attending Twelve Step meetings. That was not the only thing that changed. She had also broken contact with her sponsor and other people she had gotten to know in recovery. Maddie had stopped journaling and stopped reading about recovery. In short, Maddie had ended all of the recovery routines she had learned the previous year. Her sponsor said she was surprised her slip had not come sooner.

Do Others Slip?

We know that most sexual addicts have experienced at least one slip since entering recovery. In one survey, participants were asked if they had ever slipped and if so, how often. Thirteen percent said they had never slipped. Twenty percent indicated they had one or two slips,

---

99. Disclosure of sexual acting out should be facilitated by a Certified Sex Addiction Therapist (CSAT).

20 percent had three to five slips, and 8 percent had six to ten slips. Twenty-one percent of the respondents said they had experienced more than ten slips.[100]

Number of Slips Experienced

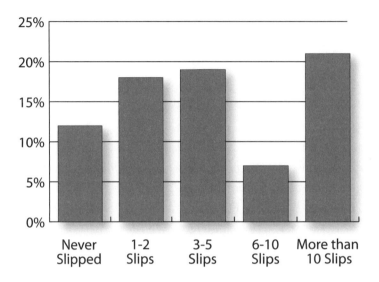

Slips

I never tell clients to expect that they will slip. Instead I tell them just the opposite. I believe there should be a very high expectation that slips will not occur. However, slips are common early in recovery. If you are in a committed relationship, I would strongly encourage you to ask your partner to read this chapter. Partners should be prepared for how they are going to respond if a slip occurs.

If the slip included being sexual with another person, the sexual addict and partner must get tested for sexually transmitted diseases. This may seem like excessive caution, but it is a necessary consequence of breaking sobriety. Partners have a right to know whether their health is at greater risk.

Someone has said that a SLIP means *Sobriety Loses Its Priority*. Slips do not just happen. They occur because something has changed in recovery. Often it is easy to spot numerous lapses in recovery routines that take place well before a slip.

Relapses

Where a slip is an isolated incident, a relapse is a return to acting out on more than one occasion during a brief period. For example, a sexual addict who slipped on a weekend and went to a massage parlor to receive sexual gratification would be considered in relapse if the same thing happened the next weekend or even the next month. Also, someone who has planned

---

100. (Magness M. , 2004)

Thirty Days to Hope & Freedom for Sexual Addicts

for a period of time to act out has also experienced a relapse even if the acting out was a single brief occurrence.

If a relapse occurs, relationship partners will want to take steps to protect themselves. For some, this may mean an immediate separation and a visit to an attorney to determine their rights. Relapses are serious events that should cause both the sexual addict and the partner to determine changes must be made if the relationship is to survive.

Dealing with Slips and Relapses

A slip or relapse should not automatically bring an end to the relationship. However, they should be treated as the serious events that they are. If no consequences result from the slip, it may be difficult for the partner to believe the sexual addict is taking recovery seriously or is remorseful for the breach of sobriety.

Relationship partners would do well to consider what their response will be if their spouse has a slip or a relapse. There are three areas that should receive focus.

1. What support does the relationship partner require to deal with the slip or relapse? This may include working with a therapist. It may also include taking a few days alone to process the pain that comes from the slip or relapse.

2. What does the sexual addict need to do to return to solid recovery and repair the breach of sobriety? It is not the relationship partner's responsibility to determine what these steps are, but there should be enough communication between the couple so that the partner knows the sexual addict is taking the necessary steps to prevent recurrence.

3. What are going to be the consequences if the sexual addict slips or has a relapse? It might be helpful to consider a range of consequences that escalate in relation to what behavior is involved in the slip or relapse. For example, consequences for a slip that does not involve acting out with people may include the sexual addict voluntarily giving up television for two or three months. A slip that involves a conversation with a former sexual partner may include fifteen to twenty hours of community service or volunteer work—but not doing something that the sexual addict would tend to enjoy. A slip or a relapse that involves being sexual with other people may include the sexual addict moving out of the master bedroom or perhaps even moving out of the house for a period of time from a week to a month. The consequences should fit the situation, be determined ahead of time, and allow for restoration of the relationship.

Sometimes relationship partners may want to enter a period of celibacy that lasts from one to three months. A therapist skilled in working with sexual addiction should be consulted to get guidance on whether this would be beneficial to the relationship. A period of celibacy may be helpful to allow the partner time to process the slip event and to feel safe in the relationship.[101]

---

101. (Magness, M. S., 2009) p. 123-130

Couple's therapy may be helpful. Working with a therapist who has expertise not only in couple's work but also sexual addiction can often make the difference in the future of the relationship. Unfortunately there are therapists who do not understand sexual addiction and might be inclined to immediately advocate for divorce if there is any breach of sobriety.

One slip, or even two or three slips, can be dealt with in a relationship if both parties are willing to give recovery and the relationship more time. The critical thing is that there be a commitment to the relationship and a willingness to work through the trying circumstances surrounding the slip.

If a relapse has taken place, the partner will want to decide whether to continue in the relationship with the sexual addict. Depending on the circumstances, the relationship partner may be encouraged to give the sexual addict one final chance, but also be ready to enforce any consequences that are agreed upon in the event of a subsequent relapse. Persons who experience a relapse often find it necessary to seek intensive outpatient care or even inpatient treatment that may last for several weeks to several months.[102]

Returning to Sobriety after a Slip or Relapse

If you experience a slip or relapse, get back into your recovery routine at once. Contact your sponsor immediately. Go to a meeting the same day. Break the isolation and spend time with other recovering people. Get to meetings early and stay late so that you can get to know the group members and learn from their recovery journeys.

One of the most helpful activities after a slip or a relapse is to do a postmortem of the event. This task is particularly effective if you have had the practice of journaling daily throughout your recovery. Previous journal entries often reveal recovery lapses that occurred before the slip. Journaling is also a great relapse prevention tool if you make daily entries and then go back and reread the entries at least once a week.

As you conduct an autopsy of the slip or relapse, start with the events that took place just prior to the slip. What was going on in your life? Had you changed your recovery routine? Did you start isolating yourself?

Continue going backward day by day and asking the same questions. Also look for stressors you may have endured and see what you did or did not do to address them. Did you have any change in your job or career? Sometimes promotions or achieving some other recognition are fuel for a slip or relapse.

You will want to consider other questions as well. What new routines should you add to your recovery to get back to where you were? Does your sponsor have any suggestions for how to get back on a firm recovery foundation? Some people find that committing to doing a 90/90 (attending ninety "S" meetings in ninety days) is one of the best things they can do to reestablish good recovery.

---

102 Appendix B lists several intensive outpatient (IOP) programs as well as several inpatient treatment programs.

The main thing you want to do is to learn from the event. If you do not learn from it, then your slip or relapse has been a total waste. But if you do learn from it, you may find that a slip can be one of the most significant growth experiences in recovery.

Is a Slip or Relapse Inevitable?

Slips and relapse are often a part of recovery. That does not mean that you should expect to have a slip. The fact is there are numerous people who enter recovery and never experience a slip or a relapse. In the survey mentioned earlier, 13 percent had never experienced a slip or a relapse. Do not expect a slip. Envision yourself continuing in recovery free from all slips.

Slips and relapses do not indicate that a person has lost their recovery. If you have had a slip or a relapse, you are still in recovery. What you lose is sobriety but not recovery. While this is serious, such occurrences can be times of great learning and of increasing resolve. No one should look forward to a slip or a relapse, but if you have experienced one, do not let this episode define you. Let this event be a wakeup call for you to make the necessary changes in your recovery program to see that it does not happen again.

"Today, I will live soberly. I will make recovery a priority and not beat myself up for past mistakes. I will learn from my mistakes and move forward into solid, lasting sobriety."

Day 27: The "M" Question

Masturbation! The word is whispered, ignored, held in reverence, and sometimes despised. The word may produce shame. "Don't touch yourself there! It's nasty!" Those words, perhaps followed by a slap, or shaming language may be the first sexual memory of a person. And for a sexual addict, this is the beginning of a lifetime of activity that both fascinates and repulses. It is a behavior that brings pleasure, shame, and often confusion.

Jordan's Story

"I remember it like it was yesterday," Jordan explained as he talked about how he learned to masturbate. *"I was in physical education class in the seventh grade. We were taking turns climbing ropes that were connected to the rafters of the gym. I noticed a funny feeling between my legs as I shimmied up the rope. I wasn't sure what it was, but it felt good. I climbed the rope two more times. The coach was impressed. I was hooked. That night I masturbated in the bathroom for the first time. I felt ashamed. I was sure I was doing something wrong."*

Why even bring up the subject of masturbation? Unless you determine your stance concerning masturbation as to what is healthy for you, you will likely continue to struggle with establishing and maintaining sexual sobriety. Should you or should you not? You may not have been given this choice as a youngster. But now in recovery, you must decide what is healthy for you.

Masturbation is very common. In a study of undergraduate college students, 98 percent of men and 44 percent of women reported having masturbated at some point in their lives.[104] Some religious organizations have strict taboos associated with masturbation, so it is a subject seldom talked about, and persons who have masturbated are often racked with shame.

Each year Hope & Freedom sponsors three retreats for men who struggle with compulsive sexual behavior. One of the features of these retreats is an open discussion about masturbation. For many men, that is the first time they have spoken the word masturbation and certainly the first time they have been able to discuss the subject in a healthy setting with other men.[105]

Does masturbation have any place in recovery? Should a recovering person masturbate? The purpose of this chapter is not to advocate for one view over another. Rather, it is to get you to think about a subject that is often defined by silence.

---

104. (Pinkerton, Bogart, Cecil, & Abramson, 2002)
105. Information about the Journey of Hope Retreats can be found at www.HopeAndFreedom.com.

Different Views on Masturbation

For some recovering sexual addicts, any masturbation is considered acting out. In fact, in Sexaholics Anonymous, the definition of sobriety is limited to no sex with self and no sex outside of a heterosexual marriage.[106] By definition, that eliminates all masturbation.

In other Twelve Step fellowships, such as Sex Addicts Anonymous, each person determines his own definition for sobriety, which means each person must personally decide whether masturbation is healthy or not. Using SAA's Three Circle Plan,[107] members decide whether each behavior is an Inner Circle behavior, meaning it constitutes a breach of sobriety, a Middle Circle behavior, meaning it is dangerous and should be avoided, or an Outer Circle behavior, indicating it is a healthy behavior.

In SAA, a person can have masturbation in any of the three circles. Some may have masturbation in two circles or even in all three circles. That would indicate a belief that masturbation may be either healthy or unhealthy depending on a number of factors. For some persons in recovery, masturbation is something they allow themselves to do within certain limits. For others, masturbation is dangerous for them, and they choose to eliminate it from their lives.

This approach to the subject is often liberating, especially if childhood religious views were dominated with puritanical beliefs and teachings. In recovery, rather than someone else dictating what is healthy and giving a list of "Thou Shalt Nots," the addict has to determine what is healthy for him. Critical thinking is central to long-term sobriety in addiction recovery. Rules are less helpful than guidelines. Rigid rule-following is a factor that has often contributed to developing an environment where sexual addiction can flourish.

People entering recovery from sexual addiction often make an immediate decision that masturbation is a forbidden activity without ever really taking time to think through how they feel about the subject. They simply impose on themselves the same prohibition that was passed on to them when they were adolescents. And if they find they are unable to break a habit that may have been a daily part of life for many decades, they feel immediate shame and believe they have failed in recovery.

For those who are adamantly opposed to masturbation during recovery, I think it is much healthier to view it as an activity that they would like to eliminate but not to make it a standard that determines whether they have remained sober. If a person has been masturbating for years, it may take some effort and some time in recovery to eliminate this habit.

For sexual addicts who are single, masturbation sometimes provides their only sexual outlet. They may determine that masturbation is healthy for them so long as it is kept within appropriate guidelines. And they can help determine those guidelines with the aid of their sponsor or their therapist. However, it is significant to recognize that sex is not a need. It is a drive. Eating is a need. Breathing is a need. But sex is not a need. Body parts do not fall off if one does not have sex.

---

106. (Sexaholics Anonymous, 1989) pp.191-192
107. (Sex Addicts Anonymous, 2005) p.16

For couples who are unable to have intercourse because of a medical problem, masturbation may be part of their joint sexual activity. In these cases, masturbation, or mutual masturbation, can be a healthy sexual expression. Note that this activity is within the relationship and is used to further the relationship rather than used as a substitute for couple's sex.

There are a significant number of people in recovery who have discovered that masturbation has been the thing that helped fuel their fantasies and perhaps even served as a prelude to other acting out behavior. This is a valid point. For some, masturbation has served as the fuel to move them toward other behaviors that have greater negative consequences. In such cases, masturbation is detrimental to recovery.

False Beliefs Concerning Masturbation

There are a number of false beliefs concerning masturbation. These include the things that were once told to young boys to try to scare them into not masturbating. "If you do *that*, you will go blind." Or, "Don't you know that if you keep doing *that*, it will make you grow hair in the palm of your hand?"

Another false belief is the idea that masturbation will stop automatically when one reaches age eighteen. There are also those who wrongly believe it will automatically stop when one gets married or enters a committed relationship. Another false belief is that it is impossible to be in good recovery and still masturbate. There are many people who are in solid recovery and allow themselves some limited masturbation within certain guidelines. So if you do not believe masturbation is healthy for you, be careful about judging someone else's recovery if they do not share your views.

"How many times per day indicates a problem with masturbation?" That question itself probably indicates the level of a problem. For this person, masturbation is something that should be examined as recovery moves forward. For this person to develop long-term sobriety, it may be that masturbation is something they will want to eliminate.

There are a number of sexual addicts whose acting out is confined to "just" masturbation and viewing pornography. This may not seem like a great problem to another sexual addict whose acting out involves other people and high-risk behavior. I have found that some of the people who have the greatest struggle with compulsive sexual behavior are those who have never acted out with people but whose acting-out behavior is "just" masturbation and viewing pornography. Fantasy-fueled masturbation can be very addictive and ultimately harmful to those who become obsessed by it.

Problems Associated with Masturbation

Masturbation may be benign to many people. But there are also some problems associated with it. These problems should be considered particularly by those who view masturbation as something they can engage in while in recovery.

The first of these problems is that masturbation sensitizes a person to their own touch. They know what they like, what makes them feel good, and what heightens their sexual excitement. This sensitization may make it difficult for their spouse to arouse them. They get so used to being sexual with themselves that they may actually prefer it to being sexual with their partner.

A second significant problem with masturbation is that it typically is driven by fantasy, objectification, pornography, the memory of pornography, or the memory of previous sexual encounters. The battleground for sexual addicts is that space between the ears rather than the space between one's legs. Entertaining sexual thoughts and fantasy accompanied by masturbation may make it very difficult for a person to change thought patterns to those that are more conducive to recovery.

Sexual addicts are very "me-centered." They look out for self first. Their greatest desire is to have what they want, when they want it, and the way they want it. Masturbation is another expression of this "me first" mentality. So if masturbation is encouraging you toward more narcissistic tendencies, is this something that is indeed healthy for you?

Masturbation is also used as medication. It is mood altering. It may be used to comfort, unwind at the end of the day, assuage loneliness, or induce sleep. Masturbation may be sought to change one's view of the day, help them tolerate difficult people, or boost self-esteem. If you use masturbation as a drug, how then is it different from any of your other acting-out behaviors?

A very significant problem with masturbation is that it further disconnects emotion from sex. Men in particular have a problem integrating sexuality and the emotions. Partners of sexual addicts often complain, "He is just after sex. He does not care about my needs at all. As long as he gets off, he is happy."

For people to masturbate they do not have to be having warm, fuzzy feelings about themselves. They do not have to communicate with someone else. Nor does it matter if they are getting along with their partner.

But healthy sexuality in a committed relationship depends on having a strong emotional connection. Deep spiritual connections are even possible in such relationships. Good sex is not the basis of a close loving relationship. Instead it is the result of a relationship where two people care about each other's needs, wants, and feelings. It is the product of two people sharing their lives and their deepest emotions. A byproduct of healthy sexuality is true intimacy.

When I work with couples, I am often asked by partners, if their spouse is a sexual addict, why there is not more sex in their relationship. Closer examination reveals that in many of these couples the sexual addict is masturbating much more frequently than they are being sexual with their partner. So it is not that there is little sex taking place in the relationship because the sexual addict is continuing to be sexual with self. There is just little mutual sex taking place between the couple.

Decision Point

In the final analysis, you must decide whether masturbation is something that is healthy for you or not. If it is going to be part of your life, you would do well to talk with your sponsor or therapist and determine under what conditions it is allowable. And if masturbation is something that you do not want to be part of your life, determine what boundaries you want to put into place to eliminate this act from your practice. Ignoring the "M" question will only put your future recovery in jeopardy.

Day 28: Hope & Freedom Recovery Points System— Recovery by the Numbers

There is no one right way of doing recovery. Your daily recovery routines may be similar to or quite different from those of others in recovery. Certainly there are some similarities. For example, attending Twelve Step meetings and working the Steps of recovery with a sponsor are foundational to recovery.

Daryl's Story

Social networking sites provided a new playground for Daryl. He has multiple profiles on each of the sites. He has found that, just like fishing, the more hooks he has in the water, the more likely he is to catch a new partner. Daryl has realized that there are many lonely people on the social networking sites who would love to be his friend and give him access to their personal photos. He has rationalized that he is single, so there is no harm in what he is doing. But he also has admitted to himself that he has not had a real relationship in over three years. The time corresponds with the beginning of his obsession with social networking sites. Daryl is now in recovery and is attending four Twelve Step meetings a week.

At the start of recovery it is suggested that you attend a minimum of two Twelve Step meetings a week. However, there are individuals who attend three, four, or more meetings each week. Some attend a meeting every day, and occasionally some may attend multiple meetings a day.

Beyond meeting attendance there are other areas where one's individual recovery may differ from that of others who are in recovery. Some people journal about their recovery every day. Others journal occasionally. Some do not journal at all.

Many people in recovery have discovered that taking care of their bodies is helpful for keeping their recovery strong. They exercise regularly, eat a healthy diet, and are careful to get plenty of sleep every night. But there are others who neglect their bodies and still seem to do well in recovery.

With so much room for individual expression and choice, how do you develop a healthy recovery plan that works for you? You have already developed a Personal Recovery Plan on Day 24. Is there a way of maintaining your individuality and still knowing that you are doing well in recovery?

I believe there is. Using the Recovery Points System along with some basic guidelines, I have found that men and women in recovery can achieve sobriety and maintain their recovery even though their plan may not look exactly like that of someone else in recovery. The Hope & Freedom Recovery Points System will allow you to create a recovery plan that fits you and still follows the fundamentals of solid recovery. On Day 30, you will be introduced to the *iRecovery—Addiction Recovery Tracker*, an iPhone app, that makes use of the Hope & Freedom Recovery Points System.

Phases of Recovery

To get started with setting up your Hope & Freedom Recovery Points System, we must review the various Phases of Recovery. This is covered in greater depth in the book *Hope & Freedom for Sexual Addicts and Their Partners*.[108]

Survival Phase

The Survival Phase lasts from six months to a year or more. If a person is in therapy, the focus of therapy is on stopping all acting-out behaviors. Sexual addicts begin attending a minimum of two Twelve Step meetings each week and find a sponsor.

Persons who have suffered a slip or relapse are also in the Survival Phase. This is a time for establishing solid sobriety and being able to identify on a calendar a sobriety date. During this phase, all immediate crises are addressed, and a preliminary plan for recovery is mapped out. To move to the next phase, all compulsive sexual behaviors must have ended and sobriety maintained for at least three months. Additionally, a sponsor must be secured.

Stability Phase

This phase begins six months to two years into recovery and lasts for a year or more. Persons in this recovery phase have a good understanding of recovery and are regularly engaged in the recovery basics. They continue to attend a minimum of two meetings each week, have a sponsor, and are actively working the Steps of recovery. Persons in this phase have typically broken through all of their denial and resistance and are making solid progress in recovery. They look forward to attending Twelve Step meetings and recognize therapy as something that is enhancing their recovery rather than a punishment for previous bad behavior.

Several significant things have happened in recovery as clients move to the next phase. First, they will have made a complete disclosure of all of their acting-out behavior to their relationship partner and will have taken and passed a polygraph exam to verify that the disclosure is accurate and complete.[109] Second, the sexual addict will be living slip free and has been free from all acting-out behaviors for at least six months before moving to the next phase.

Sustaining Phase

This Phase of Recovery begins eighteen months to three years into recovery and lasts for one year or more. Disclosure has been accomplished, and the relationship has been stabilized. Sexual sobriety is solid and growing. The focus on therapy during this Phase of Recovery is

---

108. (Magness, M.S., 2009) p. 69.
109. More information on the use of polygraph exams is found in *Hope & Freedom for Sexual Addicts and Their Partners*, p. 111.

Thirty Days to Hope & Freedom for Sexual Addicts

on deepening the addict's knowledge and broadening the foundation of recovery. Therapy may move from a weekly to a bi-weekly routine. Persons in this phase have assumed total responsibility for their own recovery.

A person is ready to move out of this Phase of Recovery after working all Twelve Steps and living free from all acting-out behaviors for a minimum of one year. By this time, his or her anger and resentments are well-managed, and the relationship with the spouse or partner is growing in the rebuilding of both trust and intimacy.

Phases of Recovery Timeline

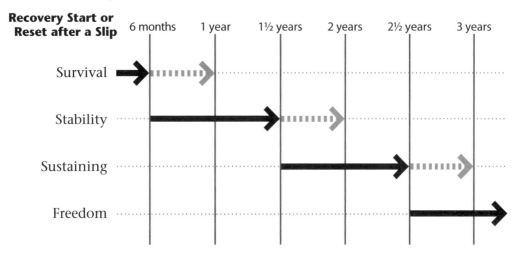

Criteria for Moving to Next Recovery Phase

To move from Survival Phase to Stability Phase
- Recovery time: minimum of 6 months
- Must have a sponsor
- Sobriety time: minimum of 3 months

To move from Stability Phase to Sustaining Phase
- Recovery time: minimum of 18 months
- Sobriety time: minimum 6 months

To move from Sustaining Phase to Freedom Phase
- Recovery time: minimum of 2 ½ years
- Sobriety time: minimum 1 year
- Must have worked all Twelve Steps

Freedom Phase

Persons in this Phase of Recovery have been in recovery for two and a half years or more. They typically spend the first six to twelve months in this phase actively working on recovery. If a person has been in individual or group therapy, they move out of therapy or use therapy sporadically to address specific concerns, work on "rough spots" in their relationships, or do periodic recovery checkups.

As clients move out of therapy, they will have been free from all acting-out behaviors for at least one year and have worked all of the Twelve Steps of recovery with a sponsor. By this time they are actively sponsoring others and are otherwise engaged in giving back to the recovery community. They have developed and implemented a strong maintenance plan for continued recovery.

Recovery Point Goal Chart

Recovery Points Needed Per Week			
Phase of Recovery	**Minimum**	**Target**	**Optimal**
Survival	70	80	90
Stability	60	70	80
Sustaining	50	60	70
Freedom	40	50	60

When you determine what recovery phase you are in, it is time to set your weekly Recovery Points Goal. A good strategy is to use the "target" column to determine your weekly goal. That way if you have an unusually busy week and fall a bit short of your target goal, you still will achieve the minimum for your Phase of Recovery.

However, if you are new to recovery, I would suggest that you consider going for the "optimal" level. Well over one hundred points are possible each week using this system. Persons who are in a committed relationship can achieve even more because points are given for couples activities. Yet, it should be noted that single persons can still easily achieve a weekly goal that will help ensure they are in solid recovery. A single person's recovery is not penalized by not being in a relationship.

Calculating Your Recovery Points

Using this system, every recovery activity is assigned a point value. All of the recovery activities are significant and should be part of your Personal Recovery Plan that you developed on Day 24. Some activities receive more points than others. Just because an item has a low point value does not mean is it not a major part of recovery.

Recovery points may be earned in four basic areas. The activities listed in each of these areas are primary activities that are foundational for any recovery program. You may find additional activities that you would like to add to your recovery program.

Recovery Activities

The heart of every sexual addict's recovery program is attending Twelve Step meetings and working the Steps of recovery with a sponsor. With each meeting you attend, award yourself seven points. Each time you meet with your sponsor to work on your recovery, award yourself another five points. However to get the points for the sponsor meetings, it must be more than a brief check-in. When persons are working through the recovery Steps with their sponsor, typically those meetings last about an hour though some of them may be briefer. (Sponsors also get five points for meetings with sponsees.)

Regardless of the Phase of Recovery that you are in, you should attend weekly Twelve-Step meetings. You will attend more at the beginning of recovery, perhaps less as you progress in your journey. But even in the Freedom Phase of Recovery you will still be attending at least one Twelve Step meeting each week.

Working the Twelve Steps (that is, doing Step work) earns you two points for each forty-five minutes of work. Step work is typically assigned by your sponsor as you progress through the Steps. Completing assignments and then reporting to your sponsor is a crucial part of recovery. Working through a Twelve Step workbook such as *A Gentle Path Through the Twelve Steps*[110] will also earn you two points.

Reaching out to other recovering persons will earn one point for each call. You may choose to make as many program calls a day as you wish. A maximum of two points per day may be earned with this activity.

Recovery-related reading also earns you points. You get one point for every thirty minutes you read recovery-related books or literature. Your reading time does not have to be continuous to earn points. For example, you could read for fifteen minutes in the morning and then fifteen minutes before bed and still earn one point.

For persons in a committed relationship, participation in a weekly recovery night[111] where recovery work continues for a minimum of two hours earns another four recovery points. If you are single, your recovery night may include journaling, recovery-related reading, working through a workbook like *Facing the Shadow*,[112] and other activities. However, you may find that you earn more points by awarding points for the individual activities rather than for participating in a recovery night. You only get points for one or the other.

---

110. (Carnes, *A Gentle Path Through the Twelve Steps: A Classic Guide For All People in the Process of Recovery*, 1993)
111. Details for establishing a recovery night are given in the chapter on Day 29.
112. (Carnes, *Facing the Shadow: Starting Sexual and Relationship Recovery*, 2005)

If you are in a committed relationship, you earn two points for each day you participate with your partner in some recovery activity. These activities may include doing a nightly communication or intimacy exercise, reading through a book together, participating in a devotional, or doing something else together that supports your recovery as a couple.

Spiritual Activities

Spiritual activities may revolve around a central major weekly event. Participation in some formal spiritual activity earns you three points. This may be attending services at temple, church, or a mosque. A structured meditation time would also qualify for these points.

Daily prayer or meditation will earn you one point. If you "bookend" the day with a prayer in the morning and then again in the evening, you get two points. Again, you may meditate or pray multiple times during the day. The maximum daily points that may be earned for prayer is two.

If you keep a recovery journal, you earn one point each day you journal. Journaling more than one time a day still just earns a total of one point for that day. If you journal a few times each week, give yourself one point for each day you make entries in your journal. Daily journaling is certainly best. Strive to earn some points for journaling several days each week.

Mental/Psychological Activities

Not everyone needs to be in therapy. And some who need it choose not to participate in therapy because of financial concerns or because qualified specialists with expertise in treating sexual addiction are not available in their area. Nevertheless, if you are engaged in therapy, you earn five points. If you are in individual therapy, award yourself five points for each session. If you are also involved in group therapy, award yourself another five points per session. Those who are in a relationship and are also doing couple's therapy receive five points for each of those sessions.

In the chapter on Day 23, affirmations were singled out as important in helping to counter the negative messages that often accompany addiction. Repeating the same or multiple affirmations one hundred times each day earns you a point. While the point value may seem low, affirmations are a significant factor in your recovery.

Hopefully you have already discovered the importance of introducing healthy fun back into your life. Every week, you should have some fun. If you do something just for fun, then award yourself one point. Regardless of how many fun activities you participate in, the maximum you can earn for fun each week is one point.

Physical Activities

In the chapters on Days 10 and 19, we talked about the importance of physical exercise and how it enhances recovery. For every twenty minutes of continuous physical exercise, award yourself two points. You get an additional point for every ten minutes of exercise beyond the first

Thirty Days to Hope & Freedom for Sexual Addicts

twenty minutes. However, you do not get any points for exercise periods that are less than twenty minutes in length.

When you eat healthily for the entire day, you get one point. You have to decide what is healthy eating for you. At first, you may award yourself a point simply for improving your diet from the norm. Eventually, you will only award yourself a point for adhering to stricter guidelines. The nutrition police are not going to be knocking on your door. Be honest with yourself.

Since getting good, sound sleep is critical to your overall health and well being, you get one point just for sleeping—so long as you sleep for at least seven hours a night. If you sleep longer than seven hours that is good but you get a maximum of one point per day for sleep. And if you sleep less than seven hours, you do not get any points.

When you have sex with your spouse you earn three points. While there is certainly no limit to how often you may be sexual with your spouse, you may only earn a maximum of six points per week in this area. As your recovery progresses and you want to continue to move more toward healthy sexuality, you will find it helpful for you and your spouse to read *Erotic Intelligence*, by Alexandra Katehakis. This is a book about healthy sexuality that is written specifically for couples in recovery from sexual addiction.

Taking care of your physical health is a positive recovery activity. When you get an annual physical exam or even when you are going to the doctor because you are ill, award yourself five points. For each dental check-up, award yourself an additional five points.

You also earn one point for a date night with the maximum of one point in this category per week. If you are in a committed relationship, set yourself a goal of having a date with your partner every week.

Make several copies of the Weekly Recovery Points Worksheet so that you can track your progress every week. Record your progress at least once each day. At the end of the week record your progress on the Recovery Tracking Chart. Compare your progress from week to week.

You may also go to www.ThirtyDaysTheBook.com to find and easy to use "fillable" PDF of the Weekly Recovery Points Worksheet.

Recovery Tracking Chart

There is an iPhone application called *iRecovery*[113] that tracks your recovery points each week. More information about *iRecovery* is given in Day 30.

After you have adopted your recovery point goal for the week, give some thought to how you are going to achieve your goal. Review your Personal Recovery Plan from Day 24 to see whether there are adjustments you want to make in your plan. Make those adjustments, and then monitor your progress at the end of the week. Were you able to follow your plan? Did you achieve your recovery point goal? What changes do you want to make as you prepare for the following week?

---

113. Available at www.RecoveryApp.com and the Apple Store. This tool is also available for iPad™. A similar tool is available for computers.

My Commitment

I am currently in the _____ Recovery Phase. I commit to a goal of achieving _____ recovery points each week. Further, I commit to giving my sponsor and my Circle of Five a report of my weekly progress.

Signed _____ Date _____

Weekly Recovery Points Worksheet

	Recovery Activity	Point Value	Points Earned
Recovery	Twelve Step Meetings (no limit)	7x	
	Sponsor/Sponsee Meeting (max. 5 points per week)	5	
	Step Work (for every 45 minutes)	2x	
	Program Calls (1 point per call made or received; max. of 2 points per day)	1x or 2x	
	Recovery-Related Reading (for each 30 minutes)	1x	
	Recovery Night (min. of 2 hours of focused work, max. 4 points per week)	4	
	Recovery Activity with Partner (max. 2 points per day)	2x	
Spiritual	Spiritual Activity (min. of 1 continuous hour)	3x	
	Recovery Prayer/Meditation (1 point for morning or evening prayer, 2 points for bookending the day)	1x or 2x	
	Journaling (max. 1 point per day)	1x	
Mental Pyshcological	Individual Therapy (for each session)	5	
	Group Therapy (for each session)	5	
	Couple's Therapy (for each session)	5	
	Affirmations (repeated 100 times a day)	1x	
	Something Just For Fun (max. 1 point per week)	1	
Physical	Physical Exercise (20 minutes min. of continuous exercise per day)	2x	
	Additional Exercise (for each additional 10 minutes)	1x	
	Healthy Eating (max. 1 point per day)	1x	
	Sleep (min. of 7 hours per night, max. 1 point per day)	1x	
	Healthy Sex (3 points per occasion, max. of 6 points per week)	3 or 6	
	Doctor/Dentist Visit (5 points for each visit)	5x	
	Date Night (max. 1 point per week)	1	
Weekly Goal vs. Points Earned		Weekly Goal	Points Earned

Recovery Tracking Chart

Each Week of Recovery

	1	2	3	4	5	6	7	8	9	10	11	12	13	14	15	16	17	18	19	20	21	22	23	24	25	26	27	28	29	30
130																														
120																														
110																														
100																														
90																														
80																														
70																														
60																														
50																														
40																														
30																														

Recovery Points Earned for the Week

Thirty Days to Hope & Freedom for Sexual Addicts

Day 29: Recovery for the Couple

Your recovery comes first. Before you focus on your partner or the relationship, make sure your recovery is solid and that you are making progress. Follow the many suggestions in this book to ensure that you have a solid recovery foundation and that you are moving forward.

A full clinical disclosure of your past sexual behavior is a necessary part of recovery. This must be professionally facilitated by a therapist who is experienced in working with sexual addiction and in conducting clinical disclosures. Disclosure puts an end to secrets and ultimately the shame that accompanies them. It also answers all of your partner's questions about your past behavior.

A polygraph exam can be a helpful tool in aiding a full disclosure to finally eliminate all of the secrets and shame. It can also be helpful for the partner to provide some basis for restoring trust. A strong word of caution is necessary. Do not use polygraph exams unless they are part of an integrated approach to therapy. I know of cases where they caused great harm because a couple tried to use a polygraph by themselves or they persuaded a therapist to try to incorporate this into therapy when they were not comfortable with doing so. A full treatment of disclosure and polygraph can be found in *Hope & Freedom for Sexual Addicts and Their Partners*.[114]

Jerome's Story

Jerome was a master of control. That is, he knew how to control others but not necessarily himself. When his partner called him on some of his addictive behavior, he would yell and curse. Sometimes he would throw things as a means of intimidation. However, he took pride in saying he had never hit his spouse. While it is true that he never hit his partner, his behavior was nevertheless abusive. Jerome believed he could only be pushed so far, and beyond that he was free to retaliate. Jerome had bought into the idea that it was alright for him to have a limit switch.

Remove the Limit Switch

Electronic equipment and tools often come with a limit switch that is built in to keep a circuit from being overloaded. Sadly, many guys have built-in limit switches when it comes to dealing with their partner. They may have been acculturated to believe they can only take so much or that people can push them only so far. They may have a limit as to what can be demanded of them at work before they tell off their boss and find another job.

In their committed relationship, they may feel that if their partner pushes them too far or asks too many questions that they are justified in retaliating with rage or by just shutting down.

---

114. (Magness M. S., 2009) p. 87

While that behavior may succeed in shutting your partner down, it will cause significant damage to your relationship. Your partner must be able to talk about feelings and hurts and even suspicions. If they cannot, they will never completely heal.

Make a decision today to remove the limit switch when it comes to your relationship. Resolve that there is nothing that your partner can say that will give you permission to exhibit your pre-recovery addictive behaviors. If you require a timeout, request ten minutes alone so that you can compose yourself before continuing the conversation. If you want a timeout, do not stomp out in a huff and slam the door like a petulant child. Instead, exercise self-control and restraint as you exit. Be certain that you make it clear that you will be back in ten minutes. Otherwise, you may trigger abandonment fears in your partner to add to the other wounds you have caused.

You may say that your patience is short. Do you have the right to be impatient? Yes. Do you have the right to use that impatience as an excuse to avoid recovery practices and continue to be abusive toward your spouse? No.

You can do something about your addiction and see early hope from your recovery program. This often results in immediate affirmation as you see the progress that you are making. However, your partner may be stuck in the morass of trauma, resulting from your previous acting out. Your patience will be necessary if your partner is to have the chance to heal.

Your Partner's Recovery

The next concern is your partner's recovery. Your behavior has injured your spouse more than you will ever be able to comprehend. A number of suggestions for your partner's recovery are given in *Hope & Freedom for Sexual Addicts and Their Partners*.[115] However, you cannot push your partner into recovery. Often a partner resents being told there is work they have to do, simply because they are in a relationship with a sexual addict.

Roseanne's Story

Roseanne first discovered her partner's secret sexual life when she received an anonymous phone call that told her to check out a photo on a website that had classified ads for "adult services." She was horrified to find a nude photo of her husband. Over the next several weeks, she assumed several identities on that website to see whether she could find out what her husband had been doing.

To her dismay, she found that her husband had been engaging in a secret life throughout their marriage. Eventually, Roseanne's husband got into recovery and has been doing well. He is sponsoring others and has achieved two years sobriety. Roseanne's problem is that she continues to have nightmares about her husband's acting out. She also cries several times a week and does not know why she is doing that. A friend suggested that she might be suffering from post-traumatic stress disorder (PTSD) and encouraged her to see a therapist who specializes in this area.[116]

---

115. Published by Gentle Path Press in 2009.
116. (Steffens & Means, 2009). This book contains a wealth of information about PTSD and how it often develops in the partners of sexual addicts.

Thirty Days to Hope & Freedom for Sexual Addicts

The partner's work does not require that they wear any label or be treated like they are the cause of your addiction. The main focus for partner's work is on the trauma caused by the sexual addict. Be patient with your spouse. She (or he) may not work her recovery on your schedule or on your terms. Your role is one of support and willingness to do whatever you can for her as she goes through the painful healing process.

Your acting out has traumatized your spouse. In fact, the trauma that you have caused your spouse hooks in to all the previous traumatic experiences your spouse has suffered over his or her lifetime. While it may not seem fair, it is as though you are the one who is guilty of causing all the past trauma. You will either help or hinder your partner's progress. Your main job during your spouse's recovery is in validating her reality. Learning to effectively validate your partner may be a challenge. It will be difficult because you will want to learn a new way of relating to your partner and then be willing to give your spouse all of the time necessary for the healing to take place.

Some of the time when you are feeling good about your journey of recovery, you hear your spouse speak about the pain that was endured because of your sexual addiction or the anger over how you have violated her. You may find yourself saying, "Doesn't she know I am in recovery?" There may be a big temptation to lose your temper and tell your partner to get over it because you are not acting out now. Part of the price you pay in recovery is giving up your "right to be right." Once a sexual addict has crossed the line with his partner and violated that person's trust, the sexual addict gives up the right to get angry and lash out at what may be perceived as an injustice. True, the spouse of a sexual addict may accuse their partner of something they did not do. They may even lash out in anger about injuries that the sexual addict caused months or years earlier. But the sexual addict should not—must not—respond in kind.

The only hope of rebuilding trust comes when the sexual addicts allow their partners to speak their minds and do not respond in kind. Only by practicing good listening skills, something that is foreign to many, do you allow the healing to begin. Look your partner in the eye, listen to what she has to say and then do one more thing—validate her!

Validating Your Spouse

Validation is a key element in rebuilding trust. What does it mean to validate your spouse? Validation is not the same as agreeing with her, though it is close. Something in the present has reminded them of your past acting out. Just as you may be triggered to have sexual thoughts by something you see or do, your partner may be triggered by an event and be plunged right back into her trauma.

Probably the hardest thing to listen to is being accused of acting out when you know that you have not. A natural response would be to say, "How dare you accuse me of that. I haven't done anything!" Can't you feel a bit of righteous indignation? Don't you want to set the record straight?

If your spouse falsely accuses you of acting out, do not become angry. Try to understand your partner's feelings. For example, you might say, "I can see how you could get angry when you see something in a movie that reminds you of the way I behaved in the past. I know I hurt you deeply."

This is not the time for an apology. By including an apology you turn the focus back to yourself. You are asking for your spouse to verbally forgive you and then change their behavior. How selfish! That is the way you used to live when you lived in addiction. Everything revolved around you.

There is not a lot you can to do to convince your spouse that you are not guilty. The best approach is to follow this formula:

1. Listen to what your partner says. Maintain eye contact and beware of showing anger, defensiveness, or annoyance in your facial expression.
2. Validate what your spouse says. "I can see how you would think that I acted out. I acted out many times in the past. You don't have any basis for trusting me."
3. Add an "and" rather than a "but." Using the example above: "I can see how you would think that I acted out. I acted out many times in the past. You don't have basis for trusting me. And this time I didn't act out. However, I can see why you might feel that I did."

If you did act out, it will not be a pleasant situation to confess it to your spouse. Remember, secrecy and shame are two of the elements that led you into the depth of addiction. Living your life in the open is different, but it is also rewarding.

If you have had a slip or relapse, you owe it to your spouse to be open and honest. As hurtful as disclosing a slip may be, it is necessary for your program of recovery. You are not in recovery if you slip and keep it secret from your spouse. Instead, you are reverting to your old behavior of living in secrets and shame. As strange as it may sound, disclosing a slip to your spouse is one of the healthiest steps that you take in recovery. It hurts. It may lead to estrangement. But the consequences of not sharing mean a return to addictive living.

One of the best ways of telling your partner about a slip is to use the FASTT check-in.[117] This is a weekly check-in where you tell your partner about your

- Feelings
- Activities in recovery
- Sobriety statement or a slip report
- Threats to your sobriety and
- Tools you used to stay sober

This tool is used *after* you have already had a full clinical disclosure with your partner.

---

117. (Magness M. S., 2009) p. 161

The Relationship Recovery Cycle

Once you and your partner are in recovery, then you can begin to look at your recovery as a couple. Couple's recovery is something that most sexual addicts want to happen sooner rather than later. However, it is the last part of the relationship recovery cycle.

Significant work is necessary for a couple to experience complete recovery. And the recovery work done as a couple typically should wait for several months before doing anything other than handling crises that may arise. Starting couple's work too soon can distract you from your greater priority of your own recovery. It is not possible to bypass your own recovery and jump right to couple's recovery.

Couple's recovery must also wait until your spouse is ready to work on the relationship. A wounded spouse does not have to be concerned with giving attention to either your neediness or the future of the relationship. Instead, the spouse should give primary focus to his or her own healing.

When the time comes to work on couple's recovery, that does not mean you have come to an end of working on your individual recovery. Those efforts must continue if your relationship is going to have a future. Just as you should be patient with your spouse in his or her personal recovery, you will want to be patient in your couple's recovery. This is a process that may take several years.

One of the ways of getting a head start on couple's recovery is to participate in a Three-Day Intensive.[118] Intensive programs are a good way to begin recovery and provide the opportunity of laying a foundation upon which trust can be reestablished in the relationship. They are hard work, but they can also be very rewarding.

---

118. A complete list of Three-Day Intensives offered at Hope & Freedom Counseling Services is found in Appendix A.

There are a few Twelve Step groups that cater to couples in recovery. The best known of these is Recovering Couples Anonymous. This organization is for couples from any background and any addiction who want to improve their relationship. In addition to this, some cities have joint SAA and CoSA meetings and other joint meetings with "S" groups and partner groups. Check with the Twelve Step organizations in your area to find out what couples meetings are available.[119]

Many couples have also found it helpful to seek the services of a therapist. Choose a therapist who has expertise in working with couples and understands sexual addiction and the trauma that is faced by partners of sexual addicts.[120] In some cases, couples find it better to pick a therapist who has not done individual therapy with either partner. That way both can build a relationship at the same time without any fear the therapist may be favoring one over the other due to a previous therapy relationship. However, there are also many cases where couples have successfully received couple's therapy from the same person providing individual therapy to the husband or the wife. The main thing to keep in mind is that you find a therapist with the appropriate expertise and one that both of you can trust.

A good resource for work with your spouse is the workbook by Carnes, Laaser, and Laaser, called *Open Hearts*.[121] This workbook can provide you a roadmap for couple's recovery, and it can give you some guidance in conversations and problem-solving. The workbook may even be assigned by a couple's therapist as an adjunct to their therapy sessions.

The Myth of 50-50 Relationships

Tamera always believed relationships should be 50-50 propositions. That is, she was willing to put in 50 percent, but she expected her partner to put in 50 percent as well. She has been in many relationships. Four have resulted in marriage, and three others resulted in living-together relationships. But none of her partners have ever given 50 percent to the relationship. Her current husband comes close at times, but she realizes that since she entered recovery, he has a hard time dealing with her past indiscretions. He believes he is doing the best he can, given the circumstances. Tamera feels this is just another relationship where her partner is not willing to give as much as she does.

In recovery the partner may well lag behind the sexual addict. Your partner may have a lot of baggage from your acting out. And they have to deal with the trauma you caused.

However, even without the strain put on relationships by sexual addiction, 50-50 relationships do not work. Each person's perception is that they are giving far more than their share to the relationship. In reality, most give less than 50 percent and expect more than 50 percent in return. So what happens if you are giving, say, 45 percent or even 48 percent in your relationship and your partner is doing the same? There ends up being a significant gap that cannot be bridged as long as you and your partner are entrenched and believe you are doing your part.

---

119. Information Twelve Step fellowships for couples can be found in the Appendix B.
120. A listing of therapists can be found at www.sash.net and www.iitap.com.
121. (Carnes, Laaser, and Laaser, *Open Hearts: Renewing Relationships with Recovery, Romance and Reality*, 1999)

For your relationship to work, you must be willing to give more than you expect to receive. And this is particularly true for sexual addicts. This may be a time when your spouse is able to give significantly less than they were giving in the past. For your relationship to make it, you must think in terms of a 60-40 or even a 70-30 relationship. It is your job to give more—much more—than you expect to receive from your spouse.

Communication

"Do we talk? He would say we talk. But usually all I get is a conversation that I call 'news, sports, and weather.' He doesn't seem to know how to talk about things that really matter." While this could also be said of some women, men typically are more challenged when it comes to having intimate conversations with their spouse.

Meaningful conversation with your partner should be a part of every day. "But all she talks about are things that really don't interest me. Who really cares if she has had a hard day at work? Her day is nothing compared to mine." Talk about a blind spot! This man would gladly engage in conversation as long as it is about him, his work, what he needs, what he wants, what he likes, or what he does not like. In other words, as long as they are talking about him, he is engaged in the conversation. As soon as his spouse wants to talk about anything else, his attention wanders, and he loses interest.

What should you do to improve the communication between you and your spouse? Would it be helpful if you were intentional about being interested in your spouse's day? How can you get beyond the "news, sports, and weather" conversation? What interests does your partner have that you have never taken the time to hear? Can you focus on things that your partner likes instead of having the conversation always be about you?

Where Is the Romance?

Women in general are much better about romance than guys. The single biggest complaint I hear from wives and partners is that their sexual addict husband is not romantic. They find it extremely difficult to understand that he is a sexual addict when they have not seen much evidence of them caring a great deal about sex.

Perhaps even harder for wives of sexual addicts to accept is that their sexual addict husband has been romantic with others when they have not seen evidence of romance in their relationship for several years. There have not been many romantic getaways, romantic dinners, love notes, or anything of a similar nature. And when the sexual addict enters recovery, I often hear wives saying, "I want him to pursue me like he has pursued others."

Early in the recovery journey, your partner may not be ready for any romantic overtures. It may be several months until the time is right for you to make any such advances. It is crucial to remember that romance must be part of your future with your spouse if your relationship is going to thrive.

Romantic gestures might include phone calls that are unexpected. You might try writing love notes and leaving them where they can be found. One of the best ways you can show you care is to plan dates that show you truly care about your partner.

Dating Your Spouse

For this section, I am going to address male sexual addicts who are married. If your wife tells you she would like to go on a date, are you likely to reply, "All right. Where would you like to go eat?" or "What movie would you like to see?" This would be a good time to rethink the term "date." A good rule of thumb would be to realize if you take your wife to dinner and/or a movie that she may not consider it a date. Sure, she might have let you get by with it before you were married. For many wives, a date is something that requires thought and planning beyond picking a restaurant or movie on the fly.

Of course, some dinners, perhaps many dinners, may be very romantic. For a meal away from home to be considered a date by your wife, it should reflect some extra effort by you. And that does not mean taking her to your favorite place for buffalo wings and football.

If you were single and had just met the woman you are married to, how would you romance her? What would you do to let her know that you were interested in her and that you wanted to spend time with her? You would probably think about her constantly and wonder what you could do to win her affection. As you progress through the recovery journey, and after your wife has had a chance to do some significant healing, it will be vital for you to look for opportunities to show her that you care about her and that you are glad that you are married to her.

Dating Ideas

The following is a list of dating ideas that have been contributed by different men who are in recovery. It is not meant to be an all encompassing list. Instead, it is designed to get you out of the dinner-and-a movie rut. If these are not available where you live, then check out the offerings in a nearby city.

- **Arboretum, botanical gardens, and nature centers.** You can find these in major cities. They are good places for an afternoon walk on the weekend or on a day when you get off of work early. The best part is that many of these are free or are priced at a very reasonable rate.

- **Bike riding.** Look on the Internet to see whether there are biking clubs in your town. These sites may give you a list of bike routes and trails in your area, as well as events that involve biking.

- **Bluegrass music.** Actually it can be any kind of music. Find the little out-of-the-way places that have a once-a-month (or once-a-week) performance by a local group. You do not have to be a bluegrass aficionado to enjoy some good banjo picking and fiddle playing.

- **Bonfire in the backyard.** Check your local ordinances first. It does not have to be very large. You can make an impromptu fire pit by using the manufactured fireplace logs on a water heater pan you can purchase at a hardware store. And don't forget the hot chocolate and smores.

- **Bowling.** You do not have to be good—just willing. Check out a bowling alley near where you live.

- **Climb a tree.** Sounds corny, but if you can find a good climbing tree nearby, it could prove to be an interesting date. And when the climbing is done, go for an ice cream cone.

- **Concerts.** There are certainly concerts by big name entertainers available. But additionally consider concerts that are held throughout the year in the school of fine arts at most universities. They will likely feature students who are studying to be professional musicians or music teachers.

- **Cooking classes.** Take a class *with* your partner. Look in the phonebook or on the Internet for currently available classes. Keep a list of these and surprise your partner with an out-of-the ordinary date.

- **Dance lessons.** Fun for the brave at heart. Thanks to the popularity of television shows about dancing, there are even more dance studios around than ever. Try ballroom, salsa, swing, or tango. Be adventuresome. Your partner will appreciate the effort even if you are not likely to be given a guest spot on television dancing with a celebrity.

- **Dinner cruises.** A surprising number of cities have dinner cruises available on lakes, rivers, or other waterways. If there are not any available where you live, plan an overnight trip to a city that offers them.

- **Drive.** Take a sightseeing drive around your state. Do a day trip or find an out-of-the-way hotel or bed-and-breakfast and spend the night. In Texas, bluebonnet time and football season are just two good times to get out-of-town. What are the special seasons in your area that would be good for taking a long drive?

- **Half-price tickets.** Many of the large performance halls sell their unused tickets at a deep discount on the day of the performance. And here is a hint worth knowing. If all you can find are single seats, choose two singles on the same row. When you get to the performance, ask if others on the row would be willing to slide one seat toward the middle so that you and your date can sit together.

- **Horseback riding.** If there are stables near you, they may offer trail rides or even individual riding lessons.

- **Hot air ballooning.** This is a pricey but memorable date. Balloons typically fly at dawn and near dusk when the air is the calmest.

- **Ice skating.** Even if you have never tried it, put on some warm clothes, take your thick socks, and escort your date around the ice. You may find yourself being out skated. And that is not so bad either.

- **Kite flying.** Spring and summer offer some wonderful opportunities for kite flying. You might even consider building a kite with your partner.

- **Continuing education and leisure-learning classes.** Take a class together. Check out the opportunities at community colleges and even at major universities. You can learn a new hobby or skill and enjoy spending time with your partner.

- **Lemonade stand tour.** On a hot summer Saturday, get a pocketful of quarters and see how many lemonade stands you can find. And every day, make it a point never to pass a lemonade stand without patronizing it. You will help make a child's day.

- **Outdoor theater.** Many cities have outdoor amphitheaters that offer concerts and plays for free or for a modest fee. In many, you can take a picnic lunch and a blanket.

- **Museums.** If you live in or near a large city, consider becoming a member of a museum for the many "members only" openings and parties. If you enter "museums" and your city name into a search engine, you may be surprised at how many museums are in the area. Besides the major museums there may be many small, somewhat offbeat museums that you could visit for a memorable date.

- **Mystery weekend.** Plan a date to a destination that you know your partner will enjoy. Tell your spouse how to pack and how long you will to be gone, but keep the rest a secret until the date unfolds.

- **Rodeo.** Some small towns have several rodeos year round. If you want a real treat, consider going to the Houston Rodeo or the Calgary Stampede.

- **Picnic.** Pick a park, set the menu, and do *all* the meal preparation yourself! Be creative. The more creative you are, the more "points" you get with your partner.

- **Private party.** Plan a party just for you and your partner and send a special invitation ahead of time.

- **Progressive date.** Prepare envelopes with clues about the date and then give your partner the clues as the date unfolds. Again, creativity counts big with this date.

- **Progressive dinner.** Plan a dinner with a different course at various international restaurants. Have fun and be creative.

- **Rafting.** You might be surprised to find that there are rafting or canoeing opportunities not far from where you live. Pack a lunch that you prepare yourself.

- **Roller skating.** There are still a few roller rinks around. You will have to search for them, but they can make for a memorable date. Even if you used to be a hot shot, be careful if it has been a while since you have skated.

- **Scavenger hunt.** Plan a scavenger hunt around your house. Leave clues that lead your partner to find a birthday gift or perhaps clues about a mystery weekend you have planned.

- **Star gazing.** In connection with some museums of natural history or science and some universities, there are star gazing parties where telescopes are provided and seasoned astronomers show novices the wonders of the heavens.

- **Theme dates.** Plan a date around a particular theme. For example, set aside a day when you watch a movie like "My Big Fat Greek Wedding," attend a Greek Festival, and then have dinner at a Greek restaurant.

- **Walking around town.** If there is a shopping district or a quaint section of town with old shops, spend a couple of hours just window shopping and browsing.

- **Water sports.** Boating, water skiing, taking scuba lessons together, or just watching the sun go down at the beach can provide you with many fun dates.

- **Zoo.** You do not have to be a kid to enjoy the zoo. In some cities, member benefits include various "members only" parties with some including the opportunity to spend the night at the zoo and listen to the nocturnal sounds.

Someone has said:
- Dialogue Daily
- Date Weekly, and
- Depart Monthly

This is a good reminder that a weekly date night will not substitute for the daily conversation and sharing that every couple needs. There should be frequent exchanges during the course of the week, preferably several of these each day. Your spouse needs to have that daily connection with you.

Departing monthly does not mean that you have to plan an expensive getaway every month. But if you can afford it, a weekend trip to a nearby city to do something your partner enjoys will help rebuild the relationship. Some state parks have cabins that can be rented inexpensively. And if money is tight, a long drive in the country would provide the opportunity for you and your partner to have a longer reconnect time than is usually afforded on a weekly date.

Establish a Recovery Night

One final thought on couple's recovery. I encourage you to periodically set aside a night in which you can devote time to your recovery as a couple. Committing one evening a week to the work you do as a couple recognizes the importance of working on your relationship.

To establish a recovery night, set aside at least a two-hour block of time one evening each week. Hopefully, you will be able to use the same evening so as to give continuity to these evenings. Turn off the television and all phones and mobile email devices. Begin the evening with you and your partner journaling about the preceding week. Think about what went well in recovery and what requires more work. The next item is to do a FASTT Check-In[122] with your partner. Other items for recovery night include working through a workbook together such as *Open Hearts*,[123] and participating in various communication and intimacy exercises. Recovery nights may also include reading a recovery book together.

Remember, good relationships do not just happen. They are the product of hard work. Your relationship is worth it. Do not give up on it just because of the extra difficulties you are encountering in recovery. As I sometimes say to couples, *Fight for your relationship! If you do not fight for it, you may lose it!*

---

122. (Magness M. S., 2009) p. 161.
123. (Carnes, Laaser, & Laaser, *Open Hearts: Renewing Relationships with Recovery, Romance and Reality*, 1999)

Day 30: Recovery as a Lifestyle

It is Day 30 and time to think about what comes next in recovery. Obviously this is not the end of the recovery journey. Staying sober thirty days is a good start to recovery, but it would be a poor finish.

How does one stay sober long-term? Have persons who have lived for many years without acting out discovered a secret that allows them to stay in recovery and not suffer slips or relapse? I believe they have.

The secret is in the word *lifestyle*. When recovery becomes a lifestyle, a person has reached the place in the recovery journey where he or she does not have to make conscious decisions to avoid acting out. He or she does not struggle daily with urges that dominate their thoughts. He or she no longer lives with a fear that sobriety may come to an abrupt end.

The word *lifestyle* was originally coined by Austrian psychologist Alfred Adler in 1929. Lifestyle includes a bundle of behaviors that makes sense to oneself as well as to others. It includes the choices one makes with regard to social relations, dress, entertainment choices, and how money is spent. Habits are developed around these choices, and those habits become an entrenched part of one's lifestyle. Attitudes and values, as well as one's world view, are also encapsulated by the word *lifestyle*.

For a decade beginning in the mid 1980s, there was a popular television show that featured the lifestyles of people who were wealthy, famous, or both. The show was a hit and was actually one of the first of the so-called "reality TV shows." People would often watch with rapt attention to see how the financial and social elites of the world lived.

It was obvious to most who watched that show that their lifestyle was not at all like the stars and celebrities who were profiled. The wealthy celebrities on that show did not live like the rest of the world. They ate different food, drove different cars, and went to exotic places on vacation. These wealthy elites not only had yachts, but their boats were often equipped with helipads or submarines. They did not eat, dress, act, or worry in the ways of ordinary people.

For such persons, their lifestyle said something about the way they spent their time, their money, who their friends were, how they entertained themselves, and every other area of life. The lifestyle of the extremely wealthy includes decisions on virtually everything in life. If they are ill, they may go to a hospital, but most likely, they will occupy a suite instead of a semiprivate room. When they travel, they use limousines and private jets. If they eat at a restaurant, they may book the entire dining room so that they can dine alone.

While it is fun to think about the lifestyle that eccentric wealthy people have, few believe they will ever have a lifestyle that is similar. The value in looking at the lifestyles of such aristocrats is realizing that everything in their lives is determined by the fact they ascribe to the lifestyle of the financial and social elites. Every choice is the result of decisions that are made that are congruent with their lifestyle.

In the same way, a recovery lifestyle encompasses every area of life. When recovery becomes a way of life, decisions automatically support all aspects of recovery. Little thought has to be given as to whether a decision supports solid recovery or not. Choices of friends, entertainment, and recreation support recovery as well as financial decisions are tempered by the fact that one has followed the path of recovery.

You can know that you have adopted a recovery lifestyle when every area of your life, as well as every decision, supports recovery. Practiced behaviors become habit. Recovery routines are automatic. The motivation for all of these decisions is intrinsic. You are doing recovery because you deserve it and so that you will personally benefit, as well as to see benefit in your relationships and in all areas of your life. When recovery becomes a lifestyle, there are so many benefits that come from recovery that it is hard to imagine life without them.

The payoff for the recovery lifestyle is freedom! You can live free from all compulsive sexual behaviors for the rest of your life. If you want this badly enough and are willing to do the difficult but rewarding work of recovery, freedom can be yours.

Recovery Lifestyle Commitment

Today _____, I commit myself to adopting recovery as a lifestyle. I recognize this means that recovery never ends. I further realize that from this point forward, every decision in life will be measured by this commitment to a lifestyle of recovery.

Signed _____

Putting It All Together

During the past thirty days, you have learned a great deal about your addiction and have gotten an understanding of how your family of origin has impacted your addiction. You have learned the value of attending Twelve Step meetings and working with a sponsor. And you have learned a number of tools and coping behaviors for dealing with intrusive thoughts. Finally, you have put together a Personal Recovery Plan and have learned to use the Recovery Points System to track your recovery.

Thirty Days to Hope & Freedom for Sexual Addicts

Beyond the First Thirty Days

The journey never ends. Prior to recovery you may not have been able to see anything in your life that you wanted to change other than your compulsive sexual behavior. Now you can see several things that you want to change. You will continue to discover things about yourself that you want to improve. Thanks to the life you now live in recovery, you are able to give attention to those things.

What is waiting for you as you move beyond the first thirty days of recovery? You will continue going to meetings and working with your sponsor. Over the next several months you will continue working the Twelve Steps of recovery.

The most immediate milestone in your recovery is stringing together months of unbroken sobriety. Sobriety milestones are acknowledged in groups with a chip or coin that carries the fellowship's motto, as well as how long you have achieved sobriety. Chips are given each month for the first six months, two or three more are given during the next eighteen months, and they are awarded annually thereafter. These often become treasured keepsakes.

The next milestone you will achieve is to work through all of the recovery Steps. When you finish working through the Steps, you will find there is no graduation ceremony. You receive no recognition other than the personal satisfaction that comes from completing one portion of a mission that will benefit you for the rest of your life.

Often when a person in recovery finishes the Steps, they begin working the Steps again with a desire to do an even more thorough job than was done the first time. Throughout recovery you will continue to work the Steps, sometimes in a formal manner as you go through all Twelve Steps with a sponsor. At other times you may work a particular Step again as you deal with some recovery issue.

After completing the Steps, it is time to give away what you have learned to others. You move into the role of sponsor. Your sponsor will tell you when the time is right for you to begin sponsoring others.

As you embark on this new part of the journey, you will find that your recovery moves to yet a higher level. Your sponsor will become your grand-sponsor and guide you as you guide your first sponsee through the Steps.

When you become a sponsor, you do not wear the hat of a recovery expert, but rather that of one recovering person showing another recovering person how to find hope and freedom. Attendance at meetings continues as you take on the added responsibility of having appointments with sponsees.

If you have been in therapy, your therapy continues. Both individual and group therapy have proven to be of significant benefit in the recovery process. Somewhere in the future you will move out of weekly therapy to something that is less frequent. Ultimately, you will move completely out of therapy, having established long-term unbroken sobriety and new thought and behavior patterns to replace the dysfunctional ones that were associated with addiction.

Today you are thirty days further down the road than when you started this book. Your recovery never ends. You never come to the end of the journey. Hopefully, you have already achieved thirty days of living free from all of your compulsive sexual behaviors.

As you embark on the next part of the journey, be vigilant. Remain alert. Each month, you will encounter new threats to your sobriety. Learn to spot them and develop a plan for dealing with each. Be persistent. Never give up. Never let up. Never quit. The journey is long, but it is also rewarding.

iRecovery—Addiction Recovery Tracker iPhone App

At the iPhone Store and at www.RecoveryApp.com, you can download the *iRecovery— Addiction Recovery Tracker* app that will help you chart the progress of your recovery. The program is designed to be easy to use and to encourage you in all of your recovery efforts. The application will allow you to personalize your recovery and let you know whether you are staying on track. Using it regularly will help prevent slips and relapses.

In this application, you will be able to establish your personal recovery profile and automatically determine which recovery phase you are in. You will be able to keep track of your daily and weekly recovery activities and have these compared to the weekly goal you select. The data you store each week is depicted graphically so that you can get a good visual confirmation of your recovery progress.

The application utilizes a screensaver that includes randomly selected recovery quotations. A daily recovery affirmation is also included as is helpful information on goal setting. Recovery alerts warn the user of deficiencies in recovery and encourage the user to adopt recovery as a lifestyle.

In addition to the iPhone version, there is a version for iPad and Android™-based phones, as well as a version that will work on your computer. A demonstration version of this application may be viewed at www.RecoveryApp.com.

iRecovery will send accountability emails to your Circle of Five and your therapist each week. As you identify other recovery activities that are important to you, you may add them and assign a point value for each. You may also change the point value of the preloaded activities if your sponsor or your therapist believes this is important. Finally, you can record behaviors that are part of your healthy living plan that includes Healthy or Green Light behaviors, Dangerous or Yellow Light behaviors, and Forbidden or Red Light behaviors.

Thirty Days to Hope & Freedom for Sexual Addicts

Appendix A:
Recovery Programs at
Hope & Freedom Counseling Services

The primary treatment option offered at Hope & Freedom Counseling Services is a Three-Day Intensive. These are particularly good for an individual or a couple just entering recovery. They are an ideal forum to deal with the crisis that may have precipitated recovery. Intensives are also good for persons who have not been able to establish long-term sobriety or who have just experienced a slip or relapse.

Three-Day Intensives are short but concentrated periods to work on recovery. They are not designed as or presented as a "three-day cure." There is no such thing. Rather, they are for doing intensive work around recovery, either to get a good foundation for recovery or to address a specific problem during recovery. Hope & Freedom Counseling Services offers a variety of Three-Day Intensives that are especially helpful for persons who live in geographical areas where specialized sexual addiction therapy is not available.

These are not the treatment option of choice for every person or couple where compulsive sexual behavior is a factor. We currently accept fewer couples than apply for this treatment program. There are a number of factors that may not make this the treatment option of choice for couples dealing with sexual addiction within a relationship.

Persons who are considering a Three-Day Intensive must be willing to work hard. They have to be willing to take extraordinary steps in restoring their relationship. For the intensive process to be successful, it requires a couple to be willing not just to participate in the three-day experience, but to be willing to work on rigorous assignments that are included each evening. The intensives are only for highly motivated individuals and couples.

A prerequisite for participating in an intensive is for both partners to be stable emotionally. Clients with untreated obsessive-compulsive disorder, bi-polar disorder, or severe attention deficit hyperactivity disorder may not be a good candidates for intensives. After persons with these disorders are stabilized with medication and therapy, they may be good candidates for the rigorous intensive process. Additionally, intensives are not appropriate for persons who are in danger of harming themselves.

Couples who are approved for participation in a Three-Day Intensive must make an unqualified commitment to stay in their relationship after the intensive. This is crucial since disclosures typically reveal additional acting-out behaviors or at least details about those behaviors. This new information often traumatizes the partner. When the pain associated with trauma starts, the typical response is to look to anything that can stop the pain, including ending the relationship.

We ask partners to make a commitment to stay in the relationship for a minimum of twelve months after the intensive, regardless of what is revealed in the disclosure. And we ask sexual addicts to make twice that commitment—to stay in the relationship a minimum of twenty-four months after the intensive, regardless of their partner's anger or disappointment. Couples must enter a contractual agreement with that goal before being allowed to participate in a Hope & Freedom intensive.

If there is significant resistance on the part of a couple or an individual, Three-Day Intensives are not indicated. We ask couples who come to intensives to be willing to devote total effort to recovery for those three days. That includes not conducting "business as usual" during the intensive. We also ask that contacts with home and family be kept to a minimum for the duration of the intensive.

Persons interested in intensives first have to complete an online application and are then carefully screened to make sure that they are appropriate for an intensive and that there is a reasonable expectation that they may benefit from the experience. The exact content of the intensive is sculpted to the specific needs of the client. All of the intensives are offered for couples and individually for single men. However, if the client is in a committed relationship, we will only work with the couple since successful recovery depends on both partners being involved in the recovery process. (Additional information about intensives, as well as applications for intensives, may be found at www.HopeAndFreedom.com.) The following is a partial list of intensives offered through Hope & Freedom Counseling Services.

Recovery Foundations Intensive for Couples or for Individuals

This intensive is designed for individuals and couples who are at the beginning of recovery. Often these intensives focus on giving the participants a broad understanding of sexual addiction and what is involved in recovery. There is an emphasis on understanding the origins of addiction and the factors that are currently contributing to sexual addiction.

Each intensive focuses on integrating recovery routines into the couple's relationship, as well as reestablishing trust in the relationship. Relapse prevention is a significant focus of these intensives. The Recovery Foundations Intensive culminates with each client drafting a Personal Recovery Plan.

Restoration Intensive for Couples

This intensive is structured for a couple where the client has been in recovery for a while but has had a slip or a relapse. Attention is given to understanding the cause of the relapse and preventing further relapses. A significant thrust of this intensive is in dealing with the issue of trust in the relationship. The couple is introduced to a process of trust rebuilding that requires significant commitment from both parties.

Survivors Intensive for Couples or for Individuals

This intensive is designed for couples where one or both partners have experienced significant trauma in the past. The trauma may be as far back as childhood or as recent as trauma that has resulted from current sexual acting out. This intensive will focus on each partner doing some significant healing around the past trauma and looking at the impact the trauma has had on the relationship. And, as with all of our couple's intensives, a similar intensive is offered for individuals.

Step-Down Intensive for Couples or for Individuals

This intensive is designed as a step-down treatment for couples where the sexual addict has just returned from inpatient treatment or from an extended intensive outpatient treatment facility. The emphasis of this intensive is on reentering public life. Clients learn to identify and deal with daily triggers, as well as learn new thought and behavior patterns to replace dysfunctional thoughts and behaviors. Relapse prevention and developing a Personal Recovery Plan round out the intensive.

Special Topic Intensives

We also offer a variety of other special topic intensives to fit the needs of various clients. These deal with a number of topics related to recovery, such as multiple addictions, couples where the husband and the wife both have addictions, recovery issues involving the family, or religious abuse.

High-Profile Client Intensive

Individuals who find themselves in the public eye face special challenges in entering recovery. If they go into a therapy office, they risk revealing their struggle with compulsive sexual behavior. To address this concern, we take the intensive to the client.

This intensive is good for any high-profile person including senior executives, professional athletes, celebrities, politicians, and actors, as well as broadcast personalities. These are offered at a discreet location somewhere in the United States or Canada. The content of the intensive is customized to fit the needs of the individual or couple. The locale allows for an extra buffer of anonymity that is not available for celebrities who enter well-known treatment centers. Additional information on these intensives can be found at www.CelebritySexAddict.com.

Additional intensives are offered to meet the special needs of physicians and clergy. These intensives are highly individualized to deal with the specific issues involved. And in cases where an extra level of anonymity is required, we offer these intensives at locations other than our main counseling office.

Preparing for Intensives

As clients get ready to come to an intensive, they are encouraged to make adequate preparations to help ensure the success of their concentrated work. First of all, clients are encouraged to spend time thinking about the events that have contributed to their scheduling the intensive. For intensives dealing with sexual addiction, it is essential to make a complete, detailed, but confidential list of all acting-out behaviors. The more detailed and complete this list, the more effective the intensive.

Clients who participate in a Three-Day Intensive are encouraged to take care of all business and family matters before beginning and then not conduct any business during the intensive. We have found that clients who conduct "business as usual" during an intensive get only limited benefit from the experience. For this reason, we strongly encourage clients to wait until they are able to devote their full concentration to continuous therapy for three days.

In order to maximize the effectiveness of this time, we make the following stipulations:

- Leave cell phones, pagers, Blackberries™, PDAs, iPods™, laptops, and other electronic devices at home.
- Refrain from conducting business during the duration of the intensive.
- Limit phone calls to one per day to check in with family or check on dependent children.
- Do not drink any alcohol for the thirty days preceding the intensive.
- Refrain from all alcohol use during the intensive.
- Do not watch television, read newspapers, or check email during the intensive.

In short, the total focus of the three days must be to concentrate on individual recovery and for strengthening the relationship. Distractions must be kept to a minimum. Nothing should be allowed to hinder the very significant work that takes place during an intensive.

We have also found it beneficial for clients to stay an extra day or so after the intensive to process with their partner what they have learned and accomplished during the preceding three days. This time can be critical as couples make plans to reenter life and consider how their relationship may be different in the future.

Aftercare Intensives

A rigorous aftercare program is essential to any recovery treatment program. As stated earlier, Three-Day Intensives are not intended to be a three-day cure. After the initial three days of work, couples are encouraged to return for periodic One-Day Aftercare Intensives. In some respects, these are mini versions of what is experienced during a Three-Day Intensive.

During an Aftercare Intensive, the couple once again has a combination of individual and couple's therapy. The Aftercare Intensives are used to check up on recovery progress, learn additional tools of recovery, work on communication issues the couple may be facing, and take a follow-up polygraph exam to verify that the acting out has not recurred. The Individual

Recovery Plan that the couple crafted during their Three-Day Intensive is reviewed to see if changes are required.

The first of these one-day follow-ups is scheduled three months after the Three-Day Intensive. They are then scheduled every six months for an additional eighteen to thirty-six months depending on the couple's need. Thereafter, we encourage couples to schedule an Aftercare Intensive annually as a checkup on the relationship and to monitor progress in recovery.

Appendix B: Resource Guide

Recovery Start Kit

For a much more extensive treatment of the first 130 days of recovery, get the *Recovery Start Kit*,[124] by Patrick Carnes. Dr. Carnes uses his task-centered approach to sexual addiction treatment to guide a person through the first crucial months of recovery. The kit is designed to be used as a part of ongoing individual or group therapy, but it can also be utilized by persons who do not have access to a sexual addiction therapist or who chose not to engage in formal psychotherapy. The kits can be purchased at a discount from Certified Sex Addiction Therapists.[125]

iRecovery Addiction Recovery Tracker

This iPhone application is designed to keep track of recovery activities and plot the user's progress. The tracking process is also designed to be an encouragement to think about recovery daily.

Main Features

- Assigns recovery points to typical recovery activities
- Charts those activities and compares progress from week to week
- Users can add their activities and assign a point value for each
- Will send weekly accountability emails to Circle of Five and therapist/counselor showing progress for week
- "Call Sponsor" button visible on every screen for immediate contact with sponsor
- Preloaded affirmations with counter
- Users can also add their own affirmations
- User defined "Red Light," "Yellow Light," and "Green Light" behaviors
- "Contacts" button takes users to list of their Circle of Five contacts
- Alerts feature rewards consistent recovery and alerts user to potential problems
- Recovery points can be customized to meet individual recovery plans as directed by counselor or therapist.
- Includes an integrated journal function and password protection

iRecovery is also available in a specific iPad application and as a version for Android-based phones as well as a stand-alone computer version.

- www.RecoveryApp.com

---

124. (Carnes, Recovery Start Kit, 2009)
125. www.iitap.com

Intensive Outpatient Treatment Programs

Center for Healthy Sex

- Intensives for men, women, and couples with the goal of moving clients into healthy sexuality

  9911 W. Pico Boulevard, Suite 700

  Los Angeles, California 90035

  www.thecenterforhealthysex.com

  310-801-9574

Hope & Freedom Counseling Services

- Individualized Three-Day Intensives for couples and for single men
- Special programs available for physicians and clergy
- Celebrity intensives take place at a resort setting in the Canadian Rockies or at other secluded places in North America

  3730 Kirby Dr., Suite 1130

  Houston, TX 77098

  www.hopeandfreedom.com

  713-630-0111

Psychological Counseling Services (PCS)

- One to five week intensive outpatient program for men, women, and couples
- With a heavy focus on individual therapy

  7530 E. Angus Drive

  Scottsdale, AZ 85251

  www.pcsearle.com

  480-947-5739

Sexual Recovery Institute (SRI)

- Two-week intensive out-patient program for men, women, and spouses

  822 S. Robertson Blvd., Suite #303

  Los Angeles, CA 90035

  www.sexualrecovery.com

  310-360-0130

Inpatient Treatment Centers

Del Amo Hospital
23700 Camino del Sol
Torrance, CA 90505
www.delamohospital.com
800-533-5266

Gentle Path™ at Pine Grove
6051 U S Highway 49
Hattiesburg, MS 39401
www.pinegrovetreatment.com
888-574-4673

Keystone Center
2000 Providence Ave.
Chester, PA 19013
www.keystonecenterecu.com
800-733-6840

The Meadows
1655 N. Tegner St.
Wickenburg, AZ 85390
www.themeadows.org
800-632-3697

Sante Center for Healing
P.O. Box 448
Argyle, TX 76226
www.santecenter.com
800-258-4250

Sierra Tucson, Inc.
39580 S. Lago del Oro Parkway
Tucson, AZ 85739
www.sierratucson.com
800-842-4487

Christian-Based Workshops

Bethesda Workshops
Workshops for men and women
3710 Franklin Rd.
Nashville, TN 37204
www.bethesdaworkshops.org
866-464-4325

Be Broken Ministries
Three-day workshops for men
1800 NE Loop 410, Suite 401
San Antonio, TX 78217
www.bebroken.com
800-497-8748

Faithful & True Ministries
Three-day workshops for men, women, and couples
15798 Venture Lane
Eden Prairie, MN 55344
www.faithfulandtrueministries.com
952-746-3880

Recovery-Related Websites

www.AWomansHealingJourney.com
For wives of sexual addicts. Takes a Christian approach to recovery. The focus is on trauma resolution.

www.CelebritySexAddict.com
Intensive outpatient programs for persons who cannot visit a therapist without becoming the subject of media scrutiny.

www.ThirtyDaysTheBook.com
This site contains the forms and worksheets that are in this workbook. They can be filled out online and then printed for your use. Your personal information is not stored.

www.GuardUrEyes.com
For Jews who struggle with compulsive sexual behavior.

www.HopeAndFreedom.com

Resources for persons wanting to learn about sexual addiction.

www.InternetBehavior.com

Provides cybersex addiction research and resources. This site also includes a screening exam for persons who think they may be addicted to cybersex behavior.

www.PhysiciansInCrisis.com

Intensive outpatient therapy for physicians who struggle with sexual addiction.

www.ProvidentLiving.com

Resources for persons who are members of The Church of Jesus Christ of Latter Day Saints.

www.RecoveryApp.com

Recovery-related applications for iPhones, iPad, and other platforms.

www.RecoveryOnTheGo.com

Brief audio books, MP3 downloads for getting started recovery.

www.RecoveryZone.com

Offers assessment testing for all addictions.

www.SAATalk.org

Gives a list of SAA meetings that take place by electronic means.

www.SexHelp.com

Dr. Carnes' website. This site also offers a screening exam for persons who wonder it they might be a sexual addict.

www.StopSexAddiction.com

For partners who wonder if the person they love is a sexual addict.

www.WoundedClergy.com

Brief intensive programs for clergy struggling with sexual addiction.

Websites That List Therapists Who Specialize in Sexual Addiction

www.iitap
The International Institute of Trauma and Addiction Professionals

www.sash.net
The Society for the Advancement of Sexual Health

Twelve Step Fellowships for Other Compulsive Behaviors and Addictions

Alcoholics Anonymous
www.aa.org

Cocaine Anonymous
www.ca.org

Crystal Meth Anonymous
www.crystalmeth.org

Debtors Anonymous
www.debetorsanonymous.org

Food Addicts Anonymous
www.foodaddictsanonymous.org

Gamblers Anonymous
www.gamblersanonymous.org

Marijuana Anonymous
www.marijuana-anonymous.org

Narcotics Anonymous
www.na.org

Nicotine Anonymous
www.nicotine-anonymous.org

Overeaters Anonymous
www.oa.org

Spenders Anonymous

www.spenders.org

Shopaholics Anonymous

www.shopaholicsanonymous.org

Workaholics Anonymous

www.workaholics-anonymous.org

The Twelve Steps of Sex Addicts Anonymous[126]

1. We admitted we were powerless over addictive sexual behavior—that our lives had become unmanageable.
2. Came to believe that a Power greater than ourselves could restore us to sanity.
3. Made a decision to turn our will and our lives over to the care of God as we understood God.
4. Made a searching and fearless moral inventory of ourselves.
5. Admitted to God, to ourselves, and to another human being the exact nature of our wrongs.
6. Were entirely ready to have God remove all these defects of character.
7. Humbly asked God to remove our shortcomings.
8. Made a list of all persons we had harmed and became willing to make amends to them all.
9. Made direct amends to such people wherever possible, except when to do so would injure them or others.
10. Continued to take personal inventory and when we were wrong promptly admitted it.
11. Sought through prayer and meditation to improve our conscious contact with God as we understood God, praying only for knowledge of God's will for us and the power to carry that out.
12. Having had a spiritual awakening as the result of these steps, we tried to carry this message to other sex addicts and to practice these principles in our lives.

---

126. Copyright by the International Service Organization of Sex Addicts Anonymous. Used by permission.

About the Author

Milton Magness, D.Min., is the founder and director of Hope & Freedom Counseling Services in Houston. He is a psychotherapist and Certified Sex Addiction Therapist. He is the author of *Hope & Freedom for Sexual Addicts and Their Partners*, also published by Gentle Path Press, several audio books found at www.RecoveryOnTheGo.com, and several iPhone applications including *iRecovery*, the addiction recovery tracking tool that goes with this book (found at www.Recovery-App.com).

He is also the president of *The Society for the Advancement of Sexual Health* (SASH), the international professional organization for sexual addiction therapists.

Dr. Magness has studied with Dr. Patrick Carnes, the foremost authority on sex addiction, and has done specialized study in the area of cybersex addiction. He has led national workshops on cybersex addiction and has conducted a multi-state research study that focused on cybersex behavior and recovery among self-identified sex addicts. He is a frequent speaker at both professional and public events.

In addition to his Three-Day Intensives, Dr. Magness conducts numerous retreats each year. He offers specialized retreats for men as well as Leadership Retreats for successful couples who want to be able to interact with couples like themselves in a recovery process that offers both support and anonymity.

Dr. Magness focuses a significant portion of his practice in working with senior executives and other high profile individuals such as celebrities, physicians, and successful entrepreneurs. He also has intensives specifically for clergy who struggle with compulsive sexual behavior.

While his main website is www.HopeAndFreedom.com, Dr. Magness has specialized websites for clients who are part of various populations, including:

- www.ExecutivesInCrisis.com,
- www.PhysiciansInCrisis.com,
- www.WoundedClergy.com,
- www.CelebritySexAddict.com, and
- www.StopSexAddiction, for persons whose partner/spouse is engaged in compulsive sexual behavior.

Should you wish to contact Dr. Magness with questions about this book or for information about Hope & Freedom Counseling Services, you may write to him at milton.magness@hopeandfreedom.com.

Dr. Magness lives in Houston, TX, and Canmore, Alberta, Canada.

Bibliography

www.sash.net.

www.iitap.com.

Adam, Kenneth and Alexander Morgan. *When He's Married to Mom*. Fireside, 2007.

Alcoholics Anonymous, Fourth Edition. 2001: Alcoholics Anonymous.

Argente, J., N. Caballo, V. Barrios, M. T. Munoz, J. Pozo, J. A. Chowen,. "Multiple Endocrine Abnormalities of the Growth Hormone and Insulin-Like Growth Factor Axis in Patients with Anorexia Nervosa: Effect of Short- and Long-Term Weight Recuperation." *Journal of Clinical Endocrinology and Metabolism*, 1997, Vol. 82, No. 7: 2084-2092.

Bantle, Christian, and John P. Haisken-DeNew. *Smoke Signals: The Intergenerational Transmission of Smoking Behavior*. Berlin: German Institute for Economic Research, February 2002.

Canning, Maureen. *Lust, Anger, Love: Understanding Sexual Addiction and the Road to Healthy Intimacy*. Sourcebooks, 2008.

Cannon, Walter Bradford. "The emergency function of the adrenal medulla in pain and the major emotions." *The American Journal of Physiology* (Appleton), 1914: 356-372.

Carnes, Patrick. *A Gentle Path Through the Twelve Steps: A Classic Guide For All People in the Process of Recovery*. Hazelden, 1993.

—. *Don't Call it Love*. Bantam, 2000.

—. *Facing the Shadow: Starting Sexual and Relationship Recovery*. Gentle Path Press, 2005.

—. *Out of the Shadows: Starting Sexual and Relationship Recovery*. Gentle Path Press, 2001.

—. "Recovery Start Kit." Gentle Path Press, 2009.

—. "Recovery Zone Lecture." 2008.

Carnes, Patrick, Mark Laaser, and Debra Laaser. *Open Hearts: Renewing Relationships with Recovery, Romance and Reality*. Gentle Path Press, 1999.

Carnes, Stefanie. *Mending a Shattered Heart*. Gentle Path Press, 2008.

Cooper, A., and L. Sportolari. "Romance in cyberspace: Understanding online attraction." *Journal of Sex Education and Therapy*, 1997: 22(1), 7-14.

Cooper, A., Scherer, C., Boies, S. C., & Gordon, B. "Sexuality on the Internet." *Professional Psychology: Research and Practice*, 1999: 30(2), 154-164.

Cooper, Al, and D. L., & Burg, R. Delmonico. "Cybersex users, abusers, and compulsives: New findings and implications." *Sexual Addiction & Compulsivity*, 2000: 7(1-2), 5-30.

Diagnostic and Statistical Manual of Mental Disorders (DSM-IV-TR). American Psychiatric Association, 2000.

Dopamine Agonist. October 9, 2009. http://en.wikipedia.org/wiki/Dopamine_agonist (accessed October 23, 2009).

Earle, Ralph, Gregory Crow. *Lonely All the Time: Recognizing, Understanding, and Overcoming Sex Addiction, for Addicts and Co-dependents*. Pocket Books, 1998.

Earle, Ralph, Marcus Earle. Sex Addiction: Case Studies and Managements. Brunner/ Mazel, 1995.

Ewing, John A. "Detecting Alcoholism: The CAGE Questionairre." *Journal of the American Medical Association*, 1984: 1905-1907.

Ferree, Marnie. *No Stones: Women Redeemed from Sexual Shame*. Xulon, 2002.

Frost, Robert. "The Road Not Taken." In *Mountain Interval*. Henry Holt, 1920.

Gambling Impact and Behavior Study: Final Report of the National Gambling Impact Study Commission. University of Chicago: National Opinion Research Center, March 18, 1999.

Glasser, William. *Positive Addiction*. Harper Colophon, 1976.

Heatherton, T, P Nichols, F Mahamedi, and P Keel. "Body Weight, Dieting, and Eating Disorder Symptoms Among College Students, 1982 to 1992." *American Journal of Psychiatry*, 1995: 1623-1629.

History of Alcoholics Anonymous. www.aa.org (accessed August 7, 2009).

Hope & Freedom Counseling Services. www.HopeAndFreedom.com.

How Much Sleep Do We Really Need? 2009. http://www.sleepfoundation.org/how-much-sleep-do-we-really-need (accessed October 21, 20098).

Jacobson, Nora, and Dianne Greenly. "What Is Recovery? A Conceptual Model and Explication." *Psychiatric Services*, 2001: Vol. 52, No. 4, pp. 482-485.

Jester, Jennifer M, Joel T Nigg, Leon I Puttler, Jeffrey C Long, Hiram E Fitzgerald, and Robert A Zucker. "Intergenerational transmission of neuropsychological executive functioning." *Brain and Cognition*, June 2009: 145-153.

June 29-30, 2009: Joint Meeting of the Drug Safety and Risk Management Advisory Committee with the Anesthetic and Life Support Drugs Advisory Committee and the Nonprescription Drugs Advisory Committee: Meeting Announcement. US Food and Drug Administration, 2009.

Katehakis, Alexandra. *Erotic Intelligence: Igniting Hot, Healthy Sex while in Recovery from Sex Addiction*. Health Communications, Inc., 2010.

Kent-Ferraro, J. "Risky business: Sex and the bottom line." *Sexual Addiction & Compulsivity*, 2002: 9(2-3), 73-86.

Laaser, Debra. *Shattered Vows: Hope and Healing for Women Who Have Been Sexually Betrayed*. Zondervan, 2008.

Laaser, Mark. *Healing the Wounds of Sexual Addiction*. Zondervan, 2004.

Latt, Noeline, Stephen Jurd, Jennie Houseman, and and Sonia E Wutzke. "Naltrexone in alcohol dependence: a randomised controlled trial of effectiveness in a standard clinical setting." *The Medical Journal of Australia*, 2002: 530-534.

Lieberman, L. *A Social Typology of Gambling Behavior*. New York: National Council on Compulsive Gambling, 1988.

Lipp, Elizabeth. *Novel Approaches to Lead Optimization.* April 1, 2008. http://www.genengnews.com/articles/chitem.aspx?aid=2550# (accessed October 23, 2009).

Magness, Milton. February 17, 2004. http://www.HopeAndFreedom.com/option,com_docman/task,cat_view/gid,28/Itemid,87.html (accessed October 23, 2009).

Magness, Milton S. *Hope & Freedom for Sexual Addicts and Their Partners.* Gentle Path, 2009.

Marcus, Bess H, et al. "Exercise Enhances the Maintenance of Smoking Cessation in Women." *Addictive Behaviors*, 1995: Vol. 20, No. 1, 87-92.

McDaniel, Kelly. *Ready to Heal: Women Facing Love, Sex, and Relationship Addiction.* Gentle Path Press, 2009.

McGoldrick, Monica, and Randy Gerson. *Genograms: Assessment and Intervention.* W.W. Norton & Co., 2008.

Parfitt, Tom. "Russia's Health Promotion Efforts Blossom." The Lancet, June 2009: Vol. 373, No. 9682, pp. 2186-2187.

Pathways to Addiction: Opportunities in Drug Abuse Research. National Academy Press, 1009.

Patton, George C, and Carolyn Coffey. "Prognosis of Adolescent Partial Syndromes of Eating Disorder." *The British Journal of Psychiatry*, 2008: 294-299.

Perry, Bruce D., Ronnie A. Pollard, Toi L. Blakley, William L. Baker, and Domenico Vigilante. "Childhood trauma, the neurobiology of adaption and 'use-dependent' development of the brain: how 'states' become 'traits'." *Infant Mental Health*, 1995: 271-291.

Prescription Drugs: OxyContin Abuse and Diversion and Efforts to Address the Problem. United States General Accounting Office, December 2008.

Ratey, John J. *Spark: The Revolutionary New Science of Exercise and the Brain.* Little, Brown and Company, 2008.

Russell, Gerald. "Bulimia nervosa: an Ominous Variant of Anorexia Nervosa." *Psychological Medicine*, 1979: 429-448.

Santayana, George. *The Life of Reason.* Scribner's Sons, 1905.

Schneider, Jennifer and Debra Corley. *Disclosing Secrets: When, to Whom, and How Much to Reveal.* Gentle Path Press, 2002.

Schneider, Jennifer. *Back from Betrayal: Recovering from His Affairs.* Recovery Resources Press, 2005.

Sex Addicts Anonymous. Sex Addicts Anonymous, 2005.

Sexaholics Anonymous. Sexaholics Anonymous, 1989.

Steffens, Barbara, and Marsha Means. *Your Sexually Addicted Spouse: How Partners Can Cope and Heal.* New Horizon Press, 2009.

Stoliaroff, Sharon. "Over the Edge-Exercise Addiction." *Running and Fitness News*, 2003: Vol. 18, No. 6.

Wegner, Daniel M, David J Schneider, Samuel R Carter III, and Teri L White. "Paradoxical Effects of Thought Suppression." *Journal of Personality and Social Psychology*, 1987: Vol. 53, No. 1, 5-13.

Wurtman, R.J., F. Hefti, and E. Melamed. "Precursor Control of Neurotransmitter Synthesis." *Pharmacological Reviews*, 1981: 315-335.

Young, K. S., E. Griffin-Shelley, and A. Cooper. "Online infidelity: A new dimension in couple relationships with implications for evaluation and treatment." *Sexual Addiction and Compulsivity*, 2000: 7(1-2), 59-74.

Young, Kimberly. *Caught in the Net: How to Recognize the Signs of Internet Addiction—and a Winning Strategy for Recovery*. 1998: John Wiley & Sons.

Index

gambling, 51, 52, 78, 80, 93, 142, 143, 149

genogram, 67, 69

God, 1, 2, 25, 34, 65, 119, 127, 128, 131, 132, 133, 135, 136, 137, 156

gratitude, 19, 133, 136, 159, 160

guilt, 62, 75, 80, 153

Halcion™, 142

Higher Power, 24, 127, 128, 132, 133, 135, 136

hope, 1, 2, 3, 5, 6, 7, 8, 11, 15, 20, 21, 22, 23, 24, 26, 27, 30, 35, 48, 131, 136, 161, 162, 163, 196, 197, 209

humility, 133

Hydrocodone, 142

inpatient treatment, 52, 76, 164, 176, 213

intensive outpatient (IOP), 51, 52, 146, 176, 213

Internet, 6, 13, 17, 26, 30, 33, 34, 43, 44, 65, 78, 79, 93, 96, 97, 103, 104, 105, 106, 107, 108, 113, 117, 139, 143, 148, 202, 203

intrusive thoughts, 109, 110, 112, 113, 115, 118, 208

iRecovery, 3, 172, 186, 191, 210

isolation, 11, 58, 65, 95, 96, 144, 152, 164, 176

journal, 59, 113, 130, 156, 166, 176, 185, 190

Klonopin™, 142

Librium™™, 142

lifestyle, 3, 54, 91, 134, 207, 208, 210

limit switch, 195, 196

ludomania, 142

masturbation, 25, 45, 69, 98, 179, 180, 181, 182

meditation, 22, 73, 113, 136, 137, 165, 171, 190

MySpace, 43

naltrexone, 77

neurochemical, 9, 39, 45, 78, 97

nicotine, 143, 144

overeating, 146, 147

oxycodone, 142

OxyContin™, 142

Percocet™, 142

Personal Recovery Plan, 90, 161, 162, 164, 165, 168, 170, 185, 188, 191, 208, 212, 213

Phases of Recovery, 186, 187

polygraph, 186, 195, 214

pornography, 6, 19, 34, 35, 39, 43, 45, 51, 55, 63, 69, 78, 79, 93, 97, 98, 104, 105, 110, 117, 169, 181, 182

powerless, 34, 36, 42, 54, 129, 152

prayer, 73, 113, 132, 133, 136, 165, 190

procrastination, 18

program calls, 3, 166, 189

psychiatrist, 75, 76, 77, 80, 146

Recovery Night, 193, 205

Recovery Points System, 185, 186, 191, 208

Reframing, 113, 114

relapse, 3, 6, 8, 19, 22, 51, 53, 146, 161, 169, 173, 174, 175, 176, 177, 186, 207, 211, 212

resistance, 16, 17, 50, 74, 186, 212

romance, 201, 202

Ropinirole, 78

secrecy, 13, 35, 152, 162, 198

Gentle Path Books that May Interest You

Facing the Shadow, Second Edition
Starting Sexual and Relationship Recovery
Patrick Carnes, Ph.D.

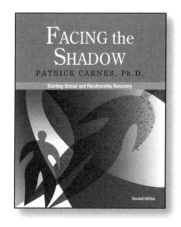

Dr. Patrick Carnes' ground-breaking book, *Out of the Shadows*, introduced the world to his research on sexual addition. *Facing the Shadow* is the innovative workbook that helps readers understand how to begin meaningful recovery from an often misunderstood addiction. This book guides readers through the first seven tasks in Dr. Carnes' researched-based Thirty Task Model of treatment—the most respected therapy model available for treating sex addicts.

325 pp
Trade Paper | $29.95
978-0-9826505-2-3

Recovery Zone, Volume 1
Making Changes that Last: The Internal Tasks
Patrick Carnes, Ph.D.

Recovery Zone, Volume One, picks up where *Facing the Shadow* leaves off, guiding readers through tasks eight through thirteen of Dr. Patrick Carnes' innovative Thirty Task Model. This book helps readers understand how to move beyond merely stopping addictive behavior. True recovery is achieved by learning to cope with difficult situations and emotions. Although there is no overnight solution for addictions, recovering people can learn how to achieve long-term sobriety by making decisions that suit their individual needs, devising a plan for living an optimal life and becoming proactive leaders of their lives.

315 pp
Trade Paper | $29.95
978-0-9774400-1-6

Connection and Healing: A 200-Day Journey into Recovery
Russ Pope, M.S., and Dan Green, Ph.D.

This guided journal provides two hundred days of inspirational writings on a variety of topics, including how to:
- reach out to family members and rebuild trust
- break habits of isolation and make the most of healthy connections
- experience the blessings of being truly known by others
- act in the true best interest of loved ones

430 pp
Trade Paper | $24.95
978-0-9826505-0-9

Gentle Path Books that May Interest You

Came to Believe: A Guide to the Second Step
Chet Meyers

In a world that seems increasingly violent, materialistic, and filled with problems, is it possible to believe in a Higher Power? Author Chet Meyers offers answers to this and other questions to help readers reframe their thinking on the nature of spirituality and faith. This is a thoughtful and nonjudgmental discussion of Step Two, *Came to believe that a Power greater than ourselves could restore us to sanity.*

90 pp
Trade Paper | $14.95
978-0-9774400-7-8

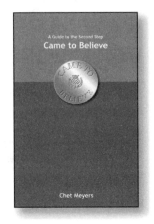

Mending a Shattered Heart: A Guide for Partners of Sex Addicts
Edited by Stefanie Carnes, Ph.D.

Hundreds of unsuspecting people wake up every day to discover their loved one, the one person who they are supposed to trust completely, has been living a life of lies and deceit because they suffer from a disease called sex addiction. Stefanie Carnes, Ph.D, brings together several authors to guide the reader through such difficult questions as "Should I stay or should I leave?" This comprehensive guide offers readers the best expertise available on how to begin the road of personal recovery.

220 pp
Trade Paper | $19.95
978-0-9774400-6-1

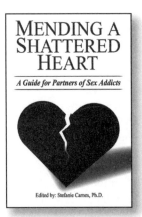

Hope and Freedom for Sexual Addicts and Their Partners
Milton S. Magness, D.Min.

Dr. Milton S. Magness offers sexual addicts and their partners step-by-step guidance on how to work through the phases of recovery. Readers learn about disclosure, celibacy contracts, relapse, and how to rebuild broken trust. This is a compassionate yet straightforward primer on how to end sexual addiction.

220 pp
Trade Paper | $19.95
978-0-9774400-5-4

Gentle Path Books that May Interest You

Disclosing Secrets: When, to Whom, and How Much to Reveal
M. Deborah Corley, Ph.D.,
Jennifer P. Schneider, M.D., Ph.D.

Nearly every book on addiction recovery discusses the need for "coming clean" with loved ones, but this is the only guide that exclusively addresses this essential step in revealing sensitive secrets. Readers will learn what, when, and how to disclose information related to sexual and other addictions, as well as who to involve and what (if anything) to tell children.

290 pp
Trade Paper | $23.00
978-1-929866-04-5

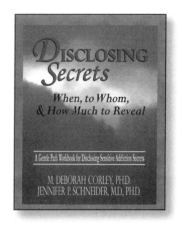

Open Hearts: Renewing Relationships with Recovery, Romance, and Reality
Patrick Carnes, Ph.D., Debra Laaser,
Mark Laaser, Ph.D.

No relationship situation is hopeless. In *Open Hearts*, readers will learn how to overcome "coupleshame," fight fair, understand their family "epics," break free from the same old battles, form a spiritual bond, and renew their early passion. This book provides hopeful and helpful guidance on transforming one's most intimate bonds.

230 pp
Trade Paper | $19.95
978-1-929866-00-7

Ready to Heal: Women Facing Love, Sex, and Relationship Addiction
Kelly McDaniel

Author Kelly McDaniel offers women compassionate yet direct assistance on how to change painful relationships. Readers will learn how to address patterns of choosing partners who are addicted to sex and substances, how to stop being involved in serial relationships, and what to do about anger and other painful emotions associated with intimate relationships.

190 pp
Trade Paper | $18.95
978-0-9774400-3-0

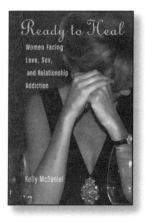

New Freedom Companies

Gentle Path Press

Gentle Path Press was founded in 1998 by Patrick Carnes, Ph.D., a pioneering researcher, clinician, and author in the field of sexual and multiple addictions. Dr. Carnes' goal was to publish innovative books and other resources for consumers and professionals on topics related to addiction, trauma, and brain chemistry. Gentle Path books provide readers with the best research-based materials to help repair the lives of individuals and families.

Dr. Carnes' cutting-edge research and writing became widely known in 1983 with the publication of his book, *Out of the Shadows: Understanding Sexual Addiction*. It was the first book designed to help addicts deal with their sexual compulsions, and to examine the tangled web of trauma, love, addictive sex, hate, and fear often found in family relationships. His research, work with patients, and writing have continued over the past three decades.

Experts and consumers alike have come to embrace Dr. Carnes' 2001 book, *Facing the Shadow: Starting Sexual and Relationship Recovery*, as his most compelling and important work to date. *Facing the Shadow* introduced readers to Dr. Carnes' revolutionary Thirty Task Model for beginning and sustaining long-term recovery.

More information on Gentle Path books can be found at www.gentlepath.com.

Institute for Trauma and Addiction Professionals

Dr. Carnes also founded the International Institute for Trauma and Addiction Professionals (IITAP), which promotes professional training and knowledge of sexual addiction and related disorders. Sex addiction affects the lives of millions of people worldwide, and practicing therapists are on the frontlines treating this epidemic. IITAP offers three distinguished certifications to addiction-treatment professionals: Certified Sex Addiction Therapist (CSAT), Certified Multiple Addiction Therapist (CMAT), and Associate Sex Addiction Therapist (ASAT).

More information can be found at www.iitap.com.

Came to Believe: A Guide to the Second Step, by Chet Meyers

Chapter 1

Your concept of God is a little small

Most individuals come to Twelve Step programs on their knees, grasping for any bit of help with various addictions, dependencies, and failed life dreams. Step One says, "We admitted we were powerless over [alcohol]—that our lives had become unmanageable." *Alcohol* is bracketed because, for many of us, the addiction or dependency that crippled us took another form—drugs, over-eating, gambling, sexual addiction, work addiction, codependency in caring for others, or addiction to abusive relationships. In one sense the exact nature of our addictions or dependencies is irrelevant. What all have in common is how they disrupt our lives, drag us down, destroy our serenity, and simply make life miserable.

In March of 1981 I had what is often called a nervous breakdown. Since then a friend has helped me see that it was actually a nervous *breakthrough*. It changed my life, a life that really needed to change. I was at the end of my rope, so to speak, as the result of being overextended in just about every aspect of living. My life was a case study in human busyness. Work addiction, volunteer activities, endless home repair projects, and codependency (a concept I had never heard of) with my wife, family, and friends had driven me to my limits and over the brink. I was suicidal, had homicidal thoughts about killing my wife and friends, and was experiencing uncontrollable compulsive-obsessive thoughts about anything and everything that could go wrong in my life. Finally, after three weeks of downward spiraling, it seemed my mind just snapped. My wife took me to the psychiatric ward of a nearby hospital where I could get some help and much needed rest.

I remember waking up in the locked hospital ward and looking into the eyes of a wise and kindly psychiatrist who had helped admit me to the hospital. My first words to him were, "How could God do this to me?" He smiled warmly and said, "I think your concept of God is a little small."

Perhaps the same is true for many of us. We grew up with rather limited images of a Higher Power that offered little help or consolation when we really got in trouble. Indeed, for some of us, the very word *God* conjures up such negative images that it becomes a roadblock to our spiritual growth. Also, as Americans, we so value individualism and self-sufficiency, there is little room or need in our lives for belief in a Power greater than ourselves. And that comes naturally for those of us who grew up in dysfunctional families or lived in unsafe environments.

If our parents or caregivers were alcoholic, drug-addicted, or otherwise out of control, we learned very quickly to rely on our own resources. The problem is that we began to rely too exclusively on our own resources. We took it all on ourselves. Indeed, it is usually not until we have realized the limits of our own powers and abilities that we even begin to consider what role a Higher Power might play in our lives. And when that happens—after we have exhausted all our own resources and perhaps desperately turn to God—we often discover that our concept of god is pretty small or inadequate. Our image of a god needs to be enlarged, and we need to let go of some of our old ways of thinking about the nature of God that we may have learned as children.

One of my favorite posters shows a kitten desperately hanging on to the end of a large rope. It says, "When you get to the end of your rope… let go!" So, first of all, let's admit that if the word *God* has a lot of negative feelings and thoughts associated with it, some of us may have to let go of that word for a while—maybe even permanently. Many of us grew up with an image of God as an old man in a white robe, with a long beard, who sat on a throne in heaven passing judgment on us and punishing us when we broke his rules. Or, we were raised in homes where our parents used religion as a means of punishing us and enforcing *their* rules. If we grew up in such environments, it is natural that "god-language" brings up painful memories we would rather leave behind. For others, who grew up in homes with no particular religious emphasis, or with parents who were atheistic, the idea of a Higher Power may seem foreign and strange. But even most atheists have a powerful image of the God they *do not* believe in. Whatever our upbringing, one way to begin working on the Second Step is to step back from our ideas about God that are not helpful and life-giving.

Rethinking what Higher Power means to us

The comedian Woody Allen once quipped, "After all, God is just dog spelled backwards."[1] This is not intended as a sacrilegious comment, but rather to remind us that words are just that—words— and that there are limits to human language. *God* is merely a word, a word for a concept and power that is difficult, if not impossible, to put into words. In the pages that follow we will use a number of different terms to refer to that concept or power—Higher Power, the Divine, the Transcendent, Universal Wisdom, Great Spirit, and others. The Sufi poet Rumi, from the Muslim tradition, often used the phrase *the Friend* to refer to his Higher Power.[2] That has a nice ring to it, and tells us right up front that for Rumi, at least, to start rethinking your image of God. To begin, try stepping back in time and understanding the concept of God that you grew up with as a child. And then, after careful reflection, if you sense that image has too many negative feelings and connotations, consider setting it aside for a while and using another word or phrase that feels more comfortable for you at this point in your life. Don't be overly concerned about *getting it right*. Just be willing to let go of old, painful concepts.

Sallie McFague, one of my favorite spiritual writers, says we need to accept the fact that *all* our images of Higher Power miss the mark.[5] They are all limited because our minds are limited and just can't figure the out Transcendent. Still, some images are more helpful than others. Some instill fear and hold us back, while others nurture us and help us grow. If your childhood image of *God* was fearful and perhaps punishing, as an adult you can choose to set it aside. If your earliest image was that of a loving and compassionate Higher Power, count yourself fortunate. Even so, be willing to have that image expanded and enriched. Above all, remember there is no specific, clear-cut, definition of a Higher Power set forth anywhere in Twelve Step literature. We must construct our own. That's why we talk about "the God of our understanding."